Presocratics

Ancient Philosophies

Created especially for students, this series of introductory books on the schools of ancient philosophy offers a clear yet rigorous presentation of core ideas. Designed to lay the foundation for a thorough understanding of their subjects, these fresh and engaging books are compact and reasonably priced, with illustrative texts in translation.

Published by University of California Press in the series:

1. *Stoicism*, by John Sellars

2. *Presocratics*, by James Warren

3. *Cynics*, by William Desmond

4. *Neoplatonism*, by Pauliina Remes

5. *Ancient Scepticism*, by Harald Thorsrud

6. *Ancient Commentators on Plato and Aristotle*, by Miira Tuominen

7. *Epicureanism*, by Tim O'Keefe

8. *Plato*, by Andrew Mason

9. *Confucianism*, by Paul R. Goldin

Presocratics

James Warren

University of California Press

University of California Press, one of the most distinguished university presses in the United States, enriches lives around the world by advancing scholarship in the humanities, social sciences, and natural sciences. Its activities are supported by the UC Press Foundation and by philanthropic contributions from individuals and institutions. For more information, visit www.ucpress.edu.

For Rhiannon and Niamh, two early thinkers

University of California Press
Oakland, California

© 2007 by James Warren

Published simultaneously outside North America by
Acumen Publishing Limited.

Library of Congress Cataloging-in-Publication Data

Warren, James, 1974-.
  Presocrates / James Warren.
    p.   cm.
  Includes bibliographical references and index.
  ISBN 978-0-520-25367-4 (cloth : alk. paper)
  ISBN 978-0-520-25369-8 (pbk. : alk. paper)
  1. Pre-Socratic Philosophers.   I. Title.
B187.5.W37   2007
182—dc22   2007003295

21   20   19   18   17
10   9   8   7   6   5   4   3   2

The paper used in this publication meets the minimum requirements of
ANSI/NISO Z39.48-1992 (R 1997) (*Permanence of Paper*).

Contents

Acknowledgements

As a new Classics student in Cambridge, the first ever philosophy lecture I attended was on the Presocratics. I had no intention at that time of studying philosophy seriously and I remember being confused by the idea that studying philosophy involved thinking about people who thought the world was made of water. But something about that lecture – given by Malcolm Schofield – must have made me come back for more.

There are a number of good books on early Greek philosophy and I have learned a lot from them. My hope is that, in a crowded field, this book manages to convey what I take to be the variety and importance of the philosophy at that time, together with an impression of how to go about thinking more deeply about these philosophers, both in terms of how to approach them in a philosophical way but also in terms of how to approach and handle the surviving, often frustrating, conflicting, and meagre, evidence. If I leave a number of interpretative issues open, that should stand as an invitation to further enquiry as well as an indication of the difficulty of drawing unquestionable conclusions about many of these philosophers. (I hope that I might be forgiven, therefore, for the often lengthy strings of further references in the notes. I thought it important to point readers in the direction of the various competing interpretations should they want to pursue a given topic.) There are, of course, many things I would have wanted to explore in greater detail. Nevertheless, I hope that readers might be encouraged by what I have included to go and think more about what I have not had space to discuss.

One of the irritations of working on these early philosophers is that it becomes necessary to deal with a variety of different numberings of the various fragments and testimonia as different editors and translators impose their own orderings. I have therefore decided to give references to the Diels–Kranz edition wherever possible with the thought that, although Diels–Kranz do not provide translations into English, all good later editions and translations either use their numbering or include at least a concordance to Diels–Kranz so the appropriate text can be found without too much difficulty.

Thanks are due, as ever, to my students for telling me when I was not making much sense and to my colleagues for showing me how to think and write about ancient philosophy. Drafts of various chapters or of the whole book were read and commented on by Jenny Bryan, Eric James, Sara Owen, Kelli Rudolph and the anonymous readers for the publisher; my thanks to them all. Special thanks also to Jason Lucas for the map on p. xv. Most of the work for this book was completed during sabbatical leave for the Michaelmas term 2005 and the Lent term 2006; warm thanks to my faculty and college colleagues who covered various duties for me. Thanks also to Steven Gerrard, who suggested that I should write this book as part of Acumen's *Ancient Philosophies* series and kept faith with the project as it progressed.

This book is dedicated to two people who ask lots of questions. I hope they never stop.

JIW
Cambridge, December 2006

Sources and abbreviations

The following texts are the ancient sources referred to, and serves as a guide to the abbreviations used in this volume.

Aet. (= Aëtius), 1st/2nd century CE collector of philosophical views
    See H. Diels, *Doxographi Graeci* (Berlin: de Gruyter, [1879] 1965) and
        Mansfeld & Runia (1997).

Aristophanes, *c.*446–*c.*388 BCE, Athenian comic dramatist
    Clouds = *The Clouds*

Aristot. (= Aristotle), 384–322 BCE, philosopher
    De an. = *De Anima* (*On the Soul*)
    De caelo = *De Caelo* (*On the Heavens*)
    EE = *Eudemian Ethics*
    Gen. an. = *De Generatione Animalium* (*On the Generation of Animals*)
    Gen. et. Corr. = *De Generatione et Corruptione* (*On Coming to Be and*
        Passing Away)
    Met. = *Metaphysics*
    Meteor. = *Meteorology*
    NE = *Nicomachean Ethics*
    Phys. = *Physics*
    Pol. = *Politics*
    Rhet. = *Rhetoric*

Cic. (= Cicero), Roman statesman, orator and writer
    Acad. = *Academica*

De nat. deorum = *De Natura Deorum* (*On the Nature of the Gods*)
Tusc. = *Tusculan Disputations*

Diog. Laert. (= Diogenes Laërtius), 3rd century CE author of *Lives of the Eminent Philosophers*

Dionys. *ap.* Eus. *PE* = Dionysius, 2nd century CE bishop of Corinth, quoted in Eusebius's (2nd–3rd century CE bishop of Caesarea) *Praeparatio Evangelica*

DK = H. Diels and W. Kranz, *Die Fragmente der Vorsokratiker* (6th edition, Berlin: Weidmann, 1951)

Epicurus, 341–270 BCE, philosopher, founder of Epicureanism
Letter to Herodotus

Galen, 129–*c*.199 CE, doctor and philosopher
PHP = *De Placitis Hippocratis et Platonis* (*On the Beliefs of Hippocrates and Plato*)
De medic. empir. = *De Medicina Empirica* (*On Empirical Medicine*)

Herodotus of Halicanassus, 484–*c*.425 BCE, historian and ethnographer
The Histories

Hesiod, *c*.700 BCE, Greek poet
Theog. = *Theogony*
Works and Days

Hippocrates, mid-5th–early-4th century BCE, doctor to whom many ancient medical writings, the "Corpus Hippocraticum", are traditionally attributed
On the Nature of Man
On Regimen

Hippol. (Hippolytus of Rome), 170–*c*.236 CE, Roman bishop
Ref. = *Refutation of all Heresies*

Lucretius, 1st century BCE, Roman Epicurean poet
DRN = *De Rerum Natura* (*On the Nature of Things*)

Plato, *c*.429–347 BCE, philosopher
Alcib. I = *First Alcibiades*
Parm. = *Parmenides*
Phaedo
Phaedr. = *Phaedrus*

Phileb. = Philebus
Prot. = Protagoras
Rep. = Republic
Symp. = Symposium
Tim. = Timaeus

Plut. (= Plutarch), 1st–2nd century CE biographer and essayist
    Adv. Col. = Adversus Colotem (Against Colotes)
    Per. = Life of Pericles

Ps. Plut. (= Pseudo-Plutarch)
    See *Doxographi Graeci* (Diels 1879) and Mansfeld & Runia (1997)
    Strom. = Stromateis (Miscellanies)

SE (= Sextus Empiricus), 2nd century CE Pyrrhonist sceptic
    M = Adversus Mathematicos (Against the Professors)
    PH = Outlines of Pyrrhonism

Simpl. (= Simplicius), 6th century CE philosopher and commentator on Aristotle
    De caelo = Commentary on Aristotle's On the heavens
    In Phys. = Commentary on Aristotle's Physics

Stob. (= Stobaeus), 5th century CE anthologist

Themistius, 4th century CE philosopher and orator
    Or. = Orations

Theoph. (= Theophrastus), c.370–285 BCE, pupil and successor of Aristotle

Timon on Philus, c.320–230 BCE, Pyrrhonist and satirical poet

Xen. (= Xenophon), 428–c.354 BCE, Athenian general and writer
    Mem. = Memorabilia
    Symposium

Chronology

Dates for many of these philosophers and writers are only approximate. "*Floruit*" indicates the likely period of their mature philosophical activity.

BCE

*c.*700	Hesiod composes *Theogony* and *Works and Days*
*c.*600	**Thales** *floruit*
585	Eclipse, said to have been predicted by Thales
*c.*580	**Anaximander** *floruit*
*c.*550	**Anaximenes** *floruit*
*c.*540	**Xenophanes** *floruit*
	Pythagoras *floruit*
*c.*500	**Heraclitus** *floruit*
499	Ionian revolt against Persia
494	Persian sack of Miletus
490	Persian Wars: Battle of Marathon
480	Persian Wars: Battle of Salamis
*c.*480	**Parmenides** *floruit*
479	Persian Wars: Battle of Plataea
469	Socrates born
*c.*460	**Anaxagoras** *floruit*
	Empedocles *floruit*

c.450	**Zeno** *floruit*
	Melissus *floruit*
	Democritus born
450	Great Panathenaia, probable dramatic date of Plato's *Parmenides*
441–39	Samos revolts from Athens, Melissus a Samian general
c.440	**Leucippus** *floruit*
430–29	Plague in Athens, death of Pericles
c.430	**Diogenes of Apollonia** *floruit*
	Philolaus *floruit*
c.428	Plato born
423	Aristophanes' *Clouds* first performed
399	Death of Socrates
384	Aristotle born
c.360	Death of Democritus
c.347	Death of Plato
c.335	Aristotle begins teaching in the Lyceum
c.320–230	Timon of Philus
322	Death of Aristotle
285	Death of Theophrastus
106–43	Cicero

CE

c.50–c.120	Plutarch
1st–2nd century	Aëtius
	Clement of Alexandria
2nd century	Sextus Empiricus
	Dionysius of Corinth
129–c.199	Galen
2nd–3rd century	Eusebius of Caesarea
	Hippolytus of Rome
3rd century	Diogenes Laërtius
4th century	Themistius
5th century	Stobaeus
6th century	Simplicius

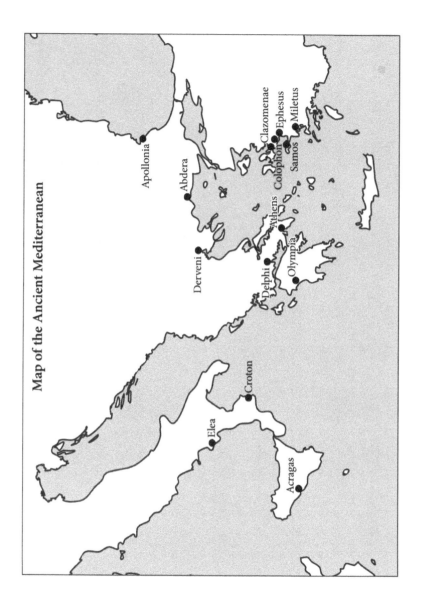

Map of the Ancient Mediterranean

ONE

Introduction: reading Presocratic philosophy

Our primary interest in what follows will be in thinking about early Greek philosophers' views on such topics as the nature and origins of the world, our knowledge of it and how we should act within it. We shall also be interested in thinking about the arguments they offered for these conclusions. But there are some crucial questions and difficulties to be addressed before we can begin, since they bear on the nature of our evidence for early Greek philosophy and the nature of the context in which the early Greek philosophers lived and worked. These factors shaped first the production and then, in turn, the transmission of the philosophy we shall go on to consider, and therefore deserve to be given serious attention.

What is "Presocratic" philosophy'? What does this book include and what does it leave out?

The term "Presocratic" is a modern classification not found in the ancient sources themselves and, although it is still commonly used, some scholars have argued that it ought to be allowed to fall into disuse.[1] Not only is it chronologically inaccurate, since some of those philosophers usually classified as "Presocratic" were contemporaries of Socrates and others, notably Democritus, probably outlived

1

him, but it is potentially misleading in other ways. A full account of all Greek thought in the period up to the death of Socrates in 399 BCE would include a far wider cast of characters than do standard accounts of Presocratic philosophy. It would include not only the Greek cosmologists, but also doctors, poets such as Hesiod, political thinkers such as Solon and Thucydides, teachers of rhetoric and other intellectuals of many different interests, few of whom would conventionally be referred to as "Presocratics". There is no reason to think that a global account of Greek thought to the end of the fifth century BCE could not be written, but it would be a daunting task and I shall not attempt it here. One reason for this refusal is that there are Greek sources who have left us a relatively clear and plausible account of what they took to be the development and history of Greek philosophy. In following their lead, we might indeed produce just one selective history among many possible others, but it would at least have the virtue of following what classical and later ancient writers took to be a plausible and enlightening account. We should note first, therefore, that the Greeks themselves are responsible to a large degree for the production of an account of their own intellectual development and also, it must be emphasized, for the selection of a certain group of thinkers and a certain set of speculations that they chose to single out as "philosophy" rather than, say, "history" or "medicine" (see Nightingale 1995). Of course, we ought also to be aware of the presence of other thinkers and sources of influence outside the cast of characters in the standard modern collection of evidence about Presocratic philosophy, H. Diels and W. Kranz's *Die Fragmente der Vorsokratiker* (usually referred to as DK, first edition by Diels in 1903). However, although they did not refer to anyone as a "Presocratic", ancient writers nevertheless often identify a specific phase in the development of Greek philosophy before Socrates and give a narrative account of its development, characterizing it as driven by some shared general concerns, principally concerns in "natural philosophy": the study of the nature, origin and processes of the natural world. While it would be foolish to follow this ancient historical account slavishly and without critical distance, it would equally be foolish to discount it, either as an informative description of how some ancient philosophers saw their own philosophical heritage or as a plausible – if partial – account of a genuine historical reality.

A further characteristic of these ancient accounts is that they tend to identify phases within the development of philosophy before Socrates, often pointing to Parmenides as an important break in the tradition and the inauguration of a new phase of "post-Parmenidean" cosmologies. In brief, this story of Presocratic philosophy begins with Thales and the other Milesians, who are principally interested in the question of what is the original material principle out of which all things in the universe are made or from which all things originate. (This is sometimes referred to as the *arkhē*: the Greek word for "beginning", which can describe a temporal beginning but also a first principle or cause.) Each Milesian offers a different candidate and goes on to offer a description of how the universe and the workings of the natural world can be explained in these terms. Next, a new movement is inaugurated by Parmenides and the "Eleatic philosophers" Zeno and Melissus, perhaps also inspired by Xenophanes. They are radical monists, claiming that only one thing exists, and also produce arguments that deny the possibility of plurality, coming-to-be and passing-away or change. After the Eleatics come various pluralists – Empedocles, Anaxagoras, Democritus – who accept certain Eleatic strictures such as a ban on any absolute coming-to-be but nevertheless seek to explain the processes of the natural world in terms of the interactions between a set of fundamental existents. They return, in other words, to the Milesian project of natural philosophy but with a more sophisticated metaphysical view generated in reaction to Parmenides and his followers.

This is a very influential story, particularly because it derives to a large extent from the work of the two greatest ancient philosophers, Plato and Aristotle. They both saw that it was important to engage with the work of their philosophical predecessors and, although there were earlier moves to produce accounts of the works or collections of the views of early philosophers, it is the Platonic and Aristotelian tradition that is to a large extent responsible for the view we have inherited of the early period of Greek philosophy (see Mansfeld 1986).[2]

Plato's presentation and reception of early philosophy is complicated further by his choosing to compose philosophical works in the form of dialogues, often set during the lifetime of his own philosophical inspiration, Socrates, and often involving as characters some of the important intellectuals of the time.[3] It is unlikely, for example, that we should ascribe the views of the character "Parmenides" in the dialogue of that name to the real historical Parmenides. Even so, it is hard to imagine that these characters are meant to bear no relation to the historical people concerned, and it is undeniable that Plato's depiction of his predecessors played an important role in creating a history of Greek philosophy and in emphasizing the role of face-to-face discussion, argument and disagreement in its development.[4] Aristotle's treatises offer a more systematic and less dramatic treatment of his predecessors but always in the service of the promotion of his own preferred view. Sometimes he chooses to present these earlier thoughts as partial or mistaken attempts to grasp the full account that he himself provides, so his discussions of his predecessors often come early in his treatises, setting the scene for the explanations to come. See, for example, *Physics* 1.2–9, *Metaphysics* A 3–10, *De anima* 1.2–5. These texts are of critical importance to our understanding of early Greek philosophy for a number of reasons. They are important sources of information about the theories themselves. Further, Aristotle's insistence on the usefulness of gathering together previous views about a given philosophical question was an important stimulus for the production of "doxographic" texts: ancient works that record different philosophers' views on a given question and that are another important source of information. This work was begun by Aristotle's successor as head of the Lyceum, Theophrastus. Also, in later antiquity a number of lengthy commentaries on Aristotle's works were produced. When those commentators – writers such as Simplicius and Philoponus – came to comment on the sections of Aristotle's works that deal with early Greek philosophy, they often tried to elucidate Aristotle's point by including quotations and discussion of those early philosophers. Often, these commentators' works are our principal sources of these fragments and texts. So whatever view we take of Aristotle's reliability as a reporter of early Greek philosophy, his importance to the survival of our evidence is beyond question.[5]

The role played in the transmission of early Greek philosophy by Aristotelian sources, and indeed other sources that are themselves interested in promoting their own philosophical view, has an important consequence. Since accounts such as these, and other writers influenced by such accounts, are themselves often the most important sources of our information about the earlier events they relate and explain, we can fall into the danger of a self-justifying explanatory circle. Our evidence fits the story we are offered fairly neatly, but this is of course because that same evidence has been chosen precisely to do so. Xenophanes, as we shall see, was considered by some later writers to have been a precursor of later sophisticated forms of scepticism. Certainly, later sceptics such as Sextus were fond of citing parts of Xenophanes' work that seem to cast doubt on our chances of achieving clear and sure understanding. What we know about Xenophanes, therefore, is likely to fit with this picture precisely because much of our evidence for Xenophanes is provided by people trying to paint a certain picture of their own philosophical history.

This ancient history of ancient philosophy might well capture some of the processes involved in the complicated story of philosophical thought before Plato. However, although I shall follow the general outline of its course, there are some important weaknesses in its narrative that need to be addressed. First, in emphasizing certain trends in physics and metaphysics, this history misses out or underplays some other important elements to be found in many of these early philosophers, such as the various discussions of questions of what we would call ethics, epistemology and theology. The early Greek philosophers were undoubtedly concerned with ethical and epistemological questions, as was Socrates, and Socrates himself, at least as portrayed by Plato and Xenophon, is not averse to sometimes turning his thoughts to questions of natural philosophy. Even so, Socrates is generally – and perhaps rightly – seen as representing a major change in philosophical concerns.[6]

We face the demanding task of having to deal with two histories: the history of how early Greek philosophy came to be viewed as it was by the philosophers of the classical period and later; and, if we can, the history of early Greek philosophy itself. In what follows, I have tried to assemble an account of early Greek philosophy that retains some of the ancient idea of a narrative of influence between one philosopher and another. I have, for the most part, restricted my interest to writers and thinkers who would be conventionally termed "Presocratic", without any particular commitment to the importance of that term besides its traditional convenience. My interest extends beyond questions of physics and cosmology into what, in the face of often very limited evidence, we might say about their related epistemological, theological and – to a lesser extent – ethical interests, in part because these are areas of enquiry that are captured now by the notoriously difficult to define practice of "philosophy".[7] Medicine, history, political theory and the like were no doubt also being explored and discussed at this time, sometimes by these very same "philosophers", but I shall leave it to others to give an account of those developments. I have also chosen not to extend my story to include the group of thinkers often referred to as "Sophists", such as Protagoras, Gorgias, Antiphon, Prodicus and the like.[8] Their interests are primarily political and ethical, and they often focus on questions of persuasion, rhetoric, justice and power. Although there are clear continuities between their thoughts and some of the philosophers I shall consider – Democritus, for example – they can also be seen as marking a new and distinct philosophical moment, and the most illuminating context in which to place them is among the familiar discussions of Athens in the classical period: its historians, playwrights and poets, and, most notable of all, Socrates himself.[9]

How do we know about early Greek philosophy?

There are a number of further difficulties to be faced by anyone attempting to offer a history of early Greek philosophy and also by anyone who is not so interested in the history of philosophy as such, but nevertheless wants to find reliable sources of information about the ideas and arguments of early Greek philosophers. First, we have to contend with the usual absence of sources and barriers of language and culture that plague any investigation of an ancient society. Often, the translation and interpretation of the remains of these early Greek philosophers is extremely contentious, not only for the reasons that make any translation from ancient Greek difficult, but also because with so little surviving of many of these thinkers it is often difficult to test a particular understanding of a term or phrase by comparison with other instances or uses by the same author. Further, philosophy at this period has not developed a set of shared and commonly understood technical terminology for certain concepts or ideas. The translations I offer here are my own, but readers should be warned that when it comes to the interpretation and translation of Presocratic philosophy there is very little that is not subject to doubt and debate.

Secondly, much of early Greek history can be accessed only through the histories created by successive generations of Greek writers.[10] The same goes for the early history of Greek philosophy. We have no complete works by these early philosophers, and most of what we do have of their works is in the form either of "fragments" – quotations in later ancient writers and other surviving small sections of what we take to be the original works – or else "reports" or "testimonia" – second-hand information from later writers who sometimes had access to much more of the original text than we have. In DK this distinction is marked by labelling testimonia as "A" sources and fragments (printed in larger type) as "B" sources.[11] Each philosopher is given a number according to a rough chronological order. Historians are familiar with working with a distinction between "primary" and "secondary" evidence in constructing interpretations of the past and these two categories are closely analogous to the "fragment–testimony" distinction. There are some important complications, however, for the historian of Greek philosophy. Most importantly, it is not always clear what is a fragment and what is a report. Ancient authors were not always entirely clear or scrupulous about marking what is a quotation and what is not and, furthermore, were not entirely averse to altering the wording of an early philosopher even when they intended to "quote" him. Further, even those pieces of information we are happy to accept as fragments have already been chosen and excerpted from a larger work by an intervening source. This is an essential point to keep in mind whenever reading and thinking about these texts, but it is all too easy to forget about when using collections of fragments or reports in modern textbooks and editions.[12]

For example, DK 21 A 33 is a report about Xenophanes from the Christian Hippolytus of Rome's late-second–early-third-century CE work, *The Refutation of all Histories* (*Ref.* 1.14.1). It is a claim about Xenophanes' view on the possibility of knowledge "Xenophanes first declared the incomprehensibility of all things, by saying …" (B34, 3.4). The reference at the end shows that at this point Hippolytus supported his claim with a brief quotation from Xenophanes' poetry, lines 3 and 4 of fragment DK 21 B34: "For even if someone should particularly happen to say what has occurred, all the same he would not himself know it. But opinion covers all." What weight should we give to this report? There is certainly some anachronism in play since the term Hippolytus uses that is translated here as "incomprehensibility" is *akatalēpsia*, a technical term in the epistemological theory of the Stoics, which was developed more than two hundred years after Xenophanes' time. We might therefore be concerned that Hippolytus has failed to be sensitive to the possibility that Xenophanes' concerns may not have mapped neatly onto this later set of ideas. What about the quotation? It is certainly a genuine piece of Xenophanes' poetry, but in this case we can compare Hippolytus with another source, the second-century CE sceptic Sextus Empiricus, who chooses to give us the two preceding lines as well. Sextus quotes the four-line snippet (which forms DK 21 B34) three times in his *Against the Professors* (*M*) at 7.49, 7.110 and 8.326.

> And as far as what is clear, no man has seen nor will there be any man who knows about the gods and what I say about all things. For even if someone should particularly happen to say what has occurred, all the same he would not himself know it. But opinion covers all.

Immediately, we might wonder if the preceding lines limit the scope of what Hippolytus took to be a statement about our most general inability to reach the truth, since Xenophanes seems to be talking about theological questions and the topics covered in his work. And once we have become worried about Hippolytus' selective quotation, it is hard not to become concerned that Sextus too may be playing the same sort of game. What were the next two lines of Xenophanes' poem? Sextus himself notes that there were two competing interpretations of what Xenophanes means, both using these four lines as evidence. Some people took him to say that no one has any sure access to truth, while others took him to be recommending that we make do with a certain kind of understanding, here called "opinion", and give up on a more certain or more accurate sort. We might like to think that ancient writers could be useful guides to the thought of these early philosophers, but it is clear that they were often just as divided in their interpretations as modern scholars. And we are in the unfortunate position of often relying on authors such as Hippolytus and Sextus not only for reports about these philosophers, but also for the transmissions of the texts themselves. Great care needs to be taken, therefore, in assessing our evidence and we should remember in particular that "primary" texts too, with very few exceptions, have passed through some process of selective quotation.

How was early Greek philosophy produced and communicated?

Histories of philosophy often make claims of the form "Plato was influenced by Parmenides" or "Aristotle responded to the arguments of Plato". Often this is justified by explicit statements to that effect by the philosophers involved, whether in the work being considered or in some other source of information such as their private correspondence. Similar claims are made about early Greek philosophers and, indeed, have been since the history of Greek philosophy began to be written in classical Greece. They are important for the presentation of a kind of tradition or narrative of philosophy's development, and I shall make some such claims in what follows. But, at least for the earliest phases of what is conventionally imagined to be the history of Greek philosophy, it is not immediately clear what such claims amount to because it is not easy to see how philosophers exerted influence over one another when they often came from different parts of the Greek world and were working in the absence of any institutionalized philosophical or academic network. There were no formal schools of philosophy in this period and no philosophical conferences. For some commentators, no doubt, claims of influence are justified simply by an interpretation of the remaining fragments of these philosophers' works and comments by other ancient authors, whether or not there is any direct supporting evidence. So, for example, one might say that it is evident that Democritus' atomism is in part a response to Zeno's paradoxes of divisibility, even though there is no direct evidence that Democritus himself said that it was, simply because of the clear relationship between their ideas. It makes immediate and satisfying sense to infer some influence or relationship between the two.[13]

What basis do we have for any such claims about early Greek philosophers? To answer this, and before we press on and consider what these early Greek philosophers did think and say, it is important to place them into some kind of context. We can approach this task by asking some more material questions about the context of the dissemination of ideas and works in the period of early Greek philosophical history (roughly 600–430 BCE). How did these philosophers find out about one another's ideas? How widely were these ideas disseminated and in what form? In trying to answer such questions I hope to illustrate the general context in which philosophical ideas and works moved about the Greek world.

The ancient sources themselves are not altogether helpful in accounting for relationships of influence between philosophers. Much of our information comes from later ancient authors who were already working within a model that saw Greek philosophy in terms of traditions of thought handed from one philosopher to another as master to pupil. They often simply refer to some philosopher being a "pupil" (the term they use translates literally as "hearer") of another. This mode of thinking certainly has its roots in a view of philosophical influence being based in direct personal contact but there is little reason to accept any of these claims unless we have other independent reasons to think that the philosophers involved did indeed know each other.[14]

Explicit references to one another in the works of these philosophers are relatively rare, even given the fragmentary nature of much of our evidence. Generally speaking, ancient philosophers often couched their frequently serious disagreements with one another in general terms by citing "those who say that ..." or using some similar formula rather than naming names. Others simply argued an alternative view, perhaps borrowing the odd apposite phrase from a rival and turning it to their own ends. Some references are telling, however, because they remind us that these writers often saw themselves competing with a wider group of authorities than we might initially imagine. In particular, they remind us that they were competing not only with other philosophers but also with poets – especially the traditional authorities, Homer and Hesiod – and with other experts too, including doctors.[15] Heraclitus, for example, abuses Xenophanes along with Hesiod, Pythagoras and Hecataeus (DK 22 B40). Xenophanes himself has no time for Homer and Hesiod (DK 21 B11). The author of the Hippocratic treatise *The Nature of Man* (§1) has little time for those who support the argument of Melissus, and the author of *On Ancient Medicine* is similarly scathing about Empedocles. But such cases are still quite rare. More common are reports of such attacks: Xenophanes may also have attacked Thales and Pythagoras (Diog. Laert. 9.18); Democritus, we are told, joined Plato in thinking that Protagoras' relativism was confused (DK 68 A114, B156). It is hard to think that these authors were not at least sometimes reacting to one another, but they do not often make a feature of naming or explicitly tackling specific opponents or arguments. As a result, claims about influence or disagreement must often rely on our interpretations of the content of the respective philosophies rather than on any clear external evidence.[16]

One further important feature of philosophical production at this time needs to be recognized. Some early Greek philosophers were happy to produce works in prose and others were equally happy to compose in verse. The reasons for the coexistence of the two forms are complicated and it is best when approaching this question to think first in terms of what a particular choice of form would contribute to the philosophical agenda of each individual philosopher rather than to attempt to offer more generalized explanations in terms of geographical location or a consistent development over time.[17] A range of factors combine to form the overall picture. There is, as we have already noted, a complicated relationship between early Greek philosophy and other authoritative texts composed in various forms, including poetry such as that by Homer and Hesiod and also prose works such as the Hippocratic treatises and, later, rhetorical and sophistic works. In addition, we should note the probable performance context of many of these philosophical works and the gradual emergence over time of a tradition of philosophical writing that could be embraced or rejected. Each philosopher could choose a medium to fit his particular needs and the content of his message, and in doing so he positioned himself in relation to the competition and his predecessors. In choosing to write in prose, for example, Melissus is presumably orienting himself once more towards the tradition of prose treatises on nature such as those composed by Anaximander, even though it is clear that the prime inspiration for the content of his work is Parmenides' poem.

Despite there being little direct evidence of contact between early Greek philosophers we can nevertheless build up a persuasive picture of intellectual life and the traffic of ideas, at least for the period of the middle-to-late-fifth century BCE.[18] Let us start by looking closely at two well-known episodes from Plato's dialogues of what we might call the mechanics of transmission of early Greek philosophy. Between them, they can illustrate some of the most likely means by which the ideas of early Greek philosophers were publicized and became disseminated.

Plato's *Phaedo* is set in 399 BCE. In it, Socrates explains how he came to know about the details of Anaxagoras' philosophy. The passage is well-known, particularly for the explanation that Socrates gives for his dissatisfaction with Anaxagoras' views, but I want to take from it certain details about the availability and access to Anaxagoras' work that Socrates mentions (see Pepe 2002).

Socrates says that he had become perplexed about the right kind of explanation to offer in questions of natural philosophy. In his youth, he confesses, it seemed right to attribute the growth of people to their intake of food and the acquisition of the right sort of matter. He also admits to having accepted various explanations for differences in size: one man is larger than another "by a head"; a ten-cubit length is longer than an eight-cubit length because it has had two cubits added; and so on. He further admits that he no longer finds such explanations satisfactory. As part of this process of rethinking he recounts the story of his encounter with Anaxagoras. Anaxagoras' philosophy initially appealed because it seemed to refer causal explanations to some sort of intelligence, but on closer inspection Socrates was disappointed by the lack of use made by Anaxagoras of this explanatory principle. We shall consider the details of Anaxagoras' philosophy later (see pp. 119ff.), but for now let us concentrate on some of the details of Socrates' story. The episode refers to two distinct means by which Socrates came to know about Anaxagoras' philosophy. At first his interest was kindled when, he says, "One day I heard someone reading aloud (in Greek: *anagignōskontos*) from a book of Anaxagoras and saying that it is Mind which arranges and is responsible for everything" (97b8–c2). After offering a lengthy description of the hopes this stirred up in him, Socrates then explains: "I got hold of his books with great eagerness and read [for this Plato uses the same verb: *anegignōskon*] them as quickly as I could so that I could find out as soon as possible what was for the better and what for the worse" (98b4–6).[19] So Socrates first hears someone reading, or perhaps performing, some of Anaxagoras' work but manages to catch only some of the content: enough for him to imagine Anaxagoras as the kind of natural philosopher he would admire. Later he manages to get hold of the works himself and study them more thoroughly.

Evidently, for someone like Socrates, literate and educated, it was economically and practically possible to acquire the books of Anaxagoras. It is difficult, of course, to date when this episode is supposed to have taken place but, given Socrates' famous reluctance to travel outside his home city, we are to assume that it took place in Athens.

It seems to be later than the phase of Socrates' youthful acceptance of explanations that make no reference to the value of the product of any causal interaction, since Socrates is by this time pleased to find someone like-minded in the Anaxagoras he hears about. He has already, therefore, begun to find simple material explanations less satisfying than he once did. Let us say, then, that Socrates is at least twenty years old. Taking his date of birth as 469 BCE, that gives us a *terminus post quem* of 449. Anaxagoras' period of activity in Athens (if we believe Demetrius of Phalerum in Diog. Laert. 2.7) can be dated to the middle of the fifth century BCE.[20] I think it is likely, therefore, that Socrates heard someone talking about Anaxagoras' work at a time when Anaxagoras himself had already left Athens, but perhaps quite recently. The fact that Anaxagoras had spent some time there, perhaps very recently, is sufficient to explain the presence of someone in Athens discussing his thought and also the apparent availability of the text of his work. But it is also clear that whomever Socrates heard, it was not Anaxagoras himself giving a lecture, but someone else.[21]

We would like to know more about who this person was. Socrates gives no indication about his status and no clues about the context in which he heard the reading. But for the remainder of his story to be plausible, we must imagine that Socrates did not on this first occasion hear enough about Anaxagoras to know that his hopes for a certain kind of teleological explanation were going to be dashed. He heard some of Anaxagoras' work, or perhaps some parts or claims taken from it, but not the whole thing. Bearing all that in mind, we are left with possibilities ranging from a public recitation, some of which Socrates heard while walking past (perhaps a recitation specifically designed to advertise the availability of copies of Anaxagoras' books), to a more private gathering at which Anaxagoras' work was read or performed, much as we imagine some kinds of poetry being performed at elite meetings. There are some clues that might help further. Socrates first hears someone reading "from a book" (*ek bibliou*: 97b8) but later gets hold of Anaxagoras' books (*biblious*: 98b4) (see Sider 2005: 19–21). Perhaps the original recitation was from one part of the work, or else from a précis or condensed version, while

Socrates later acquired the full work, which ran to more than one papyrus roll. If that is right, then we can imagine the original occasion less as a performance of Anaxagoras' work in its entirety and more as a trailer or advertisement for the work as a whole, perhaps focusing on the central arresting theses, the role of *nous* ("Mind") undoubtedly being one.

The second part of the story gives Socrates the occasion to study Anaxagoras in more detail through a proper look at the text itself. Socrates does not tell us here how he acquired the works, nor whether they were costly or difficult to find. We might suspect that the casual way in which he tells his friends that he got hold of them suggests that it was relatively easy. This suspicion is supported by Socrates' comment in the *Apology* (26d–e) that Anaxagoras' books are available "in the market place from time to time for a drachma at most". We do not know whether Socrates himself purchased Anaxagoras' books or merely borrowed them.[22] Still, texts were clearly available. Socrates quite easily found copies in his relative youth and they were still occasionally available at the time of his trial in 399 BCE. They could, however, be pricey: a drachma is about the daily wage for a skilled labourer at this time and Socrates is probably underestimating the likely cost of the book (see Sider 2005: 12–13).

Anaxagoras had spent a considerable period of time in Athens when it was reaching the height of its influence, drawing intellectuals of various sorts from all over the Mediterranean, many of whom people Plato's dialogues. These works often portray visits to Athens by Sophists and orators such as Gorgias and Protagoras, who, in the dialogue named after him, is accompanied on his visit by a host of other intellectual celebrities (*Prot.* 315a–d). These visits seem to have been sufficiently infrequent to cause a stir among the Athenian intellectuals keen to meet the visiting thinkers (at *Prot.* 310e–311a, Hippocrates is very excited to hear of Protagoras' visit; Hippocrates was still a young boy when Protagoras last came to Athens).

In the second of the episodes I want to look at in more detail, the philosopher Parmenides travels to Athens, accompanied by Zeno. Whether or not this is a historically accurate meeting is irrelevant for our purposes; what matters more is that it was plausible to Plato's audience to think of someone like Parmenides travelling across the Mediterranean and spending time in Athens and for someone like Zeno to have given a personal performance of his work.

The opening to Plato's *Parmenides* gives us another snapshot of intellectual commerce in the fifth century. Parmenides and Zeno have come to Athens at the time of the festival of the Great Panathenaia and are staying at the house of the Athenian Pythodorus (*Parm.* 127b–c). We are also told that the two have brought Zeno's book to Athens for the first time and that Zeno is finishing a performance of his work when Socrates arrives at Pythodorus' house. It is reasonable to assume that the visit by the Eleatic pair has been arranged to coincide with the Great Panathenaia, a major civic and religious festival that took place every four years and involved dramatic and musical competitions, processions, athletics and, evidently, performances and recitations of various forms of literary and technical works including medical works, the likes of Herodotus' *Histories*, and even Zeno's prose treatise of paradoxes.[23] (The likely date of this episode is the Panathenaia of 450, when Socrates was 18 or 19 years old, perhaps not far in date from Socrates' exposure to Anaxagoras' thought.) We are certainly to imagine that Zeno had been giving other performances of his work in addition to this private performance for his host, Pythodorus, and certain select friends. Pythodorus, for one, is said to have heard Zeno's performance already (127d) and, we learn elsewhere, he had paid Zeno for his instruction the princely sum of 100 minae (Plato *Alcib. I* 119a; this is equivalent to 10,000 drachmae – enough to buy many copies of Anaxagoras' work).[24] The performance seems to consist in a recitation of the book, which is then followed by a discussion prompted by a question from Socrates, the resulting conversation forming the rest of the dialogue. It is unclear whether this kind of question-and-answer session commonly followed such performances or whether Socrates is unusual in demanding a more dialectical engagement with Zeno himself. All the same, this is a private gathering among friends, which forms the context for a philosophical interchange. This private gathering is itself mirrored in the dramatic setting of the dialogue in which Cephalus, a visitor to Athens from Clazomenae, asks his friends Adeimantus and Glaucon to take him and some fellow philosophers to Antiphon, who is asked to recount the story of Parmenides' visit.

The *Parmenides* episode concentrates on the direct personal exchange of ideas. Parmenides and Zeno are companions and, to some extent, master and pupil. They travel the Greek world teaching, for which they receive a handsome payment, and presenting their work to gatherings ranging from intimate *soirées* such as aristocratic symposia to public festivals.[25] Such presentations no doubt served to enhance their reputation and attract paying customers.[26] Indeed, some of the works by these philosophers may have been composed for and dedicated to a patron. But the *Parmenides* episode also adds other details to the picture from the *Phaedo* of the circulation of ideas through the medium of texts. Zeno complains that he composed his work while still young, but someone made a copy without his permission and his work began to circulate before he himself had decided whether it should "see the light" (*Parm.* 128d–e) (see Nagy 2002: 95–6). This complaint is the cue for Socrates to make a clever joke about the problems of the relationship between unities and pluralities – here the many copies of a single work – of just the sort played on by Zeno's own paradoxes, but once again the story must be plausible even if fictitious. It is a useful reminder that the copying and distribution of these texts was often outside the author's own control and certainly was not going to bring the author himself any income. Any money to be earned would come from direct personal contact, performance and tutoring. It is extremely difficult, however, to gauge the size and nature of the audience of such works just as it is difficult to know whether the authors constantly revised their works, added detail and explanation to them when giving public recitations, answered questions or added qualifications.[27] We might be tempted to imagine Athens constantly full of robed intellectuals debating the latest ideas, but it is more likely that the proportion of the Athenian population interested enough and wealthy enough to have the time for such things was very small.

These two episodes, it must be admitted, come from works by Plato, who was writing up to one hundred years after the dramatic date of these dialogues, so we might be cautious in accepting them as accurate portrayals of even the fifth century. And, it must be stressed, we would do well not to insist on the historical accuracy of any of the particular events they depict. But it is hard to think that anything significant had changed in that time concerning the means by which philosophical ideas were disseminated. We can take from them a general picture of itinerant philosophers, whose works were known by a combination of personal performance and teaching and the circulation of written texts.

Athens' cultural dominance in the middle of the fifth century made it a focal point for exchange of all kinds, the exchange of ideas included. And despite the dangers and difficulties of travel at this time there seems to have been a high degree of mobility, certainly among the more elite members of Greek society. Travel to other cities, to Pan-Hellenic festivals and religious sites, was relatively common. In addition, the often turbulent relations between the Greek city-states and the resulting conflicts would have added to movement across the Mediterranean. Indeed, war might even account for one of the more intriguing cases of philosophical influence between these philosophers. It is agreed that Melissus of Samos' work is heavily indebted to Parmenides' work, even though Parmenides came from Italy and Melissus from an island off the coast of Turkey. Within ten years or so, Parmenides' work reached the ears of Melissus and prompted him to write a work in response. We can leave for a later chapter the discussion of the philosophical nature of this influence, but for now let us wonder about how it came to be applied. Perhaps, given the picture of mobility in the fifth century, it is not implausible to think that the two men met somewhere, perhaps at another Pan-Hellenic festival. Melissus was certainly a prominent Samian citizen and features as a general during his city's revolt from Athens in 441–39 BCE (see Plut. *Per.* 26 and Thucydides 1.115.2–117 [DK 30 A3]). His dealings with Athens would, in all likelihood, have led him there at some time and, if the picture that has been emerging so far is correct, Athens would be an appropriate location to hear or acquire works such as Parmenides' poem. As the fifth century proceeded and Athens' influence spread, it must have attracted from across the Mediterranean writers and poets keen to publicize their ideas and also those interested in hearing them and studying with them. Athens' pre-eminence as a philosophical centre therefore predates the founding of Plato's Academy and Aristotle's Lyceum. It was just the place for Melissus to find out about Parmenides.

We can in this way offer a picture of the intellectual life of the mid-fifth century BCE. But we still need to ask whether the scene was any different a hundred years earlier, when the first of our early Greek philosophers were working. For the sixth century our evidence is even less rich than for the fifth. We are mostly left with reports from much later authors, many of whom are undoubtedly creating or propagating more or less fictional stories about the lives of these earliest thinkers. There are plenty of stories of them travelling or meeting and being taught by various characters, none of which can be relied on to any great extent. It is clear nevertheless that in this period the cities of Asia Minor, the west coast of modern Turkey, enjoyed many of the characteristics that later made Athens such a successful cultural centre. Cities such as Miletus were wealthy and well connected with the Greek cities to the west as well as with Phoenicia and Egypt to the south and Lydia and Persia to the east. Indeed, it is reasonable to think that this location, which exposed the population of Miletus to goods and ideas from various cultures, coupled with economic prosperity and the attendant leisure it provides, is one of the factors responsible for the growth in new kinds of speculation.[28] It is therefore not altogether surprising that three of the earliest thinkers identified by the ancient sources as members of a philosophical tradition – Thales, Anaximander and Anaximenes – were all from this city. No doubt there is a certain momentum created once someone is thought to have instigated a new approach to thinking about the world, which, coupled with a general tendency to competition and dissent, would quickly generate a series of competing theories all hoping to outdo one another. Some have also suggested that a growing sense of debate about questions of political authority, perhaps fuelled by an emerging new wealthy but non-aristocratic class, contributed to the growing air of speculation and a search for explanation (Lloyd 1987: 78–83; Osborne 1996: 315–18). Contact between these Milesians will quite probably have been direct and personal. Miletus, although relatively impressive, was not a large city by modern standards and we can imagine that any prominent thinkers would have known each other. The sixth century is also a period of increasing use of written and inscriptional texts and, we can suggest, a growing spread of literacy.[29] Even so, we should not overestimate the role played by written texts; there were certainly occasions for travel and the Pan-Hellenic festivals and competitions had been taking place since at least the eighth century BCE, providing opportunities for reaching beyond the confines of one's own city and for face-to-face meetings with people from across the Mediterranean.[30] Any written texts these early thinkers produced, again most likely combined with public performances of some kind, would in this early period presumably have had a limited circulation. Xenophanes apparently would perform his own poetry (Diog. Laert. 9.18) and tradition has it that Anaximander was the first to produce a written treatise (Themistius *Or.* 36.317 [DK 12 A7]). Of course, once later generations had become convinced of their importance, copies, selections, quotations and summaries would be acquired and retained by antiquarians and historians, but there is little reason to imagine any widespread dissemination of ideas in solely written form at an early stage. Even later, there was no guarantee that a work would remain available throughout antiquity. In the sixth century CE, Simplicius explains that he needs to cite extensively from Parmenides' poem since copies are rare (Simpl. *In Phys.* 144.25 [DK 28 A21]). Nevertheless, we might note there are some stories (however unfounded) in later ancient writers about the circulation of texts by early philosophers. Heraclitus is said to have deposited a copy of his work in the temple of Artemis in his home of Ephesus, hoping that this would deter all but the most serious and dedicated readers. We are also told that Socrates was given a copy of Heraclitus' book by Euripides and that it was first brought to Greece by a man called Crates.[31]

The end of the sixth century brought a period of significant instability to the region as Persia and the Greek cities began to come into conflict. The Ionian cities eventually revolted against the Persians in 499 BCE and the region was in turmoil for some five years until the Persians' eventual victory.[32] The Persian victory cost some cities dearly: Miletus, for example, was sacked and much of the city had to be rebuilt. Coupled with the growing influence of Athens, the problems in Asia Minor probably contributed to a reorientation of philosophical influence further west, to Athens and the cities of Italy, but the north and east of the Aegean still produced important figures in the fifth century, including Melissus and Democritus. The story of Xenophanes' decision to move from his native Colophon in Asia Minor to Italy and Sicily also has a ring of truth to it, even allowing that it offers a convenient link between him and the next in this perceived tradition of philosophers, Parmenides (See Diog. Laert. 9.18 [DK 21 A1]). Pythagoras is said to have made a similar move from his native Samos to Italy.

This, in brief, is the picture we have of the way in which these various thinkers worked and found out about one another's ideas. The ideas themselves have made them interesting to people from antiquity to the present and it is to those ideas we should now turn.

TWO

Ionian beginnings

Thales of Miletus, the "first philosopher"

"Philosophy", declared Bertrand Russell, "begins with Thales" (1961: 25).[1] Many ancient writers would have agreed, and it is presumably their decision to start the history of Greek philosophy with Thales that is reflected in Russell's judgement. This honour was also awarded to Thales by none other than Aristotle who, in turn, is responsible for a great deal of our picture of the interests and theories of the very earliest Greek philosophers. For his part, Diogenes Laërtius also accepts that Anaximander, Thales' pupil, founded the "Ionian" tradition of philosophy, which takes in Anaxagoras, Socrates, Plato and the Academy, but adds Pythagoras as another source for the "Italian" tradition of Parmenides, Democritus and on to Epicurus (Diog. Laert. 1.13–15).

We shall come to consider Aristotle's treatment of Thales very shortly. Before we do so, it is important to pause and note how difficult it is to draw a strict and satisfying distinction between Thales and what we know of even earlier Greek thought. This difficulty is not only due to the usual problem of a lack of sources; it is also based in the thought that Thales may count as the first Greek philosopher only on the basis of a conception of the history of Greek philosophy we have inherited from writers such as Aristotle who were themselves keen to carve both an ancestry and clear area of thought and authority for their own discipline. In any case, what we know of earlier Greek accounts of the universe in the form of poetic works such as Hesiod's *Theogony* and the Orphic hymns or prose works such as Pherecydes' *Theology* and also Near Eastern works suggests that the speculations of the "Milesian philosophers" are as much the continuation and development of a longer tradition of ancient thought as the beginning of something altogether new.[2] Evidently, the close relationship between Orphic or other theological accounts and cosmology continued through to the fifth century. One of the most intriguing and exciting recent discoveries in ancient philosophy, a papyrus excavated from a fifth-century tomb at Derveni in Northern Greece, is a philosophical commentary on an Orphic poem. It gives an allegorical interpretation of a poetic theogony explaining in the process a detailed cosmological account using ideas heavily reminiscent of a number of known Presocratic thinkers, including Heraclitus (who is quoted), Anaxagoras and Diogenes of Apollonia.[3] The persistence throughout antiquity of stories about the early philosophers' travels to Egypt and the Near East undoubtedly reflects some notion of a dependence of their ideas on other older cultures and traditions and quite possibly preserves a kernel of truth.[4]

Indeed, Aristotle too is prepared to look back even beyond Thales. After his first discussion of Thales' ideas (*Met.* A 3, 983b18ff.), he considers the first "theologians" of nature who – according to some – were the first to approach these questions. Perhaps they were, Aristotle concedes, but what they had to say is very unclear. In any case, Aristotle's choice of terminology is revealing. These "theologians" were presumably, like Hesiod, prepared to invoke divine, probably anthropomorphic, agents in their accounts. Such agents are notably absent from early Ionian cosmology, perhaps reflecting a deliberate decision on the part of Thales and the others to move away from cosmologies based on divine genealogies and anthropomorphic gods.[5] From Thales, at least, we have some clear indication of interest in what Aristotle is happy to call "philosophical" matters. Aristotle introduces him as the paradigm case of a shared method of enquiry, which he traces through most of early Greek philosophy, up to and including the atomists.

> Most of the first philosophers thought that the only sources (*arkhai*) of all things were in the form of matter (*hylē*). From this all things are and come to be and into this finally all things perish, but this being remains while changing in its properties. They say that this is the element (*stoicheion*) and this is the source (*arkhē*) of all that exists, and because of it they think that nothing comes to be or passes away, as though this sort of nature were always preserved ...
>
> (*Met.* 983b6–13)

> But they do not all say the same thing about the number and form of such a source (*arkhē*). Thales, for example, the leader and originator (*arkhēgos*) of this kind of philosophy, says that it is water. Perhaps he got this idea from seeing that everything is nourished by what is moist and that heat itself comes from it and lives by it (thinking that the source (*arkhē*) of all things is that from which they come to be); perhaps he said it for that reason, plus the fact that the seeds of all things are naturally moist, and water is the source (*arkhē*) of the nature of moist things.   (*Met.* 983b18–27)

This is a very important and influential passage.[6] It begins by outlining what Aristotle took to be the general project of early Greek philosophy as the search for the *arkhē* (or, in the plural, *arkhai*) of all things. This term, which I have translated as "source", is difficult to render well in English, since it can mean a beginning and origin not only in a temporal sense, but also in an explanatory or causal sense. It is also the word used to denote a political office or power of control. Aristotle understands the early Greek philosophers to be involved in an enquiry into what is the most fundamental and everlasting matter out of which all things are composed and into which they all eventually decay, which is itself present throughout the various intermediate processes of change. We might imagine this as an enquiry into what is the most fundamental stuff out of which everything is made. In that case, these early Greek philosophers are engaged in what we might recognize as a physical or perhaps even metaphysical enquiry, concerning themselves with questions of the nature and mode of existence of all things and attempting to account for them in terms of the modifications of something that is ontologically fundamental. Of course, much of Aristotle's explanation rests on his own conceptions of the correct method of physical enquiry and the correct method for explaining change. Aristotle groups the Milesians together as all supposing that the specification of the matter (*hylē*) of all things could exhaust what was required for a full understanding of nature and change. He can then declare that all these early philosophers share the common fault of omitting other essential explanatory factors: the other three of what we call Aristotle's "four causes", namely "form", the "efficient" or "moving cause", and the "final cause" or goal of a process of change. Yet despite their failings, Aristotle is nevertheless willing to present his own philosophy as the culmination of a tradition of thought that these early philosophers instigated.

The other important note of caution is that the explanation offered here of Thales' reasons for saying that water is the *arkhē* are the result of Aristotle's own speculative reconstruction. Aristotle, it appears, does not have Thales' own account of his process of reasoning and must rely on a certain amount of guesswork. That guesswork is based on the notion that somehow all things – and, most importantly, all living things – originate in water. Perhaps Thales had therefore offered some kind of cosmogonical account, or a description of the development of the cosmos and the various things in it from water. The overall impression is that Aristotle has had to produce his own interpretation and reconstruction of Thales' thought in order to fit him into his framework for the history and development of this species of metaphysical investigation. For all we know, Thales may have been much less interested in ontological claims about what is the fundamental material component of all things than in a naturalist's idea that all living things originated – perhaps long ago – in water.[7] Certainly, many of the early Greek philosophers considered it necessary to give some account of the origin of life and in doing so may well have been following a tradition of which Thales was also a part.

Thales is also noted for two further views that were thought sufficiently interesting by our sources to be worth discussion.[8] First, he is said to have claimed that the earth "rests on water", floating like a log on a pond.[9] Once again, the apparent stability of the earth became one of the phenomena for which any self-respecting natural philosopher had to have an explanation and here Thales is seen as giving the first, albeit naive, philosophical contribution to the debate by referring once again to his *arkhē*: water. As Aristotle is quick to note, Thales apparently felt no need to explain what, in turn, the water rested on. Secondly, Thales is supposed to have inferred from the ability of magnets to induce motion in themselves and in certain other rocks through repulsion and attraction that certain conventionally labelled "inanimate" objects also contain souls (Aristot. *De an.* 405a19ff. [DK 11 A22]).[10] It is even possible that he drew the stronger conclusion that everything in the universe contained soul or, in the words of another report, that "everything is full of gods" (Aristot. *De an.* 411a7 [DK 11 A22]).[11] If this is indeed a correct account of Thales' view, we can infer something about his method of argument. He begins with the observation of certain magnetic phenomena. He then, we might guess, adds the idea that only those things that are alive, or that possess a soul, are able to originate motion in themselves or in other things. From these premises, the conclusion naturally follows that magnets must be alive or possess a soul. And if one form of rock possesses a soul then there is no reason to think that any other kind of rock should not also. Perhaps he even thought along the lines of the following argument: if even a rock – which one might easily think is apparently the most inanimate sort of thing – can be seen to possess the properties of an animate being, then surely everything else must also.

Our other information about Thales is consistent with the picture of him as someone interested generally in explaining natural phenomena rather than a metaphysician. We are told that he was able to predict an eclipse (probably that of 585 BCE) and that he once predicted a bumper olive crop and was able to corner the market in olive presses, making a considerable profit.[12] Both stories, whether or not they are accurate, show a particular interest in astronomy and the awareness of regular astronomical and meteorological cycles.[13] His predictions are derived not from traditional cultic and religious practices of divination but from observation and something verging on a mathematical understanding of the order and motions of heavenly bodies.[14] Indeed, this interest in the heavens is emphasized by Plato, who uses Thales as the paradigm image of a philosopher so engaged in studying what is above his head that he ignores what is at his feet. In Thales' case, this other-worldliness led to him falling into a well: a nice illustration of Plato's general claim about the philosopher seeming out of place in the everyday common-sense world (*Theaetetus* 174a [DK 11 A9]). No doubt, as Thales' position as "the first philosopher" became more entrenched, such anecdotes would have accumulated around him simply as reflections of popular ideas of what "a philosopher" is like. He even acquired the status of being listed as one of the seven sages of early Greece, alongside such luminaries as the Athenian political reformer Solon, and purveyors of wise and noble maxims such as Cleobolus of Rhodes and Chilon of Sparta.[15] (This status as one of the "wise" is the reason why Diogenes Laërtius refuses to class Thales as a "philosopher" – literally, a lover of and, by implication, a seeker after wisdom – strictly speaking, and instead calls Anaximander the first Ionian philosopher; see Warren, 2007.)

Anaximander

Miletus must have been an exciting place in the sixth century BCE. Its prosperity and location made it an economic and cultural force in the Mediterranean and soon it became the home of natural philosophy. Not long after Thales, two more natural philosophers offered their own competing accounts of the universe. The first of these, Anaximander, is responsible for what is perhaps the oldest surviving fragment of Greek philosophical writing. Our information about him fits him neatly into the framework outlined by Aristotle, since he too seems to have offered an *arkhē*, from which all the cosmos was formed. The fragment, preserved by Simplicius, who in turn is probably depending on Theophrastus, is introduced as follows:

> Anaximander ... said that the *arkhē* and element (*stoicheion*) of things that are is the boundless (*apeiron*). (He was the first to use this term.) But he says that it is neither water nor any other of the supposed elements, but a different and boundless nature from which come all the heavens and all the cosmoses within them. From the things from which comes the coming-to-be of things that are, into those same things comes passing-away according to necessity: "For they pay the penalty and recompense of injustice to one another according to the ordering of time." (Here he is speaking in rather poetic terms.)   (Simpl. *In Phys.* 24,13ff. [DK 12 A9])

As with many supposed fragments, both the authenticity and the extent of the quotation are subject to some dispute, but the fact that Simplicius draws attention to Anaximander's chosen form of diction implies that at least some of the preceding lines use Anaximander's own words.[16] (Anaximander did not write in verse. Simplicius presumably means to draw attention to the picturesque and – to his mind – metaphorical use of the language of justice and recompense in a cosmological account.)

If Anaximander himself is responsible for the specification that his chosen *arkhē* is not water, then it is tempting to see this as a deliberate and hostile response to Thales. And it is clear that Anaximander offered a much more sophisticated account than his Milesian predecessor in a number of ways. First, from this small fragment we can detect a concern with the specification of some kind of law-like interchange between things that come to be and pass away. The reference to justice and injustice is most plausibly thought of as a description of relationships of ongoing interchange between things, all of which must eventually be repaid. It might be difficult to see precisely what Anaximander means because it is put in the most general terms. Simplicius assumes that he is thinking of a basic cosmology involving earth, air, water and fire: the four "elements" that became prominent in the work of Heraclitus, Empedocles and many other later philosophers, including Aristotle.[17] This is probably an anachronistic reading of Anaximander, but the other pieces of evidence do not provide a clear alternative. Other candidates for the basic stuffs in his cosmology include the "opposites": the hot and the cold, the wet and the dry, and so on.[18] Other sources show that he was interested in the interchange between heat and moisture as a means of explaining meteorological and cosmological phenomena.[19] But whatever the identity of the major players in Anaximander's cosmology, it is clear that he insisted that all interchanges between them are temporary and governed by rules of exchange. All air, for example, that is converted into water is done so at a certain "exchange rate", and over time it will eventually be returned: water will in time "repay its debt" to air.

The relationship between these things that pay recompense to one another and the *arkhē*, the "boundless" (*apeiron*), is left unclear. Simplicius is keen to see some degree of interchange between the *apeiron* and the elements within the world, making the *apeiron* the source of all worlds and that into which all worlds will perish. In this picture, the *apeiron* is also in constant motion, perhaps in a constant state of creating the elements via some process of "separation" (*apokrisis*) and receiving them once again; in this way the reciprocal exchange between the elements would be replicated by an exchange of the elements into and out of the surrounding *apeiron*. The boundlessness and immortality of the *apeiron* can guarantee that this process will never be exhausted and allows the simultaneous generation of innumerable worlds. There are, however, reasons to be suspicious of this picture: it sounds close enough to the later atomist idea of infinite worlds in the boundless void to raise concerns about it being an authentic Anaximandrean view. We can be fairly sure that Anaximander thought that the boundless contains more than one heaven (presumably meaning the visible stars and planets), and that each heaven contains a cosmos or world. But it is not clear whether there are simultaneously many such worlds or whether there is a constant succession of worlds, since other evidence suggests only that our world had a beginning, not necessarily that it will come to an end.[20]

We can, however, be reasonably confident about some character-istics of the *apeiron* (see Gottschalk 1965). It surrounds the world in which we live. It is described in terms some of which are more familiar from descriptions of traditional gods: it is immortal and everlasting, it does not age and is in constant motion. Further it somehow "steers" all things. Perhaps Anaximander did intend this to carry connota-tions of deliberate control and planning by the *apeiron*, imagining it to have some cognitive powers. Alternatively, the *apeiron* "steers" not in any deliberative way but rather simply by imparting the motion required to drive, for example, the turning of the heavens (cf. Aristot. *Phys.* 203b3–15 [DK 12 A15]). As the term "boundless" suggests, it is indefinite in extent. But it is also unlike any of the opposites for which it is the source, a necessary condition of its being the source of all the many various elements that compose a world.[21] Since, for example, it is the source of both fire (hot) and air (cold), it can itself be neither hot nor cold. Similarly, we can imagine that it is neither heavy nor light, neither dry nor wet. But it would be wrong to take this indefiniteness too far; there is no reason, for example, to think that Anaximander's *apeiron* is not some sort of body or material stuff.

If this interpretation is somewhere near the mark, then Anaxi-mander's *apeiron* is certainly a very striking cosmological and metaphysical hypothesis. We can also appreciate the reasoning that may have led to this point. The *apeiron* is an attempt to explain the observed variety and change in the world by offering a single ultimate source and cause of all the different and opposed elements in the world. The role that this cause has to play in turn dictates its various characteristics: its inexhaustibility and immortality, its dif-ference from any of the opposites or elements it creates. The precise mechanics of how some portion of the *apeiron* becomes separated off and changed into one or other of the distinct elements are obscure, but these omissions ought not to detract from the impressive bold-ness of Anaximander's view.[22]

Anaximander also turned his attention to more specific questions about the structure of our world and the arrangement of the heavens. He had a fairly detailed astronomical account of the relative distances of the sun, moon and stars from the earth, specifying various ratios of size, and accounted for their visible light by claiming that these are small pockets of fire visible through holes in the dark celestial spheres.[23] He also offered an account of the origin and development of living things in the world, explaining original zoogony in terms that make it a part of the general processes by which land and sea were created through the gradual drying by the sun of the early moist world. Strikingly, he also asserted that animals such as human beings emerged as part of the very same process of drying. Fish are an earlier development of this same process since they are more closely affiliated to water. The first human beings somehow developed within certain fish before they burst out fully formed and therefore able immediately to reproduce and rear their young.[24]

There is one further claim for which Anaximander has become famous. Thales explained the earth's apparent stability by claiming that it floated on water. Anaximander tackled the same problem but offered a solution of a wholly different kind. Here is Aristotle's report:

> There are some, including Anaximander of the ancients, who say that the earth stays still because of similarity. For it is no more appropriate for something set in the middle and placed similarly in relation to the extremes to move up than down or to either side. It being impossible to generate a simultaneous motion in opposite directions, it necessarily stays still.   (Aristot. De caelo 295b10–15 [DK 12 A26])

The most likely reconstruction of Anaximander's argument sees it as an application of what came to be termed the principle of sufficient reason.[25] The earth remains motionless because it is positioned equidistant in all directions from the outer heaven. For it to move in any direction, there must be some reason for it to move in that direction rather than any other. But no sufficient reason exists; there is as much reason for it to move in a given direction as for it to move in quite the opposite direction. Therefore, it does not move in any direction. Some have complained that this would work only if the earth is thought to be spherical, as it is in a similar argument in Plato's

Phaedo (108e–109a), and we know that Anaximander considered the earth to be cylindrical: having a height one third the diameter of its round surfaces. But this is not so: any object with at least one plane of reflective symmetry will fit the argument.[26] What is most remarkable about Anaximander's argument, if this is the right reconstruction, is that it depends on no empirical evidence or on any particular general principle derived from observation. Rather, the argument relies on an entirely *a priori* notion about what is necessary to provide a reason for anything whatsoever: if some event E, rather than something different, E^*, is to occur then there must be sufficient reason *for* E *rather than* E^*. It is a principle that can be applied quite generally, not merely in cosmology, and is an important part of a general conception of the world that sees what happens in it as in principle explicable: each effect has some cause that makes it, rather than something else, happen. Whatever happens, there must be *some reason* for it to happen and we can then begin to enquire into those reasons, confident that there is some explanation to be had.

Looking beyond the wild speculations, the combined picture from the various pieces of surviving evidence is that Anaximander gave one of the earliest clear examples of an attempt to describe the variety and presence of animal life as part of a more general process by which the cosmos as a whole came to be, constantly applying the same general forces of opposing elements and gradual physical change. He appears to have given a detailed systematic cosmological account, avoiding the need for intervention from anthropomorphic divine forces, of a world driven by regular and – in principle – wholly comprehensible forces. As such, he is certainly to be admired for the instigation of something recognizable as a "scientific" worldview and also for putting this account in the form of a treatise that could be read, debated and disagreed with by others.

Anaximenes

The next of the Ionians is Anaximenes, who often receives less attention than Anaximander, perhaps because he has been overshadowed by his predecessor's bold and arresting claims.[27] It is true that Anaximenes' worldview is in many ways deeply indebted to Anaximander, but it also has some important new characteristics that deserve our attention.

First, Anaximenes rejected the notion of the *apeiron*, replacing it with his own *arkhē*: *aēr*. Like Anaximander's *apeiron*, Anaximenes' *aēr* surrounds the cosmos and is infinite in extent. (*Aēr* is also Anaximenes' explanation for the earth's stability: the flat earth is held up by supporting *aēr* below. See Hippol. *Ref.* 1.7.4 [DK 13 A7] and Aristot. *De caelo* 294b13ff. [DK 13 A20].) In offering what seems to be a more familiar stuff as the source and origin of the cosmos, Anaximenes is trying to provide a more satisfying account of the relationship between this infinite surround and the cosmos within. His major cosmological advance was to posit a clear and definite mechanism by which this *aēr* is transformed into the various more familiar components of our world, thereby tying our world and the *arkhē* together, since *aēr* can be placed within a simple system of elemental changes. This is Simplicius' account, which follows closely after his account of Anaximander:

> Anaximenes of Miletus, the son of Eurystratos, was a friend of Anaximander. Like Anaximander, he too thought that there was a single underlying nature, but unlike Anaximander, he thought it was not undefined, but rather definite, calling it *aēr*. He said that things differ in being through rarity or density. When *aēr* is rarefied, it becomes fire, when condensed it becomes wind, then cloud, and – further on – water, then earth, then stones, and other things are formed from these. *Aēr* also causes eternal motion, through which change also occurs.　　　(Simpl. *In Phys.* 24, 26ff. [DK 13 A5])

The similarities to Anaximander are evident, but the differences are also marked. Above all, the careful stipulation of a series of states of *aēr* as it is rarefied or condensed allows Anaximenes to support his general claim that there is indeed a single stuff that can be identified as the underlying origin of all things. The notion of arranging the basic components of the world as though on a single scale of density and rarity is striking and significant. If it is at all plausible, then it does indeed suggest that all these apparently different or opposed things (think of how different water is from fire) are in fact unified in some way. Just how they are unified is a different question: perhaps we might think they are all themselves composed from some single substance; perhaps they are unified in some different way, such as being part of an essentially dynamic system of transformations. The question will be explored further in different ways by the philosophers to come, but it is Anaximenes, I suspect, who ought to be credited with inspiring such thoughts rather than Anaximander and his much more mysterious *apeiron*.[28]

Of course, there are some gaps in the account that we might wish to explore. Anaximenes seems to want to insist that *aēr* is both a privileged stuff, such that it can be identified as the *arkhē* of all other basic components of the world. But he also seems to place it as one among a series of equal stuffs, including fire, wind, cloud and so on. What reason, in that case, can he give for making *aēr* his *arkhē* rather than, say, fire? Why pick on this to be the surrounding, infinite and ever-moving stuff? One question we would like to answer to help with this difficulty is: did Anaximenes consider the air we are familiar with, the air within our world, to be what we might term "pure" *aēr*? If we do indeed come across *aēr* within the world as one of the various basic stuffs, then the dilemma we have just sketched becomes more acute. Why pick on it as the most important of the range of elements (cf. Graham 1997: 26–31)? On the other hand, if he insists that *aēr* really is to be found only outside the world, then we return to the problems we might have felt with Anaximander's *apeiron*. In this case, there seems to be no direct support for this hypothesized *arkhē* from the observed processes of our world. Perhaps we might be impressed by an account that describes fire, wind, water and rock all as gradual transformations of one another, but there is no obvious reason why we need to posit a new and additional substance to "underlie" this process in some way; from what we can see, air becomes cloud becomes rain: a series of direct transformations with no evident intermediary.

Many of these questions can be illuminated by considering another crucial role for *aēr* in Anaximenes' philosophy. Choosing aēr as his *arkhē* allows him to offer the first explicit account of one of the central pressing questions of philosophy: what is the explanation of the evident and significant difference between animate and inanimate things? His answer involved drawing a close connection between *aēr* and breath (*pneuma*), and between soul (*psychē*) and *aēr*.[29] An important piece of evidence, most likely a paraphrase of Anaximenes' own words, reads: "For example, our soul (*psychē*), being *aēr*, controls us and breath (*pneuma*) and *aēr* surround the whole cosmos" (DK 13 B2). Aëtius, who quotes this, then comments: "*aēr* and *pneuma* mean the same thing" (cf. Schofield 1997: 65–6). There are therefore two symmetrical claims being made: first, Anaximenes asserts that a soul, whatever it is that makes us alive, is in fact *aēr*; secondly, he asserts that the *aēr* that is to be found outside the world is what we would call breath. He is therefore both describing our souls in the terms of his general conception of the basic components of the universe and also describing the grand cosmic principle in terms familiar from human life. If, indeed, *aēr* is a kind of warm breath closely associated with life, then this fits nicely with the general cosmological description we have already seen. *Aēr* is not to be identified with the general air about us, but with a special form of warm, animating, rare stuff. It has a special rarity, warmth and perhaps' even a certain moistness: characteristics that link it clearly to fire, water and air but that are not shared in this particular combination by any other basic cosmological stuff. Further, the close link between *aēr* thus conceived and life reinforces Anaximenes' claim that it is a motor force in the universe. It is *aēr* that imparts motion and therefore change on a cosmic scale just as, presumably, the presence of *aēr* should be thought responsible for the characteristic forms of change and motion associated with being a living thing. Other evidence shows that Anaximenes wanted to link processes of heating and cooling to his scheme of rarefaction and condensation on the basis of observed changes in a person's breath: as things condense they cool and as they become rare they heat up. Again, he assimilates closely the phenomena associated with the maintenance of a living human being with large-scale cosmological processes.

It is worth emphasizing the importance of this move. Anaximenes' world displays all the drive for systematization and unification that we saw in Anaximander. But it expands and applies this unity even to include an explanation of the place of living things, human beings in particular, within the cosmos at large. It is a daring claim to be able to encompass and explain animate beings in just the same terms and using just the same basic apparatus as can be used to explain cycles of the weather. That said, it would not be right to think that Anaximenes is concerned to reduce living things in some way to mere locations of material change. He is simultaneously willing, it seems, to apply to his preferred *arkhē* descriptions that make it, if not itself animate, then at least an animating force. Some commentators were even prepared to assert that Anaximenes thought that *aēr* is a god (Cic. *De nat. deorum* 1.26, Aet. 1.7.13 [DK 13 A10]).

Pythagoras

Alongside Anaximander, Diogenes Laërtius' second originator of a long philosophical tradition is Pythagoras. Pythagoras originally came from the Ionian island of Samos, but at some time around 530 BCE moved to live in southern Italy, where he seems to have gathered a group of followers and to have been active in the political life of the various Greek cities in that area. Beyond this, however, it becomes extremely difficult to say anything with much conviction about the specifics of his philosophy.[30] The long-lived Pythagorean tradition has obscured much of the original nature of his teaching and sources throughout antiquity are too eager to ascribe various later philosophical and mathematical theories directly to Pythagoras. Plato was clearly impressed by something he found in Pythagoreanism (perhaps via the later-fifth–early-fourth-century Pythagorean Archytas) and many of the applications of ideas such as the geometrical account of the universe found in his *Timaeus* or the confusing metaphysics of limit and the unlimited in the *Philebus* may have been inspired by, if not borrowed from, contemporary Pythagoreanism.[31] This mixture of Platonism and Pythagoreanism is probably what lies behind references to Pythagoreanism in much of Aristotle; he saw Pythagoreanism and Platonism as intimately linked and was keen to reject both.

There is some general consensus, however, that certain philosophical views can be ascribed to Pythagoras and his immediate followers. Evidence from other Presocratic philosophers shows that he quickly became a well-known figure of some intellectual reputation, enough for him to be criticized by Heraclitus (DK 22 B40, 81, 129) for possessing "much learning" (*polumathiē*) but no wisdom. One of Xenophanes' poems suggests something of the content of his teaching: "Once, when he came across a puppy being whipped, they say he took pity on it and spoke as follows: 'Stop beating it, because it is the soul of a friend of mine. I recognised it shouting'" (DK 21 B7). Xenophanes has no intention of being sympathetic to Pythagoras here and we are, no doubt, meant to find Pythagoras' behaviour, and his explanation for it, ridiculous. Nevertheless, one of the enduring notions of Pythagoreanism is the idea of reincarnation or, better, *metempsychosis*. At death, a soul leaves the body to be born later into another body. Such ideas can be found also in Plato and Empedocles, and they also share the notion here parodied in Xenophanes that the soul may migrate into bodies of different species. Pythagoras' precise conception of the nature of the soul remains obscure, however.[32]

The other relatively securely attested aspect of early Pythagoreanism is its use of curious codified sets of questions and answers (called *akusmata*), the learning and recitation of which appear to be a central part of Pythagorean group practice. These precepts and rules, often given in the form of a question and answer, concentrate on moral and religious, particularly ritual, issues and are sometimes extremely obscure (e.g. "What is most just? To sacrifice"; "Put on the right (i.e. not left) shoe first"). Others are concerned with cosmological questions (e.g. "The rainbow is the reflected splendour of the sun"). Some mention things that are closely associated with the Pythagorean tradition generally, including more evidence of an interest in harmony and ratios and also an interest in number. For example, the answer to the question "What is the oracle of Delphi?" is "Tetraktys", which is the term they used for an arrangement of ten units into a triangle, formed from rows of 4 then 3 then 2 then 1 units (see Burkert 1972: 166–92; also Inwood 2006: 234–5). The precise significance of this arrangement is, again, unclear, but it certainly suggests an early interest in arithmetical and geometrical relationships, albeit one closely tied with ritual practices. It also shows the seeds of notions later associated with Pythagoreanism, such as the claim that the universe is somehow composed of numbers and exhibits important geometrical relationships in, for example, the movements of the heavens or the musical harmonies.

Pythagoreanism certainly developed through the sixth and fifth centuries. The Pythagorean Philolaus, who probably belongs to the generation after such philosophers as Anaxagoras and Empedocles, outlined a detailed cosmology that is clearly indebted to earlier Pythagorean interests in number and harmony (see pp. 175ff.). There also is some evidence of a schism in Pythagoreanism during the fifth century between one group, the "*akusmatici*" who emphasized the ritual and religious aspects of the movement and the "*mathematici*" – the side to which Philolaus clearly belongs – who also pursued technical and mathematical interests. Yet even in its very earliest phase in the later sixth century, however, it would be wrong to see Pythagoreanism simply as a curious religious sect entirely divorced from the rest of early Greek philosophical speculation.[33] It may have emphasized ritual aspects to a much greater degree than we can discern in, for example, Anaximander. But Anaximander's concern with the ratio of the sizes of the earth and the various heavenly spheres and his reverent description of the *apeiron* is not so unlike early Pythagoreanism's combination of cultic practices with an interest in the relationships of triangular or square numbers, and it is worth reminding ourselves that ethical and religious ideas were part and parcel of the very earliest Greek philosophical speculations and continued throughout Greek philosophy to be intimately connected with cosmological and mathematical enquiry.

THREE

Xenophanes

Xenophanes of Colophon is principally of interest for his contributions to two areas of thought: theology and epistemology. It is also important to recognize how the two areas are linked. We shall begin by looking at the fragments that relate to his discussion of the gods and then turn to his claims about the possibility of knowledge and the proper method of enquiry. Then we can ask if his theological claims can illuminate the general method he proposes.[1]

Diels and Kranz divide his work into a number of sections: the elegiac poems (DK21 B1–9), the satirical works or *Silloi* (B10–22), and the fragments *On Nature* (B23–41), all of which are in verse but in differing metrical forms. However, we have no reason to think that he did not intend his works to offer a single and unified account of the world. Certainly, the "elegiac poem", B1, apparently composed for performance at a symposium, an after-dinner male drinking party, stresses the need for proper respect for and conduct towards the gods, a theme that also appears prominently in some of the more obviously philosophical fragments. It also recommends that a good after-dinner performance should not recount tales from mythology of battles between Titans, Giants and centaurs, since these serve no useful educational purpose (lines 19–23). Concerns about the ethical content of much traditional poetry are also expressed in other fragments.

Gods and men

We can start by noticing that Xenophanes begins his theological enquiry by pointing out how the depictions of the gods vary from culture to culture. This might look like the opening of what we could call a relativist argument, but Xenophanes does not intend it in this way (DK 21 B16):[2] "Ethiopians say that their gods are snub-nosed and black; the Thracians say that theirs are pale and have red hair". How much are we entitled to conclude from this observation alone? Very little. It is merely a description of current belief and has little by itself to offer in advancing the enquiry into whether any of the various depictions are correct or nearly correct or wildly mistaken. For his part, Xenophanes seems never to consider the possibility that there are no gods at all. He is interested instead in what the gods – assuming that there are gods – are really like. Some might infer from the anthropological observations that the gods are "nothing but" human constructions and that not only do human beings create gods in their own image, but different races and cultures create gods in their own specific image. Xenophanes would probably endorse only part of such a view. He agrees that the image of the gods is a cultural invention, but he has no time for a stronger inference that we should therefore be sceptical about there being gods in the first place. But it is important to recognize that the evidence of cultural variation alone would, in any case, not support a strong atheistic claim. If anything, we might conclude that the one thing all these cultures do agree on is that there are gods; their disagreement is over the details. Xenophanes, therefore, sensibly takes from these observations a fairly weak conclusion. If we assume that all these different cultures are attempting to offer depictions of the same things, that all the cultures are offering these depictions as depictions of "the gods" and not just "the Ethiopians' gods" or "the Scythians' gods", then it cannot be the case that the Greeks, the Ethiopians and the Scythians are all correct. The same gods cannot all resemble the different inhabitants of all these nations. This is the stage at which Xenophanes' line of argument parts company with relativism, since relativism, considered in very general terms, would presumably move to conclude that each culture is correct about their own particular set of gods. What the gods are like, therefore, would be "relative to" the culture in question: it would be true relative to the Greeks that the gods look like Greeks and also true relative to the Scythians that the gods look like Scythians. This is unlike Xenophanes' line of argument since relativism rules out there being a single answer to the question "But what are the gods like?" Instead, the answer to this question will depend on various factors, including some concerning the particular person asking the question. If you are a Greek asking the question, the answer will be different from that if you are a Scythian. But both the Greek's answer and the Scythian's answer are correct. Xenophanes presses on to offer a single answer to the question of what god or the gods are like and so rejects this relativist move.

If *we* want to press on, therefore, the next point to recognize is that at most only one of these competing depictions can be correct and perhaps none of them are correct. This is the most that simple observations of conflicting beliefs can show. Of a set of conflicting beliefs (that is, incompatible beliefs about the same object or objects) only one at most can be true. But, as things stand, there is nothing to prevent a chauvinistic Greek from seeing this conflict as confirmation of the Greeks' superiority. Convinced that his own conception of the gods' appearance is correct, the fact that other people think of the gods differently merely underlines how generally inferior they are.

A further comment by Xenophanes certainly suggests that he wishes to resist such a move and to persuade us that in fact none of these various options is correct:

> But if oxen, horses, or lions had hands or could draw with their hands and create works as men do, then horses would draw images of gods just like horses, and oxen images just like oxen and they would make the bodies of the gods like those they themselves had. (DK 21 B15)

Strictly speaking, this merely reinforces what the last set of observations of human cultures has already established.[3] However, the rhetorical force of this speculation about the theological views of non-rational animals serves to persuade us that, just as it would be ridiculous to think that horses, say, are right about what the gods are like when they draw equine gods, so too it would be ridiculous to assert that any one of the human conceptions is correct. If we recognize that speculations about animals' gods, ridiculous though they are, have any kind of plausibility then we have already begun to accept an account of why different groups produce different conceptions of the gods. In entertaining a thought about what a horse's god would be like, we have accepted a general account of the mechanism by which images of the gods are formed: different groups do indeed create gods in their own image. The anthropological observations on their own are insufficient to secure this claim, even if they might naturally suggest it. By asking us to think for ourselves in a more speculative fashion about what animals' gods would be like, Xenophanes manages to push us towards an explanation of why different groups generate their different views.

The second line of thought that seems to underlie these observations is the idea that not only is it impossible for all of these views of the gods to be true, but there is also no reason for any one of them to be true at the expense of the others. Let us consider once again a chauvinist Greek who, faced with Xenophanes' observations about the Scythians' gods, merely shrugs his shoulder and declares, "Well, that's the Scythians for you!" Presumably we can imagine a chauvinist Scythian having much the same sort of reaction when faced with the Greeks' gods. Now we have a second conflict of beliefs, this time about who should stand as the arbiters of the disagreement about the nature of the gods. The Greek thinks that Greeks should decide, no doubt in favour of their own view. The Scythian thinks he should decide. And, we might add, if a horse could join in presumably he would think that the horses should decide. Once again, they cannot all be right and at most only one of them is right.

It should be easy to see how the discussion is likely to proceed. There are three options. First, we could simply reach a stalemate in which each side obstinately refuses to consider anything other than its own superior judgement. As yet, there is no reason being offered for this claim of superiority. (If the Greek, for example, did come up with a reason why we should prefer his view – for example, on the supposed basis that Greeks are more intelligent and therefore more likely to be right – then we can go on to examine this claim, questioning now the grounds for his claim of superiority.) Secondly, the various sides might decide that since the discussion is likely to run on and on and never reach a conclusion, this is a good reason to think that the question of the nature of the gods simply cannot be resolved. In that case, they should all abandon their various prior beliefs and instead register a new lack of certainty. Thirdly, they might decide that the reasonable path is to recognize that none of their prior views is correct and that therefore they ought to start a new enquiry into the nature of the gods, this time trying to avoid letting their view be coloured by the peculiarities of their own particular cultural circumstances.

The third option is the one pursued by Xenophanes. But before we follow him into that enquiry, we should pause to notice that, packed into the short fragments we have considered so far, there are some significant points not only about the practice of theology but also about how we might deal with conflicting beliefs most generally. It is no accident, then, that Xenophanes was seen by later ancient writers as paving the way for some of the sceptical movements to come. In the most developed form of ancient scepticism, that exemplified by the work of Sextus Empiricus from the second century CE, scepticism is a method of enquiry that begins by noticing disagreements or conflicts of beliefs or appearances (*diaphōniai*) and then proceeds by various sophisticated forms of argument to weigh up the various sides in any given dispute and then recognize that there is no more reason to prefer one side of the conflict to the other. Sextus recommends that then we ought to suspend judgement on the matter and simply leave it as yet unresolved, an attitude that, he claims, will lead us to a tranquil life no longer disturbed by trying to get the right answer to questions such as the true nature of the gods.[4]

Xenophanes himself would not have agreed entirely with Sextus about the importance of suspending judgement, although even Sextus recommends this only after all possible avenues have been pursued in search of a convincing account. Xenophanes instead proposes a continued search and, if necessary, the acceptance of a provisional or reasonable if not entirely proved conclusion. Even so, we have already seen enough to understand what later writers such as Sextus saw in Xenophanes.

Xenophanes' positive theology proceeds on the basis of two premises, which are not explicitly stated in any of his fragments but can plausibly be seen as the background to what he goes on to say. The first premise we have already noted. Xenophanes is sure that there are gods, or at least that there is a god. His enquiry is therefore directed at what this god or these gods are like. The second premise is implied by another of Xenophanes' assertions: "Homer and Hesiod attributed to the gods all those things which bring criticism and censure among humans: theft, adultery, and deceiving one another" (DK 21 B11).[5] The poets Homer and Hesiod, generally considered to be authorities about many topics and perhaps about the gods in particular, tell us of gods who act in ways that would bring reproach if copied by human beings. Again, at it stands this is merely a true observation. To turn this into an argument we have to expand the thought by adding the assumption that gods would not act in ways that would bring censure among human beings and therefore the portrayal of the gods by Homer and Hesiod must be incorrect. In pointing to Homer's and Hesiod's depiction of the gods' ethically dubious behaviour, Xenophanes is again at the beginning of a tradition in Greek philosophy, this time of rational theology and, in particular, of criticism of traditional depictions of anthropomorphic gods behaving in ways very reminiscent of the mortal Homeric heroes. Xenophanes will notably be followed by Plato, who, in a lengthy discussion in the *Republic* as part of the recommendations for his ideal state, has Socrates recommend strict censorship of the Homeric poems, particularly their depictions of the gods (Plato *Rep.* 379a–85c).

Some support for this addition is offered by our previous discussion. Xenophanes appears to be concerned to discover the true nature of the gods. He has already registered some views about the gods' appearance and now turns to consider the gods' behaviour. He notes that it would be odd to suppose that the gods act just as they are said to do by Homer and Hesiod since, in that case, they would either be generally less ethically honourable than most human beings or, perhaps, we would have to assume that the required standards of behaviour among the gods are more lax than those among human beings. Neither of these possibilities is very plausible. The second premise driving Xenophanes' theological enquiry therefore seems to be some sort of claim about the gods' superiority to human beings. There are gods and they are better than us. This superiority is conceived as being displayed, we have to assume, also in the gods' behaviour towards one another. They do not commit adultery or deceive one another as human beings do since they are better than us. This is quite a robust set of starting assumptions and, as far as we can tell, Xenophanes nowhere offers any support for them. Perhaps he uses them merely as plausible assumptions that his audience would share despite their inconsistent acceptance of Homeric descriptions of the gods or perhaps he felt that the assumptions were self-evident and in no need of further justification.

Xenophanes' own preferred account of god is given in four separate fragments. It makes good sense to discuss them together.

> One god: greatest among gods and humans, dissimilar from mortals in body and in thought. (DK 21 B23)

> All of him sees, all thinks, all hears. (DK 21 B24)

> But without exertion, he shakes everything with the thinking of his mind. (DK 21 B25)

> Remaining always in the same place, unmoving, it is not fitting for him to travel here and there. (DK 21 B26)

The second line of B23 ("dissimilar from …") continues a view that began to emerge from the previous critical fragments. God, or perhaps the greatest god, does not resemble any mortal in appearance nor in thought. This does not mean that god has no body, for example, since Xenophanes is thinking of his god as seeing and hearing, and it is unlikely that he thought this could be done without a body of some sort. Rather, Xenophanes here confirms the thought he wants us to extract from his consideration of culturally variable conceptions of the gods: the wide variety of beliefs are all mistaken and human beings are mistaken in thinking that god resembles them precisely in their bodily appearance. We learn precious little else about god's physical form, and later ancient interpretations that state that Xenophanes' god is spherical or identical with the universe as a whole or with the heavens cannot be supported from evidence within the fragments themselves.[6] The second claim makes a similar point about god's thinking and is perhaps linked to the criticism of Homeric depictions of the gods' behaviour: a god should not think in the same way that mortals do; it should not share mortal plans, ambitions, emotions, jealousies and so on, and gods ought not to quarrel with one another as human beings do. But a god still does think in some fashion; god is not wholly unlike human beings. Xenophanes must also refer here to a distinction between a god's understanding of the world and our limited human abilities (see B18 and 36 and the discussion below).

The first line of B23 is tricky. Xenophanes is describing "one god" and making it superior not only to human beings but to other gods as well. Who or what are these other gods? Other fragments refer both to gods (B18) and also to a single god (B38) so we might wonder whether Xenophanes is a monotheist or polytheist or simply inconsistent. Perhaps Xenophanes thinks that there is a hierarchy of gods with one single supreme god whose abilities he describes in B24–6 (what is sometimes called "henotheism"). Other interpretations are more inclined to insist that Xenophanes is in fact a monotheist, claiming that the phrase in B23 is "merely a convenient tag", a formula borrowed from epic poetry that just means "the greatest of all things". This seems unlikely. If it were true then Xenophanes would be guilty at least of being sloppy and potentially misleading, precisely where we would expect him to be very careful about his theological claims. There is no reason to dismiss the idea of a plurality of divinities, even if Xenophanes elsewhere concentrates on one principal god.[7]

Having learned that this god is not like human beings in two important ways, next we learn more about what god is like. Xenophanes explains his cognitive powers, his causal responsibilities and his location and lack of movement. In all three cases he emphasizes the difference between this god and human beings. It is important to recognize, however, that Xenophanes does not move entirely from the Homeric picture to embrace instead a theology more like the later Christian version. Crucially, Xenophanes' god is never said to be omniscient, nor omnipresent, nor benevolent. Certainly, his understanding of the world seems to be far superior to that of human beings since there is no part of him that is not able to see, think and hear, and the gods are said to have kept various truths from human beings, at least at the outset (B18). But god does appear to be able to "shake all things" without effort (B25). Whether this amounts to the idea that god governs the entire functioning of the universe or that he is responsible for physically moving all things, perhaps meaning that he is responsible for the motion of the heavens and the large-scale movements of water, air and the like, is once again unclear. We should presumably recognize the apparent incongruity between the physical implications of the act of "shaking" with the purely mental means by which god achieves it, an incongruity that further highlights how different god must be from human beings. Nevertheless, the concern to preserve the effortless power of god also lies behind the insistence that god must not need to move about to exert his influence on the world. His influence can be exerted at any distance so it would be "unseemly" for him to need to charge about as the Homeric gods do, flying first to Olympus to talk to Zeus and then back to Troy to take care of some favourite hero.[8] The overall picture of Xenophanes' god reveals what Xenophanes takes to be the essential attributes of any divinity: effortless power and superior cognitive and causal abilities. There is, however, no claim that god exerts his power in a benevolent fashion. Even when we learn in B18 that the gods have decided not to reveal all things to us, there is no implication that this is somehow for our own benefit or out of malice. Although, for example, B38 tells us that god was responsible for the creation or perhaps the nature of honey, we are given no rationale for understanding how or why god generated the world. Throughout, Xenophanes intends instead to emphasize the difference between gods and human beings, insisting the gods and their actions should never be thought of in human terms.[9]

Enquiry and belief

We have already seen that Xenophanes does not think that all human beliefs are reliable. Theological beliefs, in particular, are likely to be adversely affected by a person's circumstances and cultural context. Xenophanes extended this view to cover a wide range of beliefs and even went so far as to note certain limitations on all human beliefs. A number of fragments relate directly to epistemological concerns and draw attention to the vast gulf between human and divine access to understanding. Fragment B34 is the longest of these and expresses sure limits to human beings' chances of attaining knowledge. No doubt statements such as this were the basis of Xenophanes' later being hailed as an early sceptic:[10]

> No man has seen what is clear, nor will there be anyone who knows about the gods and all the things I say about every-thing. For if someone should happen to say precisely what is the case, still he would himself not know. Rather, belief covers everything.[11]   (DK 21 B34)

We should note that Xenophanes first disclaims any access to the clear and certain truth about all the matters he has addressed in his work and to theological questions in particular. This might sound disastrous since, after all, like the other experts with whom he is competing, Xenophanes is surely trying to win fame and an audi-ence by offering an arresting and innovative picture of the world, but Xenophanes quickly points out that no one else will ever be able to know the truth either.

In the second pair of lines Xenophanes gives his reason for this pessimism. There are two possible interpretations of these lines, one an "internalist" reading, the other an "externalist" account.[12] On the former, "internalist" interpretation of these lines, the interpretation offered by Sextus Empiricus at *M* 7.51–2, Xenophanes comes close to anticipating part of what Meno later turns into a paradox in the Platonic dialogue that bears his name (see Plato *Meno* 80d7–8) by pointing to a formal requirement for a new belief to count as a piece of knowledge.[13] Even if, says Xenophanes, someone did happen on the truth he himself would not know that he had done so. Having beliefs that are true is not enough; for them to qualify as knowledge something extra is required that is provided only if the believer in question further knows *that his belief is true*. (Simply believing that it is true is also not enough since we would then need to consider how to justify the belief that this belief is true; there is an obvious danger of an infinite regress here.) On this view, Xenophanes expresses a relatively sophisticated account of the nature of knowledge. There are two requirements. Knowledge must involve (i) possession of a belief that is true, and (ii) the additional awareness that the belief is true. The second requirement is what causes Xenophanes' pessimism since, even if we could chance on the right answer, he thinks we would not also know that it is right. This might also account for his pessimism particularly about matters of theology and the sorts of questions he has addressed in his work, for how *could* we confirm a view about god, or about the fundamental processes of nature?

The alternative, "externalist", view sees no explicit expression in these lines of the specific requirement that we must in addition know that something is true before we can claim possession of what is true and clear. Instead, the difference between knowledge and belief is to be explained by reference to the method by which we acquire a piece of information. Xenophanes states that even if someone should chance on the truth and form a true belief about, for example, god, he would nevertheless fail to *know* that fact about god. Why? There are cases, such as the question of the nature of god, in which a person who has lighted on a true belief could not see or directly observe the object in question. If Xenophanes thought a direct acquaintance with some object necessary for the acquisition of knowledge about it, then in the case of god we must be limited to belief. The manner in which the belief about gods is acquired – even if it happens to be a true belief – is simply not the right sort of method for acquiring knowledge. Unfortunately, the necessary means of generating knowledge rather than mere beliefs is not possible for the whole range of topics that Xenophanes has been discussing, which is why "belief covers everything".[14] On this view, importantly, it is not necessary for the person concerned to be aware that the belief has been acquired in the right way for it to qualify as knowledge; the relevant distinction depends entirely on the external circumstances in which the belief was acquired.

Whichever interpretation is preferred, we are offered a contrast between, on the one hand, belief or speculation (*dokos*) and, on the other, knowledge of what is clear and true (*to saphes*). Human beings are limited, at least concerning the topics of Xenophanes' poem, to the former. The term I have rendered as "belief" (*dokos*) reappears in a verbal form: "Let these be believed to be like the truth ..." (DK 21 B35).[15] Here it is clear once again that we must settle with *dokos* but the sure implication is that we can have better and worse beliefs. Xenophanes has already told us that he cannot claim absolute certainty for what he says, but nevertheless encourages us to accept what he says as in some way like the truth.[16] This poses the question of what grounds Xenophanes might offer for classifying beliefs as better or worse likenesses to the truth and here we have to do some speculation ourselves.

The theme of epistemological progress also appears elsewhere: "Indeed, the gods did not show everything to mortals from the beginning, but in time, by searching, they discover better" (DK 21 B18). The gods (note the plural) did not reveal everything in the beginning: a comment that does not necessarily imply that Xenophanes believed that the cosmos had a beginning, but only that the human race developed at some point in time (see DK 21 A37; also B29, B33). As a qualification of his general epistemological pessimism, Xenophanes here emphasizes the notion that progress and discovery are possible nevertheless. What human beings need is more enquiry, which, if done properly, can in time lead to improvements, presumably meaning that our beliefs will be better likenesses of the truth. Unfortunately, Xenophanes does not specify *how* we go about this enquiry, nor in this fragment does he explain what discovery would consist in. It would be very helpful to know what he means by "discovering better" here, given that elsewhere he has told us that we will not know if we ever hit on the right answer. We should also note that there is absolutely no implication that the gods have any hand in encouraging or hindering human progress, gradually revealing the truths they held back at the outset. As far as we can tell, any discoveries will be entirely the result of human effort. This too may be part of Xenophanes' message: we should not simply expect the gods to tell us the answers but need to engage in critical enquiry ourselves. For Xenophanes to be consistent with B34, he needs some notion of gradual progress in generating better likenesses of the truth that nevertheless does not rely on any notion of confirmation, since in B34 sure confirmation of such true beliefs seemed to be ruled out. Two possibilities are likely. Perhaps we improve by generating a larger and more internally consistent set of beliefs. Alternatively, perhaps we improve by assembling a set of beliefs consistent with more and more data, still without any direct external confirmation. Both possibilities can be supported from our evidence.

It is clear from our discussion of Xenophanes' theology that he rejects some beliefs on the grounds that they have no more claim to be true than other competing beliefs. Here, perhaps, Xenophanes is insisting that our beliefs on a given subject are better likenesses of the truth if they are consistent with one another. Progress in theological speculation is possible, even if there is no mechanism for achieving certainty in these matters, through the critical evaluation of different beliefs in a manner exemplified by our reconstruction of Xenophanes' theological enquiry. From that reconstruction we can extract a number of principles of enquiry: it is clear that not all these various beliefs can be true since they give competing accounts of the same god or gods; we can reject any that imply impossible things of the gods such as immoral behaviour; we can reject any that clearly display contamination from prejudices caused by the particular believers' background, and so on. His own account of divinity, we can infer, is offered as a better likeness of the truth because it captures what we generally consider to be the essential characteristics of a god (superior power, superior awareness and cognitive abilities) without adding any other unwarranted characteristics such as those in the various anthropomorphic accounts. Xenophanes nevertheless accepts that even this procedure is not guaranteed to generate the truth and, even if it does produce truths, it cannot demonstrate that they are correct. But he can nevertheless recommend it as a more promising route of epistemological progress.

Another route of enquiry prominent in Xenophanes' philosophy is empirical observation and inference based on observed phenomena. The most arresting example of this method at work is Xenophanes' famous observation of fossilized remains of sea creatures at inland locations (DK 21 A33).[17] From this he inferred that periodically the areas of land and sea must change, since these fossils could be produced only if what is now dry land was once under water. Xenophanes clearly felt he had sufficient evidence to offer a cosmological account that included a discussion of the origins of the human species (B33), a description of what we would call the "water cycle" (B30), and an answer to what by now was a necessary part of any self-respecting natural philosophy, namely the question why the earth remains stable. Xenophanes' ingenious reply is that the earth is stable because it has no bottom; the earth goes down infinitely beneath our feet (B28). Some of Xenophanes' physical theories serve to reinforce his criticisms of common theological accounts by debunking mythological views of the gods. So he, like the Milesians, tries to explain heavenly and meteorological phenomena, which would otherwise be attributed to divine agency, in terms of the natural motions of water or fire or air. One particular claim exemplifies this well: "What they call Iris (the Rainbow), this too is by nature a cloud, purple and red and green to behold" (DK 21 B32). Iris, the traditional name for the goddess identified with the rainbow is also a cloud. Xenophanes accepts that a rainbow is indeed visually spectacular and colourful, but he insists that this appreciation of its beauty is quite compatible with it not being divine, nor having anything to do with divine agency or even with some kind of communication between gods and men. It is likely that this fragment comes from a series of such claims, in which we might guess that Xenophanes offered similar explanations for a range of phenomena. Again, it is worth noting how these claims about meteorological and cosmological processes also look towards Xenophanes' concern with theological matters. He is constantly preoccupied with the relationship between gods and men, insisting above all on the differences between the two in appearance, behaviour and understanding.

We can finish our look at Xenophanes by considering this relationship between gods and men in one final fragment, which will draw together a number of the themes that have emerged so far: "If god had not made green honey, they would have said that figs are far sweeter" (DK 21 B38). This is an intriguing fragment, which provoked reactions in a number of later philosophers. The Hellenistic sceptic and follower of Pyrrho, Timon of Phlius, was a keen reader of Xenophanes and used him as a model for his own satirical poetry and even cast Xenophanes as a character who led him to see the great philosophers of the past. Timon recasts this claim with his own sceptical pronouncement: "That honey appears sweet, I admit, but as to whether it is sweet I withhold judgement".[18] Even later sceptical philosophers such as Sextus Empiricus took up this theme.[19] Xenophanes' own intention is not clear: in our source the fragment is quoted by a grammarian not for its philosophical content but for Xenophanes' use of an unusual word for "sweeter". But we can offer the following plausible interpretation. "If god had not made honey then they would think figs much sweeter." Sweeter than what? Not honey, presumably, since the hypothesis we are considering is what would be the case in a world without honey. Instead, the claim must be that in a honey-less world then we would think figs sweeter than we currently do. As it is, we do not think figs so sweet as we might, mainly because there are sweeter things around, including honey. Xenophanes' thesis, therefore, is not that honey is not really sweet, nor that figs are in fact sweeter than we think. Rather his point must be that assessments of perceptual qualities such as sweetness are often comparative and relative even if we do not always recognize that they are. So honey is indeed very sweet, but we should recognize that this is the case in comparison with other things around. Perhaps there could be something sweeter that would make us think honey less sweet. Figs are indeed not so sweet, but that is because we always assess their sweetness in comparison with something else.

The lesson here is similar to what we learned about the gods. In that case, it became clear that what people believe about the gods has as much to do with their own context as the real nature of things. Just so, our belief that honey is very sweet and figs less sweet is dependent on a particular set of circumstances concerning what other foods are on offer. That set of circumstances, apparently, is not a necessary one, since it seems to be possible for god to have made a world not containing honey. In both the theological and these more mundane spheres, epistemological progress is made by noticing how our beliefs are affected by surrounding circumstances. When enquiring into the nature of god, we would do well to try to shrug off as much of our own cultural preconceptions as possible. When enquiring into the nature of honey, however, we do not aim for a context-free view, but instead try to understand honey by recognizing and making explicit the contribution made to our beliefs by surrounding circumstances. This insight has distinct echoes in the next of our philosophers: Heraclitus.

FOUR

The oracles of Heraclitus

Heraclitus lived in Ephesus on the Ionian coast at the turn of the sixth and fifth centuries BCE. He shares many of the concerns of his fellow Ionians and so it is possible to think about Heraclitus' conception of the basic *arkhai* of the world, how the elements interrelate and so on. He also shares with Xenophanes an interest in morality and theology, and a set of concerns about the right way to understand knowledge, wisdom and expertise. But there are several striking facets of his thought that set him apart from what we know of these predecessors. The remaining fragments, when combined and interpreted as a whole, produce an overall worldview that encompasses not merely a set of claims about how the universe is, but also a view of the place of human beings within that world and, as an essential part of this, a set of thoughts about the proper manner in which we ought to think about ourselves in relation to the world in which we live. He also chose to express these thoughts in a remarkable manner: a tactic that was designed with a particular educational philosophy in mind.

Heraclitus undoubtedly exerted a profound influence on later philosophers. Indeed, it is perhaps true to say that, of the Presocratics, Heraclitus had an influence on ancient philosophy second only to that of Parmenides. For example, there are sure signs of the influence of aspects of Heraclitus' cosmology on the Stoics. More strikingly, Plato responds to and uses Heraclitean ideas, particularly the prominent notions of opposition and of change and flux, in a number of his dialogues, and it has been reasonably claimed that Heraclitus may lie behind some of Plato's views about the changing perceptible world.[1]

It is extremely difficult, however, to move swiftly from the surviving evidence of Heraclitus' views to the construction of a clear and consistent "Heraclitean philosophy", and this difficulty is an essential element of Heraclitus' own project. His work survives now as a collection of some 120 or so short fragments, usually statements of only one or two sentences in length. They are often frustratingly obscure and demand careful interpretation and sometimes significant supplementation to produce a satisfying complete thought. They are also extremely carefully composed, often containing subtle linguistic rhymes or making use of the flexibility of word order in Greek to generate balancing clauses or interesting juxtapositions of ideas. These effects are, of course, very difficult to render adequately in an English translation, but it is important to recognize their presence in the original since they provide important information about Heraclitus' probable intention in choosing a particular form for his philosophical output. Take as an example: "Greater deaths take by lot greater destinies" (DK 22 B25). This is a simple, if obscure, statement rather than an argument, so we shall have to do some work to fit it into a set of related philosophical ideas designed to persuade us of something. But, disregarding the content for a moment, the Greek reveals a careful writer at work. The Greek, transliterated into English script, reads as follows: "*moroi mezones mezonas moiras lanchanousi*". This has clearly been designed as an intriguing and aesthetically pleasing linguistic unit. We might notice: the repeated "m" introducing the first four words; the juxtaposition of the two forms of the word for "greater" (*mezones/mezonas*); the rhyming "*mezonas moiras*" and "*moroi moiras*". We have to linger over the phrase, short though it is, and consider it carefully as we might a line of poetry or an elegant epigram. In some ways, it might be incorrect to think of these as fragments as if they are short sentences culled from a longer and more expansive, now lost, context. While it is likely that there are Heraclitean writings now lost to us, it is a reasonable hypothesis that

Heraclitus' book took the form of a set of short and syntactically self-contained sayings or aphorisms. It is notoriously difficult to arrange the remaining examples into a reasonable order, since themes recur in various different contexts and no single overarching argument can be easily discerned. The different editions of Heraclitus often choose different orders for the fragments and Diels and Kranz chose to print mostly according to the alphabetical order of their respective sources, so as not to impose their own particular interpretation on the evidence. Indeed, we shall see that perhaps Heraclitus invites us to consider the order of his aphoristic statements, perhaps encouraging us to try out different combinations and orders according to the various interlinking themes across the fragments. In any case, it is an odd experience to read Heraclitus and the most reasonable explanation of this oddity is that Heraclitus has chosen a particular medium fit for his philosophical purpose.[2]

Perhaps the closest analogues in classical culture for Heraclitus' pronouncements are the oracles mentioned in both literary and historical sources. These are often short, obscure and deliberately ambiguous pronouncements that demand careful attention by the reader to the potentially multiple meanings. A casual interpretation can lead to disastrous results. Once, when Croesus asked the oracle what would happen if he declared war on Persia, he was told: "If you do, a great empire will fall". Confident in the truth of the oracle Croesus declared war, but the empire that fell was his own.[3] Similarly, Heraclitus' sayings are initially puzzling and demand decoding. Closer examination reveals a series of ambiguities or possible interpretations, each of which ought to be given due weight. The sayings themselves suggest an interest on Heraclitus' part in oracles as a model for his practice: "The lord whose oracle is at Delphi neither asserts, nor hides, but gives a sign" (DK 22 B93).[4]

Like the oracle of Apollo at Delphi, Heraclitus too neither gives a simple and clear declaration of his views, nor sets out deliberately to confuse (although many of his ancient readers found him deeply confusing and obscure).[5] Instead, he hints and provokes further thought. It is most likely that this tactic was chosen because Heraclitus is committed to the view that what matters is that each of his readers should come to their own considered understanding of things, rather than take on views simply through his own authority. It is reasonable to think that Heraclitus, therefore, has a conception of the proper method of philosophical thinking, namely that an essential part of philosophical enquiry and, with luck, of any eventual understanding that results is that it is self-driven and involves a personal engagement with certain questions. DK 22 B101 reads: "I went to search out myself". This is not a confession of some deep personal voyage of self-discovery as an end in itself. Heraclitus does not want to turn us all inwards and make us solely introspective. Nevertheless, the project he recommends is one that each of his readers must take up individually and that will involve considering their place within the world as a whole. If anything, we are asked to look outwards as much as inwards; we learn about ourselves by considering the world around us afresh.[6]

We should bear in mind this approach as we consider some of the sayings, both individually and in groups organized by theme. It should not surprise us if we often come to the view that there is a variety of possible interpretations, or that it is simply unclear from the sayings what Heraclitus' own view may have been; the work is not set out as a persuasive exposition of Heraclitus' own conclusions, stating reasons and heading off objections.

The opening

Although the arrangement and original order, if there was any, of many of the sayings is quite unclear, we can be fairly confident of how Heraclitus' work opened. This is one of the longer fragments and serves as a useful preface to the remainder of his philosophy:

> This *logos* being the case always men fail to understand (*axunetoi*), both before they hear and when first they have heard it. For, although all things come to be according to this *logos*, they seem to be unaware as they try out both the words and deeds of the sort that I set out by distinguishing each thing

according to nature and saying how it is. Other men do not
pay attention to what they do when awake, just as they do not
pay attention to what they do when asleep.   (DK 22 B1)

The general tone is recognizable as a familiar denigration of what
"other people" think or do. But Heraclitus here begins to explain why
most people are mistaken or fail to recognize the truth and simultaneously provokes the reader into enquiring further: precisely the method
needed to remedy the problem. Let us therefore use this opening as a
starting-point for tracing some themes through his other sayings.[7]

I have left one crucial word – *logos* – untranslated because the
question of how to understand what Heraclitus means by using it
here is a good example of the sort of thinking we need to do. The
Greek word *logos* has a wide range of meanings: it can refer to a
single word, or a statement, or a longer piece of connected linguistic
material (an argument or story); it can mean a reckoning, evaluation,
relation or ratio. Coming as it does here at the beginning of a work,
it would be most natural to understand it to mean the work itself in
a self-referential way; "this *logos*" would therefore mean something
like "what you are about to read". But as soon as we move a little further into the sentence we come across a further difficulty. It has long
been noted that the adverb "always" sits in an ambiguous position:
does it mean that this *logos* is always the case, or that men always fail
to understand it, or both?[8] As we read on it is clear that Heraclitus is
pessimistic about most people's chances of achieving some understanding of what he is going to talk about, but there is a temptation to
think that he also means to say that his *logos* is always the case. That
surely cannot mean that his book exists always, but something more
like the claim that what he is going to talk about is always the case.
Logos has therefore also to be understood as meaning the subject
matter of his description, not just the description itself. And with that
thought we might go back to the men who "always misunderstand":
they always misunderstand not just what Heraclitus says or writes,
but also the subject he is talking and writing about.

We should certainly not try to pin down a single meaning of
logos here or try to determine precisely what "always" qualifies. The

intended effect, it seems, is of a series of possibilities and a recursive reading of the phrase: going backwards as well as forwards, reading and rereading in the light of what comes next. We might also, for example, choose to look for help in some of the other sayings. Many of them also make prominent use of the word *logos*: "Listening not to me but to the *logos*, it is wise to agree (*homologein*) that all things are one" (DK 22 B50). The slogan "all things are one" will concern us later. For now, let us concentrate on the reference to *logos*. If we try to combine this with B1, it seems that we are indeed meant to separate the *logos* from the precise content of what Heraclitus is saying. B50 is an incitement not to be too concerned with picking apart what Heraclitus says but instead to think ourselves and to try to listen to the *logos*. At the very least, this is a clear indication that we will not get very far if we do not move away at all from the specifics of Heraclitus' own words. Again, returning to B1, we remember that many people fail to understand the *logos* even when they have heard it. Once more, we might separate the *logos* that is the content of Heraclitus' work (which we can well imagine not understanding when we first listen to it) from the *logos* that is what Heraclitus' work is an attempt to point us towards. Even this latter we might fail to understand at first, but B50 seems to want us to persevere in listening (cf. DK 22 B19).

B1 tells us that all things come to be "according to this *logos*". This could mean simply that Heraclitus' work is a correct account of the world: it accurately describes what happens. The *logos*, on this view, might be like a statement of some physical law; the statement of, for example, the ideal gas law does not itself cause the volume of a certain mass of gas to decrease as pressure increases at a constant temperature, but it does accurately describe what happens. We might charitably consider the claim in B50 that "all things are one" as something along these lines. But, looking ahead, there is precious little clear description of that sort in what we have of Heraclitus' work (although there is a reasonably clear cosmology that can be extracted from them). Some of the statements may well turn out to be true, once we think about them in the right way, but there is something odd about calling them an account of the world. Perhaps we might try to understand the phrase "according to" in a stronger sense: the *logos* is in some way the cause of all things coming to be as they do. This would make the *logos* something much more exotic than a general account and instead it becomes a more active part of the world, perhaps even the single overarching cause of all things. Nothing we have seen so far rules out this interpretation of the fragments and, indeed, it seems that certain ancient readers were prepared to see such ideas in Heraclitus. The Stoics, who themselves held that the world was thoroughly infused and governed by a rational causal principle (which they sometimes called *logos*, sometimes god) looked back to Heraclitus as a predecessor (see Long 1996a; cf. West 1971: 124–9).

Before we move on, we can add one further saying: "Although the *logos* is shared/common (*xunos*), many live as though their thought were private" (DK22 B2). Like B1, this emphasizes how most people are unaware of how things really are but live in their own private world. They do not see what is common, shared (*xunos*), and as a result fail to understand themselves and believe instead that their thought is somehow private and isolated. This is unlikely to be a comment directed at recognizably more modern concerns about introspection and the apparently first-personal nature of much of our conscious activity or even the "problem of other minds". Rather, the language of this fragment strongly recommends that we read it alongside B1. In B1 people fail to understand (are *axunetoi*) the *logos*; in B2 we learn that the *logos* is common (*xunos*).[9] The failure, which is described both in terms of the metaphor of being asleep (and therefore failing to be properly "awake" to the world around us) or else mistakenly considering something common and shared to be private, is therefore to be remedied by some kind of recognition and understanding of what is in fact common. Other sayings suggest that wisdom is not to be identified with factual knowledge or technical expertise: certainly not with the sort of expertise and authority often granted to Homer, Pythagoras, Xenophanes and the like.[10]

It is difficult to summarize the results of our reading so far, but we might offer something along the following lines: Heraclitus' account (*logos*) is meant to be generally applicable and its subject (*logos*) is something general and common too. Moreover, as B50 has already suggested, the content is also, in its most concise formulation, a generalizing one: "all things are one". A similar set of relationships describe the recommended state of understanding or wisdom, which is equated with a recognition of something common and a rejection of "private" thinking (presumably meaning a rejection both of thinking only about oneself and not the world as a whole and also of thinking that sees the world only from a particular private viewpoint). Heraclitus is prodding us, annoying us and forcing us to "wake up" and think for ourselves.[11]

Cosmology and fire

Suppose we take up the challenge and begin to ponder the *logos* of B50: "all things are one". What does this mean? For someone coming to Heraclitus from the philosophy of Thales, Anaximander and Anaximenes, it might be natural to understand this first to be a cosmological claim. Certainly it is an assertion of some kind of monism.

How are all things one? Perhaps all things are one in the same way that Thales asserted that all things come from water. Perhaps this is an assertion of material monism. Certainly Heraclitus does seem to offer a kind of physical theory based on four elements, where the world is characterized by a constant interchange between earth, air, fire and water:

> This ordering (*kosmos*), the same for all, no god nor human made, but was and is and will be always, fire everlasting, kindling in measures and going out in measures.
>
> (DK 22 B30)

> The reversals of fire: first sea, of sea then half earth half lightning. (DK 22 B31a)

> Sea is poured out and measured into the same ratio (*logos*) as it was before becoming earth. (DK 22 B31b)

> All things are repayment for fire and fire for all things, just
> as goods are for gold and gold for goods.   (DK 22 B90)

Two things emerge immediately: Heraclitus in some way privileges
fire as the most important of the constituents of the cosmos. B30
identifies the cosmos as an everlasting fire and B90 makes fire function as an analogue for currency in the various elemental exchanges
described in B31a and B31b. This pair of sayings hints at a regular
and regulated system of elemental exchange in which each element
or cosmic constituent (mentioned here: fire, sea – perhaps standing
for water in general – earth and lightning) is part of a series of transformations that take place according to strict ratios or orderings.
This is certainly reminiscent of Anaximander's description of the
injustice and reparations between cosmic constituents and Heraclitus is, no doubt, responding to such Milesian speculations.[12] It is
also likely that although fire is doubtless the most important of the
various things that compose the cosmos, Heraclitus is not committed to making it a constitutive element in every item in the cosmos.
The simile in B90 suggest that, just as when I buy a loaf of bread for
70 pence, an exchange takes place and the loaf I take away is worth
but not composed of 70 pence, so when fire becomes, for example,
sea, that sea is somehow worth or equivalent to a certain amount
of fire but is not itself made of fire. More important, certainly, is the
notion that there is a fixed and regular amount of fire that becomes a
fixed amount of sea. Even so, we can relate this cosmological account
directly to the concise formulation "all things are one", since there
is a case for seeing a material monist view here much like the previous Milesian accounts; all things are one in so far as they are made
up of these elements and these elements are unified by the cyclical
interchange and by all being transformations of one element: fire.

We might wonder whether B30 is meant to claim that there was an
original state of the cosmos in which all things were fire. Out of this
original fire all things came to be and into a similar state of total fire
all things will eventually return, perhaps with another cosmic cycle
coming after. This would add a global diachronic cyclical story to the
picture we have so far assembled of cyclical elemental transformation

that is otherwise compatible with thinking that the cosmos is a stable system maintained by a constant exchange between the elements. Here our information becomes difficult to assess since many of the sources on Heraclitus' cosmology are clearly reading him through later Stoic writers, who did indeed assert a global cosmic cycle of periodic conflagrations (*ekpyroseis*) in which all the cosmos became fire, but there is no reason to rule out a similar thought in Heraclitus himself.[13]

Why should fire be given this prominent place in the cosmology? There is also some evidence that Heraclitus may have associated fire with a governing capacity and perhaps even assigned it some directive role in the cosmos. He asserts that human souls function best when dry (by noting the erratic behaviour of drunks) and that "for souls it is death to become water" (DK 22 B77, B117, B118). No clear identification is made between souls and fire, however, and Heraclitus may in fact have had no intention to make any clear statement about the soul's physical nature (see Kahn 1979: 245–54; Schofield 1991). However, other fragments give fire something like a regulatory role: "Fire as it progresses will discriminate and grasp all things" (DK 22 B66), and "All things the thunderbolt steers" (DK 22 B64). Whether we should identify the thunderbolt, the main traditional attribute of Zeus, as a kind of fire depends on what we make of the reference in B31a to lightning as, apparently, one of the things that fire becomes.[14] But B66 certainly ascribes to fire certain powers, no doubt deliberately playing on the various possible senses of "discriminate" (physical separation, some epistemological faculty of discrimination, legal decision-making) and "grasp" (again, both physical and epistemological senses are possible).

Heraclitus' universe is in many ways similar to those of his Milesian predecessors; it involves regular and regulated elemental transformations and it singles out one particular element for a special role. Heraclitus, however, is perhaps more concerned than his predecessors to stress the dynamic aspects of this cosmological view, a dynamism reflected in his choice of fire: fire is a particularly dynamic element, needing to be constantly fed and producing a spectacular change in transforming fuel into heat and light. It is the obvious choice for someone, such as Heraclitus, who is fascinated by change and transformation.[15]

Opposition and unity

We have already seen a series of transformations on a cosmic scale that reveal an underlying unity: all things are exchanges of fire and this series of transformations creates another unity over time. But Heraclitus' sayings also display a more general concern to show unities of other, often mundane, kinds and, in particular, a concern to show surprising unities that result from apparent oppositions. No doubt, this is all part of his concern to provoke us into considering and understanding how "all things are one".

The remaining sayings offer many examples, often in seemingly banal sentences, whose immediate subjects are everyday objects or thoughts. Some are phrased in a very concise and deliberately paradoxical fashion that leaves the reader to complete the thought.[16] Others offer some more assistance. Let us begin with an example of the second group: "Sea: purest and foulest water; for fish drinkable and nourishing, for humans undrinkable and deadly" (DK 22 B61). This begins with an apparent contradiction. How can the sea be both the purest and the most foul water?[17] This is not just a paradox; it threatens to be utter nonsense. As Aristotle points out, if Heraclitus seriously wishes to assert this, he is breaking the law of non-contradiction. It simply cannot be asserted that anything is in the same respect both F and not-F; water cannot be simply both purest water and foulest water since the two properties are contraries. Aristotle would undoubtedly have a case, were this all Heraclitus says. But the next phrase specifies that the sea is purest in one respect and foulest in another: for fish it is purest and for human beings it is foulest. Once these qualifications are understood then Heraclitus commits no gross logical error (cf. Barnes 1982: 69–75; Graham 1997: 7–12).

However, we might think that Heraclitus is saved from a deep logical mistake only at the price of making his statement dazzlingly boring. The first phrase promises to reveal a profound opposition in the nature of the sea, only for that profundity to be undercut by the prosaic qualifications that follow. But there is still an important insight to be gained from closer inspection of this saying, one that starts from the process of reading we have just outlined. The profundity and/or confusion is dispelled by a careful specification of the various respects in which the sea is pure and foul. This reveals two important things. First, it is (in a way) still true to say that the sea is "purest and foulest" and that is perhaps an interesting thing to have worked out about the nature of the sea. The sea would not be what it is unless it displayed such characteristics. Secondly, and more importantly, by working through the ways in which it is first purest and then foulest, we might come to see that there is indeed an opposition in the nature of the sea, but that this opposition is grounded in a more fundamental unity. After all, it is one and the same thing that displays these apparently contradictory properties, able both to preserve and damage life. Then, two lessons would emerge: (i) it would be wrong for us to both adopt a chauvinistic or human-biased attitude to the sea and declare it to be "undrinkable" without recognizing that it is so only to us since it is quite different for fish; (ii) recognizing that the sea is, in a way, life-preserving in no way allows us now to see it as a new source of nutrition. Relativism, once recognized, does not require us to abandon our own particular perspective even if we can now recognize it as one of a number of relations. In short, and at the risk of generating yet another Heraclitean pronouncement, the saying encourages us to recognize that water is undrinkable *from our perspective* and also that from our perspective *water is indeed undrinkable.* Compare Xenophanes' argument against anthropomorphic theology discussed above (pp. 42ff.). The crucial difference between Xenophanes' argument and Heraclitus' thought is that, in Xenophanes' example, we add the premise that the very same gods cannot be both human-shaped (as depicted by human beings) and horse-shaped (as depicted by horses). In contrast, it is perfectly possible for the sea water in Heraclitus' example to be both undrinkable to human beings and also excellent for fish; in fact, this combination is perhaps an essential part of its nature. Heraclitus stresses the partiality of the human viewpoint by contrasting it with the position of god, for whom all these oppositions are unified. Indeed, it sometimes sounds as if god is identified with the unity of these oppositions, perhaps with the *logos* itself: "The god: day night, winter summer, war peace, hunger satiety. It changes as when mingled with perfumes it is named by the pleasure of each" (DK 22 B67). Other sayings similar to B61 omit the explanatory qualifications and leave the reader to do the work. For example: "The road up and down is one and the same" (DK 22 B60). This could be read as a general statement applicable to Heraclitus' cosmology in its entirety, pointing to the cyclical transformations of elements and even to the eventual consumption of the whole cosmos by fire. But even if we read it as a saying about roads, it is certainly puzzling. Surely the road up is not the same as the road down: if the Duke of York wants to march his men up the hill he will go one way and if he wants to march them down the hill he will go another. It would be disastrous if he were to think that it does not matter which way he goes. But if we add some qualifications once again, the saying becomes less paradoxical: the road up and down is *the same road*. If he marches up a hill and then down the hill he can use one and the same road: any road up is *ipso facto* also a road down; you just need to travel along it in the opposite direction. And once again, the apparent contradiction reveals an underlying unity. It is only by being one and the same road that it can be both a road up and simultaneously a road down.

Other examples work in a similar way.[18] Yet another kind gives us one half of qualifications offered in B61's claims about sea water. For example: "Asses prefer rubbish to gold" (DK 22 B9). This is on the face of it a boring statement of fact. But read in conjunction with the set of sayings we are currently considering, we are encouraged to look for something significant in the assertion and construct our own Heraclitean paradox. There are various possibilities. We might take B61 as a model and say "Rubbish is valuable and valueless: valuable to asses, valueless to human beings", or "Gold is valuable and valueless: valuable to human beings, valueless to asses". Of course, this ought not to make us give up all our gold coinage and attempt to pay for goods with rubbish instead. But it might make us realize that there is nothing intrinsically valuable about gold since it is worthless for donkeys.

Other sayings take a different approach. Instead of taking one thing (e.g. sea water) and showing opposites inherent in it, they take two apparently opposed and contradictory things and show their unity. For example: "Disease made health sweet and good, hunger satiety, and tiredness rest" (DK 22 B111).[19] We might naturally assume disease and health to be absolutely opposed and, moreover, wish to have only health and never be diseased; similarly with hunger and rest and their opposites. But Heraclitus suggests that the "positive" member of each pair of contraries has its value only because of the negative member (and, perhaps, vice versa). So health and disease in fact form an important unity: neither would be what it is and neither would be desired or avoided were it not for the presence of the other. Heraclitus is as prepared to find unities in apparent oppositions as he is to find oppositions in apparent unities.

The relationship between the opposites is variously described as a harmony and also as a kind of strife or tension. Indeed, Heraclitus is – unsurprisingly – quick to offer the paradoxical identification of harmony and strife. DK 22 B51, for example, points to the construction of a bow or of a lyre as cases of a tension that results in a stable and useful product. The arrangement (the Greek *harmoniē* can mean a "fitting-together") and tension created by the pull of the strings and the opposing pull of the frame of a lyre is precisely what is needed for a tuneful – "harmonious" – instrument.[20] Just as in the cosmic fragments we saw a willingness to talk both in terms of lawful exchange (such as that of goods for gold) and also images reminiscent of Anaximander's cosmos of constant injustice regulated by reparation, so Heraclitus is happy most generally to talk in terms both of harmony and discord when describing the dynamic tension and unity of the opposites. For example: "We should know that war is common (*xunos*) [cf. DK22 B2 above, p. 63] and justice strife and all things come to be ... according to strife" (DK 22 B80).[21] Conflict is not entirely rehabilitated by identifying it simply with concord. Rather, we are encouraged to consider how conflict and concord are related and even, perhaps, in some ways unified.

Rivers

The sayings so far are all good examples of ways in which we might understand the central slogan that "all things are one". Some of them also hint at the idea that this unity is the product of a kind of tension or strife: a dynamic process of change that results in an overall stability. But Heraclitus was often associated with a very radical doctrine of "extreme flux": the idea that the world is subject to constant and thorough changes such that nothing at all is stable for any time. This picture of the flux-obsessed Heraclitus can be traced in particular to Plato and to various followers of Heraclitus such as Cratylus, who gives his name to one of Plato's dialogues.[22] Cratylus, we learn from Aristotle, espoused a radical theory that he traced back to Heraclitus and, in turn, influenced Plato: "When Plato was young he was a companion of Cratylus and acquainted with Heraclitean views: that all perceptible things are constantly in flux and there is no knowledge of them. (Later, Plato too believed this.)" (Aristotle *Met.* 987a32–b1). Elsewhere, Aristotle explains just how radical Cratylus' view came to be:

> Cratylus ended up thinking that we should not speak but instead simply raised his finger. And he criticised the Heraclitean statement that it is impossible to step into the same river twice, for he thought it was impossible to step into it even once. (Aristotle *Met.* 1010a12–15)

Aristotle is interested in exploring the absurd consequences of taking the extreme view that the world displays no stability whatsoever. Cratylus cannot even name anything, since by the time he has spoken what he is trying to name has already changed. Nothing is even so determinate as to allow any kind of description; nothing can be communicated. Even Cratylus' wagging finger will fail to point to anything in particular since nothing is at all one way rather than another.[23]

There is no particular reason why we should think that Heraclitus himself thought that the world displayed such an extreme state of flux, and indeed Cratylus is depicted here as explicitly building on and extending an original Heraclitean idea. That original thought is most famously expressed in Heraclitus' sayings about stepping into a river, to which we have already seen Aristotle allude. Here we might find what Heraclitus had to say on the subject of flux and the core of the later slogan attached to his thought "everything flows" (*panta rhei*).

There are, in fact, a number of different formulations of the "river fragment" transmitted by our sources and there has been considerable discussion over which, if any, of these is the original Heraclitean version. It has also been suggested that various formulations of the saying appeared as a refrain through his work, suggesting that Heraclitus took this set of claims about rivers also to be a generally applicable image for his worldview as a whole.[24] The versions printed in Diels and Kranz's edition as "B" fragments are:[25]

> It is not possible, according to Heraclitus, to step twice into the same river.   (DK 22 B91)

> Into the same rivers we both step and do not step; we both are and are not.   (DK 22 B49a)

> On those stepping into the same rivers different and then different waters flow.   (DK 22 B12)

B91 is explicitly offered as a report of Heraclitus' views rather than a quotation. It is the only one of these three, we should note, that gives the famous saying that it is impossible to step into the same river twice. The evidence from Aristotle that Cratylus responded that it is impossible to do so even once might, nevertheless, count in its favour.

In any case, let us begin with B12. Its form is like that of the descriptive sayings we have already encountered (e.g. B9). The central contrast is clearly, however, between the sameness of the rivers and the difference of the waters flowing along, and this is enough to provoke some reflection. If the waters in the river are constantly changing so that, at any location along the river, there are no two moments at which the very same water is present, why do we say that it is the same river from moment to moment? The answer must surely be that rivers are interesting precisely because they are constantly moving. In fact, an essential part of what it is to be a river is for there to be constantly moving water: that is what distinguishes a river from, say, a lake. So the different waters are not a reason to be cautious about the river's permanence over time. Rather, they are a necessary condition of the river's stability. This paradox is summed up nicely in the short saying "It rests by changing" (DK 22 B84a).

Another saying (DK 22 B125) draws our attention to a barley drink, made from various ingredients that are held in suspension and mixed only when the drink is stirred. (Think of salad dressing made from oil and vinegar.) The drink remains only when its constituents are agitated; its permanence also depends on change. If we allow B91, for the moment, to be a genuine Heraclitean claim, then it should be clear that it approaches the question of the river's identity over time from the opposite position. In order to make any sense of the deliberately paradoxical and provocative claim that it is impossible to step into the same river twice we must, at least for a moment, entertain the idea that the river is to be identified with the water that constitutes it at the moment at which we step in. If that is so, then on two different occasions different water will be present and, if the river and its water are one and the same, there must therefore be a different river there.

In combination, these two fragments offer a sophisticated dialogue. B12 provokes us to reflect that the self-same river is in fact constantly changing; B91 then provokes us to find some constancy in the ever-changing waters. Neither view captures the whole truth and yet neither view is clearly mistaken. B49a is something of an amalgam of the other two: it asserts and denies that we step into the same river and then, most surprisingly, offers a further enigmatic claim about us. In addition to the river and its waters, there is a further factor involved in any attempt to step repeatedly into a river; namely, the person doing the stepping. And what do we say about the identity of a person over time? Let us imagine someone taking their first two dips into the river Cam. Clearly some things about the bather will change from one dip to another: for one thing, on the second occasion and not the first it will be true that "The bather has previously stepped into the Cam". Various other things may also have changed: the bather's hair may have grown a little; he might now be shivering and cold. A question now might arise, provoked by Heraclitus' curious assertion that "we are and are not", about how much can be allowed to change before we become unsure whether it is the same person who is taking a dip on two different occasions. Such questions of "personal identity" have a long and complicated history in philosophical thought and Heraclitus shows no signs of offering an answer here. But it is possible that he raised the question.[26] Indeed, we might speculate that Heraclitus considered personal identity in a manner analogous to the identity of a river: it is precisely by changing (at least in some respects) that a person is a person. Or, in other words, it is an essential part of being human that we change, age, grow and so on.

There is a very good case, therefore, for seeing in these river fragments the core of Heraclitus' paradoxical conception of unity and difference, permanence and stability, applicable to particular cases of things in the world (such as a river), to more general cases (the cosmos as a whole remains stable through elemental changes), and even to what might be Heraclitus' most pressing concern: human existence and the place of human beings within the cosmos.

Gods and men, life and death

We have already seen that Heraclitus is prepared to contrast the partiality of the human perspective with a divine unity of opposites (DK 59 B67). He is also evidently interested in offering some thoughts on mortality and the cycle of life and death. This has clear associations with his general cosmological perspective: the pairing of life and death and the constant renewal of human generations are other illustrations of the overarching principles of unity and stability through change. It is part of what it is to be human that we are born and die: that is what sets us apart from the immortal gods. And yet through the constant renewal of mortal human life we might be said to approach some kind of permanence and immortality (see DK 59 B20). That is at least one reasonable interpretation of part of the tantalizing DK 22 B62: "Immortals are mortal, mortals immortal, living their death, dying their life".

The other half of this confusing and provocative set of pairings also deserves thought: in what way are the immortals mortal? Perhaps "the immortals" here are the elements that for some brief period of time compose a living person and, in so doing, take on a kind of mortality. Alternatively, these immortals are indeed the gods as commonly conceived, but perhaps the point is that they are dependent for their status as immortals on there being a distinct group of mortals against which they can be compared. In this way, the immortals themselves turn out to be dependent on and defined by mortality. In other fragments, life and death are compared with the daily cycle of waking and sleeping, again drawing close links between the rhythm of human life and the cycle of the cosmos (DK 22 B21, 26 and B88).[27]

As we might expect, despite the many references to god, or to particular gods such as Apollo and Zeus, Heraclitus offers no clear and easy to understand statement of a theological or ethical view. But there are some specific claims we can extract from the sayings: he is, for example, apparently prepared to encourage a certain kind of life and to praise certain kinds of death, notably deaths in battle. He is also comfortable invoking the idea of justice, not only in the sense in which Anaximander had conceived of a "just" system of cosmological exchange but also in the more familiar sense of what is lawful or, perhaps, fair.[28] Even on the evidence of the opening fragment B1, which we discussed above, he is clearly interested in provoking in his listeners some kind of reorientation and change of perspective, encouraging them to take on a new and deeper understanding of the cosmos and their life within it. It seems that for Heraclitus this also had some kind of religious significance, altering the way in which we are to approach the gods and engage in various kinds of ritual (see DK 22 B5, B14 and B15; Adoménas 1999). Other fragments point to an interest in the evaluation of a person's life, often linking the destiny or later fate of a person's soul to the manner of his death (see DK 22 B25, cited above [p. 58], and B24) and echoing the common motif from epic poetry of the importance of fame and reputation continuing after a person's death. More generally about death and what is to come, Heraclitus comments tantalizingly: "Things await men as they die which they do not anticipate or conceive" (DK 22 B27). Unfortunately, it is never made clear precisely what these unexpected things are, and no doubt we are to draw the now familiar lesson that we should not expect any direct teaching from Heraclitus in any case. Moreover, perhaps Heraclitus feels unable to offer any more clarification for another reason: simply because he is himself still alive and has not yet any direct experience of what is to come. He is sure only that the conventional accounts of the afterlife are likely to be mistaken and warns us – in a characteristically paradoxical fashion – to be prepared for the unexpected.

FIVE

Parmenides

Parmenides of Elea, a town on the west coast of southern Italy, is perhaps the most celebrated of all the early Greek philosophers. His fame and importance derive from his one known work: a poem in the hexameter metre used also by the Homeric epics, which was perhaps entitled *On Nature* or *On What Is.* There is no doubt that he was also very influential in his own time, and caused quite a stir in the Greek intellectual world. He is the first of our philosophers whose followers are themselves well-known – the paradox-monger Zeno of Elea and Melissus of Samos – and who can be said to constitute some sort of philosophical movement. Parmenides cast a tremendous shadow over all succeeding Greek philosophy, not only of the period before Socrates, but long after too. Plato names one of his dialogues in Parmenides' honour, and the philosophical problems first emphasized by Parmenides exercised Plato, Aristotle, and their successors.

It is easy to overstate the discontinuities between Parmenides and what had come before. He does, it seems, seek to offer a deductive argument about the necessary characteristics of "what is" without reliance on empirical information. His argument, as a result, is highly abstract and difficult, and we shall see that it has therefore both attracted and frustrated interpreters ever since.[1] There is evidently a new turn towards a self-conscious application of principles of logical analysis and argumentation that has not previously been centre-stage. However, Parmenides is in other ways still firmly within the tradition of philosophical speculation inaugurated in previous generations (cf. Graham 2002; 2006: 148–85; Nehamas 2002). He is steeped in the poetic literature of Greece and chooses to produce a work in the form of Greek hexameter poetry. His work is also full of mythological motifs, personifications and religious imagery that is reminiscent of Homeric epic, Hesiod's theological poetry and other literature well known to Parmenides' audience. Further, although the early part of his poem, the so-called "Way of Truth" has attracted the bulk of later interest, it is clear that Parmenides also set out a cosmological account not unlike those of his predecessors. He gave an account of the basic constituents of the universe, how they interact to form such things as the visible heavenly bodies and so on. In all this he is steadfastly following what by now had become a familiar trail. Just how this cosmological account is meant to fit with the "Way of Truth" is another puzzle we shall have to consider, but it is worth keeping in mind throughout that Parmenides saw fit to offer such a systematic and detailed cosmology, whatever he thought about its chances of being a true account.

Even so, the conclusions of the "Way of Truth" are so startling that there is little wonder that they have attracted so much attention. The argument concludes by denying that there can be any change, any coming-to-be and perhaps any plurality and difference at all. If the argument is sound, reality must be unchanging, perfect, homogeneous and everlasting and our common apprehension of a world full of difference, change and plurality is very mistaken. Not only does this pose a challenge for our everyday acceptance of the world we perceive, but it places a serious obstacle in the path of any natural philosopher wishing to give an account of the world about us. All accounts of that sort, however they explain the world, involve explanations that accept that some things change, some things come to be and so on. If Parmenides' poem is right, then all such projects are hopelessly misconceived. It is no wonder, then, that Parmenides' work seems to have sent shockwaves through early Greek cosmology. The "Way of Truth" is a challenge to any cosmological account. It is all the more puzzling, therefore, that Parmenides himself includes just such a cosmological account in the same poem.

The conclusions themselves are striking enough, but perhaps even more interesting is the way in which they are reached. The "Way of Truth" rules out coming to be and change in a challenging way, not on empirical grounds (since it contends that the senses are terrible guides to reality, as can be seen once we check his conclusions against how the world seems to us) but on *a priori*, non-empirical grounds. The poem offers a picture of reality deduced by strict logical argumentation from what are taken to be necessary truths. Its contention is not just that it *happens* to be the case that there is no coming to be or change, but that it *must* be this way. To avoid these conclusions some new tactics need to be found. It is not enough to point to some empirical evidence, since Parmenides' argument would simply reject that as compelling. Nor will it do simply to come up with a better and more complicated cosmological story. We need to tackle his arguments and find some flaw in the derivation or object to one of the premises. Parmenides' poem is an attempt to talk philosophically in a new way about how the world must be. He would be worth reading only for that, regardless of the nature of his conclusions.

A map of the poem

Let us start with a basic map of his poem.[2] It is conventionally divided into three parts.

1. *The Proem.* An unnamed young man, the narrator of the poem, tells of his journey to see a goddess. He travels with a divine escort beyond the human world to meet her and is offered by her a revelation. Most of the poem is his account of her address to him.
2. *The "Way of Truth".* The goddess explains how all mortal opinions are radically mistaken: they all make a profound logical mistake, confusing being and not-being. The goddess reveals what reality is truly like, by showing how to be consistent in

one's thoughts about what is. Reality turns out to be unchanging, eternal, motionless, perfect and single. There is only one thing. Of course, monism as such is not a new idea; Thales himself was a monist of a sort and Heraclitus too is very keen to impress on us the idea that "all things are one". But Parmenides' monism is of a very radical kind: only one thing exists, and anything that is not identical with that one thing does not exist. In other words, Parmenides is prepared to tell us that all the familiar furniture of the world is unreal. His message is not that all of it is somehow unified or somehow made of one fundamental substance. Rather, the "Way of Truth" ends with the disconcerting conclusion that everything – including ourselves – that we usually take to exist, in fact does not exist.

3. *The "Way of Opinion"*. Then the goddess gives a more familiar cosmological account of how the cosmos we perceive came to be. She uses two principles: light and dark or light and night. Only a small proportion of the "Way of Opinion" section survives. Parmenides was, evidently, cited by later philosophers more for the conclusions in his surprising "Way of Truth", although it is worth remembering that some later writers were happy to attribute some of the cosmological theories from the "Way of Opinion" to Parmenides as if they were indeed parts of his own favoured physical account.

The proem and the choice

The mares that carry me as far as my desire reaches formed an escort, when they took and led me to the much-famed road of the goddess, which leads the knowing man everywhere unharmed.[3] There I was brought, there the much-led mares took me, straining at the chariot, and the maidens lead the path. The axle, burning in its sockets let out the shriek of a pipe (for it was driven by two round wheels at each side), while the maidens, daughter of the Sun, hurried to send me on my way, leaving the house of Night for the light, lifting the veils from their heads with their hands. There are the gates of the paths of Night and Day and around them a lintel and a stone threshold. The shining gates are filled by great doors, to which much-punishing Justice has the reciprocal keys. The maidens addressed her with soothing words and cleverly persuaded her swiftly to push the bolted bar from the gates. As they opened, the gates made a yawning chasm in the door frame, swinging in turn the bronze posts in their sockets, fitted with rods and pins. Straight through there the maidens drove the chariot and horses along the broad path. And the goddess welcomed me kindly, took my right hand in hers and thus addressed me, saying … (DK 28 B1.1–22)

Parmenides provides an elaborate setting for his philosophical poem and throughout the work, even in the famous deductions in the "Way of Truth" he combines his argument with poetic imagery and metaphor.[4] He is concerned to use and manipulate vocabulary and themes familiar to his audience from other works and other genres, perhaps to ease their understanding of the work and certainly to mark his own place within a wider Greek intellectual tradition. The opening describes how the unnamed narrator was escorted by the daughters of the sun, carried in a horse-drawn chariot, to the gates of night and day. There is an elaborate description of the gate, and how the daughters of the sun gain entry for the narrator. Clearly, he has been admitted to a place of great importance, far from the experience of most mortals. He is met by the goddess who greets him and explains what he is to learn. This is only the first of a number of journeys in the poem: the goddess casts her own description of reality and the method by which we should come to see reality as it truly is as a road we have to stick to. Travelling and thinking are closely connected: both are conceived as having a direction and a goal and having to stick to a path. The narrator's journey, which is in many ways like other epic heroes' journeys to the underworld, takes him to a place fit for him to receive the goddess's message. That message itself takes him on a journey along the path of the "Way of Truth" and then along the confused path of the "Way of Opinion".

There has been some discussion about the precise direction of the journey to meet the goddess. Have the daughters of the sun brought him into the light, which might suggest the kind of "enlightenment" he is to receive? Or, more likely, have they come into the light to fetch him and then take him away back to the place guarded by the gate? Whichever of these we favour, why does Parmenides take such pains to construct this elaborate setting and how does it add to the philosophical message of his poem? In some mythological accounts this gate is the entrance to the House of Night, which is where night and day alternate. As one leaves the other returns. So beyond the gate is a place where it is neither day nor night. This would seem to be appropriate given that the poem is going to try to persuade us to rethink entirely our belief in change, difference, time and so on. It is delivered in a place where night and day, the primary markers of change and time, no longer apply. It is also likely that Parmenides intends us to see the journey and experiences of the narrator as some kind of initiation. He is being let into some very arcane secrets indeed: nothing less than the true nature of reality. Perhaps it is necessary for him to be removed from the mortal world in order to receive this message clearly and without impediment. An important conclusion of the goddess's argument will be that the world we are used to is deceptive and illusory. Further, the truth is not something that could be learned from any mortal source. Men are so confused that only direct divine revelation can reveal the truth. Once the truth is revealed, it can be recounted in the form of this poem. So as we read Parmenides' poem and as we come – he hopes – to accept his conclusions, we similarly remove ourselves from the world of senses and the world of most men.

The poem continues with the goddess offering a critical choice.

> Come and I will tell you (and listen and pass on my words):
> there are only two routes of inquiry for thinking. One: that
> it is and that it cannot not be; this is the path of Persuasion
> (for it attends on truth). The other: it is not and it is neces
> sary that it not be. This latter I say to you is a completely
> un-learnable way, for you could not know what is not (for
> that cannot be done) nor could you say it.   (DK 28 B2)

The argument of the poem is structured as a journey. The goddess offers a choice of two paths of enquiry but immediately rules out one of the paths. Only one is left, and that is the path we travel in the remainder of the "Way of Truth", following the various signposts left along the route as we find out more and more about the consequences of sticking rigorously to this path. Path 1 is marked "IS"; path 2 is marked "IS NOT". These are exclusive: there is no possible overlap between them. They are also exhaustive: there is no third possibility. The goddess tells us that path 2 – "is not" – cannot be taken; so we are left necessarily with path 1. (Other mortals, we shall discover, mix up the two paths.)

We should notice immediately what kind of starting-point we have been offered. There is nothing about *arkhai* or elements or some original primordial state of the universe as we might have expected from other works of this kind. Parmenides' goddess is evidently trying to start at the most abstract and general level, talking not about anything even so specific as the most general physical constituents of the world. The most pressing questions we would want to ask at this stage are the following:

- What "is" or "is not"? What is the subject of the verb "is" here?
- What does "is" mean here?

Our problems are compounded by a linguistic difficulty. Greek does not need to express a separate subject with a verb. Although in English "is" will not do as a complete sentence and we need to add some sort of subject ("it is", "the tree is" or something similar) Greek feels no such need; the single word *estin* can be a complete phrase. Usually, when a subject is not explicitly stated, it is clear from the context what subject we are supposed to understand or supply. But since this is the very opening of the enquiry, no suitable subject is available. In that case, for now let us assume that when the goddess says "is" we are to understand her to mean this in a very general sense. We might read her as saying by "is", "[it] is", where [it] stands for "anything you like". These are, remember, paths of enquiry. So we can further specify that the [it] here is "anything you might be enquiring into", or thinking about. When we are faced with a decision between the two paths of enquiry, we are faced with the following dilemma: for anything you might want to think about, that thing, [it] either "is" or "is not". (Sometimes, for grammatical reasons, I will have to use "[what] is" instead; this too is meant as a general place-holder for any proposed object of thought.)

Understood in this way, we can begin to see why the path "[it] is not" is denied by the goddess. If we are enquiring into something, we must be enquiring into something that is. Why? Because, if that thing is not then it is not there to be thought about or pointed out.[5] This is the point of the last two lines: you cannot say "[what] is not"; nor can you point out "[what] is not". These last two lines are perhaps the most important in the poem since they give the reason for rejecting the path of "[what] is not". The goddess will appeal again and again to the ban on "[what] is not" as we follow the "Way of Truth", and this is the place where that ban is justified.

Therefore, it is of the greatest importance for the goddess's argument that this justification should be sound. It is also, in that case, a prime target for any objections to her argument. If this justification is faulty, then the major starting-point for her deduction is removed. If the objection works, then everything that follows is undermined. The objection is obvious: surely we can talk about or point out something that is not.

Remember that we decided the best way to understand the idea of "[it] is" was to take the goddess to be talking about any possible object of enquiry of thought. But surely there are plenty of possible objects of enquiry of thought that are not. If so, then her reason for rejecting the path of "[it] is not" is false. What can I think about that "is not"? I can think about a unicorn, a blue banana or a perpetual motion machine. None of these things "are", but I can think about them. I can even invent things, make things up in thought that have never been thought of before. (Notice that we have not yet specified precisely what we mean by saying that something "is" and "is not". The goddess has said nothing specific about a particular meaning for the "is" in "[it] is", so we are entitled to be similarly open in raising our objection.)

The goddess's response would probably be as follows:

> When I said you cannot think of what is not, I also intended the complementary claim that whatever you can think of is. I am not sure whether you think that these various possible objects of thought you come up with "are" or "are not". If you are to object to me, then you must think that they "are not". But then you seem to be contradicting yourself, saying that there "are" these objects of thought and also that they "are not". Perhaps you mean to say that all of these things "are" since you are saying that they can be thought about. Very well. All these things on your list, for the moment at least, can be allowed to be (I say "for the moment" because as I go on you will discover that the strict application of this choice will rule out not only blue bananas but common yellow bananas from being also. In fact the whole of the world you perceive turns out not to be.) In any case, if you can think of a thing, then let us allow for the time being that it is. But you should take care always to be consistent and never to let in anything that "is not".[6]

This interchange ought to prompt us to try to get clear about precisely what we mean by "is" or "is not", since the goddess is urging us to make clear what we mean by saying that we can think about something that "is not". The goddess thinks that mortals are in general confused over this. Here we begin to address our second question: what does "is" mean here? Again, there are some linguistic problems to bear in mind. The Greek verb "to be" (the present infinitive form is *einai*; the form for "it is" is *esti* or *estin*) has a number of functions.[7] "It is" can mean:

(i)   It exists. (Call this the "existential sense".) "It is" in this sense can function as a complete statement.
(ii) It is true; "it is" can be used to assert that a proposition is true, that things are as described. (Call this the "veridical sense".) "It is" in this sense can function as a complete statement.

(iii)   It is somehow or it has some property (as in "It is red"). This is an "incomplete" use of "it is" (sometimes the verb is described here as a "copula") since it needs some other component, called a predicate or complement, to complete the sense. (Call this the "predicative sense".)

If we want to press our objection against the goddess, we need to say that she is not only *failing to distinguish* them, but is in fact *confusing* them in a way that makes some of the steps in her argument invalid. The goddess wants there to be a very strict division between what "is" and what "is not". When we imagined her response to our objection that it is possible to think of something that "is not", she was insistent on us deciding one way or another whether the proposed object of thought "is" or "is not", maintaining that this is a clear and exclusive choice. Armed with our set of different ways in which we can use the verb "to be", we might try to resist this pressure.

We can begin by making a concession to the goddess. Perhaps she is right to say that it is impossible to think of or point to something that *does not exist at all*, in any sense whatsoever. Try to think of something that does not exist at all. You cannot. If you succeed in thinking about something, then *by that very fact*, there is something there to be thought about. If you have a thought at all, then there is something you are having a thought about. Just so: something that does not exist at all *cannot* be thought about. But we need not agree that it is impossible to think about something that "is not" in one of the other senses of "to be". For example, taking the veridical sense, it is depressingly easy to think something that *is not true*. Similarly, taking the predicative sense, it is possible to think about something that *is not*, for example, *white*. We can now restate our objection: bearing in mind the various senses of "to be", I can think about and point out something that "is not" in some of those senses (perhaps the veridical and predicative senses) which "is" is another sense (perhaps the existential sense). For example, if I think of my cat wearing a top hat it is both true to say that I think of something that is (I do have a cat) and also true that I think of something that is not (he is not wearing a top hat; it is not true that he is wearing a top hat).

The "Way of Truth"

Let us keep this objection in mind and keep glancing back to it as we proceed along the "Way of Truth". This section of the poem is preserved more or less completely. "There remains one account of a route: that it is. On this route there are many signs, that it does not come to be and does not perish, whole, one-limbed, un-shaking and complete" (DK 28 B8.1–4). The goddess tells us there are signs to guide us. As we go along we shall learn more about "[what] is" – that if [it] truly is, then [it] must also have the following characteristics: it must neither come to be or pass away; it must be whole, single, perfect and so on. Provided we stick to the path we shall pass along each of these sections. This is a way of showing what it means to be consistent in the way we think about "[what] is". A consistent application of the rule that you cannot speak of "[what] is not" amounts to a strict following of the path. If we try to think of anything that fails these tests, we are trying to think of something that is not, which involves some not-being. Remember that we imagined the goddess saying that only "for the time being" would she be happy with us thinking of unicorns and the like, provided we meant to think of them as things that are. These will all fail one or more of these tests for being something that is. Of course, so will all the other things we think exist, not just these mythical or imagined things. All sorts of things we would not originally suspect of involving "[what] is not" will fail one of these tests, since they come to be, or pass away, or change.

> Nor was it nor will it be, since it is now all together, one, continuous. For what birth for it would you look for? From where did it grow, and how? I shall not allow you to say or think: from what it not, for it cannot be said or thought that it is not. And what need would force it to grow later rather than earlier, beginning from nothing? So either it must be completely or not be. (DK B8.5–11)

We can now begin the first of the goddess's arguments, which uses the idea that it is impossible to allow "[what] is not" to deduce that "[what] is" must never have "come to be". By "come to be", the goddess must mean primarily something like "begin to exist". We might at first think that there are plenty of things that come to be in some way or another – people are born, houses are built – but all of these are shown to be misconceptions by the time we reach the first of the signposts along the route. The method the goddess uses is the template for all the following arguments. Its logical form is called a *modus tollens* or "denying the consequent": the goddess shows that "[what] is" cannot come to be, because if it had done so then we would be committed to thinking about something that is not, which violates the guiding principle she set out at the beginning. The form of this argument is repeated through the "Way of Truth". The goddess takes a possible property or characteristic of "[what] is" (here the property of coming-into-being) and shows that if "[what] is" really is, then [it] cannot have that property. Having that property involves us trying to conceive of not-being, which is impossible. So nothing comes into being from what is not and, we begin to realize, we must reject as possible objects of thought anything that comes to be.

We can set out the argument as follows:

1. If [it] comes to be, [it] comes to be from "[what] is not".
2. [It] does not come to be from "[what] is not" because "[what] is not" cannot be thought of.
3. So [it] does not come to be.

Step 2 is a restatement of the principle that it is impossible to think of what is not, and has already been the subject of some discussion. We have already lodged an objection to that principle. The rest of the work in this argument is done by the conditional in step 1, which claims that anything that comes to be must do so from "[what] is not". It is this necessary involvement of "[what] is not" that rules out any case of coming to be.

Why should we accept step 1? What does the goddess mean? We are still talking very generally, so [it] can still be any possible object of thought or enquiry. Take a mundane example: a sandwich. Sandwiches are not everlasting things. They are made and they are eaten or decay.

Still, I think I can think and talk about a sandwich. But the goddess wants me to think like this: when I say, "I have made a sandwich", implicit in that statement is the claim that *before* I made the sandwich it was true to say "the sandwich is not; it does not (yet) exist". It is argued that although we might not directly be thinking about "[what] is not", such an attempted thought is implicit in our commitment to the truth of claims that say that something comes to be. This sort of implicit acceptance of "[what] is not" is the kind of thing that the goddess thinks all mortal opinion is subject to, and it is an example of us failing to stick consistently and rigorously to the path of "[what] is".

This interpretation might be supported by what the goddess says (DK 28 B6) about the mistakes made by most mortals. They "know nothing, wandering two-headed" (line 5). They are "carried along, blind and deaf, a bewildered, undiscriminating crowd" (lines 6–7). Tellingly, they are said to be people to whom "'[it] is' and '[it] is not' are the same and not the same" (lines 8–9). This last point seems to be the basis for their portrayal as confused and wandering, failing to stick properly to the path of "[it] is". Their failure is not so much that they fail to make the proper distinction and discriminate between "[it] is" and "[it] is not", but that they fail to do so consistently. If asked, no doubt, they would agree that the two are not the same, but it is all too easy – according to the goddess, at least – to demonstrate that they muddle them up. A simple claim, such as the claim "I made a sandwich", shows just how easily mortals can implicitly try to think of something that is not. Our most basic assumptions of there being a world in which many various things come to be and change are thoroughly infected by such confusions. It is, of course, a deliberate irony for the goddess to say that we mortals are deaf and blind; we are deaf and blind precisely because we take the world we see and hear to be true. This is presumably one reason why the goddess needs to remove the poem's narrator from the world he is used to, the world of change and of alternating day and night, before he can be ready to accept her truth.

What can I say in reply? First, I might say that of course there was no sandwich before I made the sandwich, but that does not mean that the sandwich came to be from nothing. Rather, it was made out of pre-existing things: some slices of bread, ham and cheese. All the same, the goddess will insist, there was no *sandwich* there, was there? Not unless you want to say that the pre-assembled ingredients in the fridge somehow already constitute a sandwich, and in that case it would be false in the first place to say that you "made" a sandwich; it was already there. In more general terms, the goddess must rule out any other possible source from which [it] comes to be other than "[what] is not".

Our earlier distinction between senses of "to be" might help. We might allow that it is impossible for something to come into existence out of nothingness (we can call this "no *genesis ex nihilo*") but not that it is impossible for one thing to come out of another. Thinking again about my sandwich, we might say that the sandwich did not come to be out of "[what] does not exist" (the existential sense) but it did come to be out of "[what] is not a sandwich" (the predicative sense). And when I think or talk about "[what] is not a sandwich", I am not thinking or talking about nothing at all; rather, I am think- ing about something that is not a sandwich but is something else; namely, the set of ingredients I use – the bread and so on. In other words, this is an objection to step 1 of the goddess's argument:

1. If [it] comes to be, [it] comes to be from [what] is not.

The goddess ought to be clear about what she means by "[what] is not" in this conditional. While it is true that when, for example, a sandwich comes to be it must do so from what is not *a sandwich*, it is not true that when a sandwich comes to be it must do so from what is *nothing at all*.[8] And we have already lodged an objection to her step 2 along similar lines: if it shows anything, it shows only that it is impossible to think of things that do not exist *at all*. It does not show, for example, that we cannot think of something that "is not a sandwich".

We have skipped over this argument quite briskly, but it is worth noting that this set of issues exercised Greek philosophers for some time after Parmenides. We shall see, for example, that many of those who came after him explicitly sign up to a ban on coming to be out of non-existence or *genesis ex nihilo*; that is the one conclusion that all subsequent pagan Greek philosophers seem to accept. It is also clear that many later philosophers, including Plato, agree with the principle that it is possible to know only "[what] is". But just how to counter the goddess's argument is not so clear. The suggestion I outlined depends on accepting that there are these different senses of "to be" that the goddess simply confuses, but that is itself rather controversial. It is certainly not clear that any Greek philosopher articulated such a distinction and it is also not clear that this distinction is a necessary one. A distinction between these three senses of "to be" seems to accept that there is a notion of "existence" quite separate from the notion of possessing properties or bearing predicates, as if the question of whether something exists or not can be settled quite separately from the question of what properties or predicates something has or what sort of thing it is. It is plausible to think that for many Greek philosophers this distinction would have been quite alien and it therefore not surprising that Parmenides' principles had such a lasting legacy. For them, it is strange to separate questions of existence from questions about the properties of any given item. For them, to be and to bear predicates are inseparable: to be is to be something or other.[9]

We should also notice that "the argument from not-being" is not the only argument offered in these lines against the possibility of coming to be. The goddess offers a supplementary argument based on the rhetorical question: "And what need would force it to grow later rather than earlier, beginning from nothing?" (lines 9–10). This is a version of a principle that we have already seen appealed to by Anaximander (p. 32). The goddess asks what reason or need would compel something to come to be *at some point rather than another*. There must, in other words, be some sufficient reason for the coming to be to begin when it does, rather than at some earlier or later point. If someone were to stipulate that [it] comes to be at time t, the goddess will ask: what was any different about time t than the earlier time t_{-1}? Or the even earlier t_{-2} for that matter? The goddess evidently thinks that her question cannot be answered, and that this gives a further reason for rejecting the thought that anything comes to be.

Again, we have to do some work to understand the force of this argument. On the face of it, it seems rather weak. If we return to my example of a sandwich, it is clear that we can give all sorts of reasons why the sandwich was made at this point in time and not earlier or later: it was lunchtime, I was hungry and so on. The argument is more persuasive if it is aimed at some sort of original coming to be: just what we have labelled *genesis ex nihilo*. In this case, we are precisely imagining something coming to be out of nothing whatsoever. So it is not clear why such an event should occur at some time rather than another since we have stipulated that there is nothing existing prior to the coming to be that could act as a cause, trigger or parent. Some support for the idea that the goddess has this specific case in mind might come from lines 12–13. There she rejects the idea that, even once there is something that has come to be, anything else could come to be besides it. This could be part of a progression of thought. First the goddess gives a supplementary argument based on the demand for a sufficient reason why anything could come to be out of nothing at all. Then she gives a further argument to show that even if that first hurdle could be negotiated it would still be impossible for anything else to come to be alongside anything else that is. Nothing can spring out of nothingness, and there can be no one-by-one accumulation of existents.

The goddess feels sufficiently confident in her arguments that she next announces that she has shown that nothing either comes to be or passes away (lines 13–14) and restates her general principles of the exclusivity and exhaustive nature of the choice between "[it] is" and "[it] is not". That "[what] is" should not perish was one of the signposts (line 3) but it is hard to see any argument for this additional conclusion in what we have been given so far. All the same, it is not difficult to see what the argument would be, once we recognize that the case of passing away would just be a mirror image of the case of coming to be. The argument would be something like this:

1.* If [it] passes away, [it] passes away into [what] is not.
2.* [It] does not pass away into [what] is not because [what] is not cannot be thought of.
3.* So [it] does not pass away.

And we can have a similar discussion to that we had about the case of coming to be, now asking about what I should say now about the sandwich I have just eaten for my lunch.

The goddess has produced a pair of principles: there is no coming to be from nothing and no passing away into nothing. These are the first two signposts along the route and already we can see how, if we want to be consistent and not try to think of anything that is not, the possible range of things for us to think about has been drastically reduced. Unless we can find some flaw in the argument so far, anything we thought we could retain as something that is must now pass the twin tests of neither coming to be nor passing away. It cannot come to be or pass away, otherwise it involves not-being and must be discarded as a possible object of thought. Even with our objection based on distinguishing various ways in which we can say that something "is", there is a sense in which the goddess has a very good case. In so far as these are arguments against the idea of *genesis ex nihilo* and of passing away into absolute non-existence, they are compelling.

Now the goddess moves to the property of indivisibility, which is closely related to homogeneity. In fact, the goddess deduces the indivisibility of "[what] is" from its being "no more in one respect, which would prevent it from holding together, and no less in another respect" (DK B8.23–4). For this reason, "[what] is" is homogeneous: no part is any more or less than any other, and therefore it cannot be divided. The idea here is that any differences in the degree of being in "[what] is" must be disallowed because unless that were the case [it] would not be "full of being" (B8.24). In other words, were differences in degree allowed within "[what] is", some of it would be "more" than other parts; some parts would be deficient in being and, since we are by now familiar with the goddess's insistence on the exclusivity of being and not being, anything other than "[what] is" must be the banned "[what] is not".

Imagine an area of red paint. According to the goddess, we ought not to allow any portion to be "more red" than another for this would make some parts deficient in "being red" and therefore introduce "[what] is not". Note that this example is using "to be" in what we called the "predicative sense". If that is the goddess's intention, then it shows that anything that is must bear its properties and predicates uniformly and without variation. Note also that in this example the variation is imagined in spatial terms: some parts being redder than others. But there is no reason why we cannot also imagine the goddess to rule out any other kind of variation. Just before this section, rounding off the denial of coming to be and passing away, she has made the surprising claim that "if [it] came to be, [it] is not, nor is [it] if [it] ever is going to be" (B8.20). There have been various interpretations of this sentence, and the text itself is disputed, but one suggestion is that the goddess wants to rule out the possibility that "[what] is" is at one time rather than another, that its being spreads out or varies over time just as she wants to rule out any other variation in its being. Perhaps she is hinting at some sense in which "[what] is" exists timelessly (see Schofield 1970; Tarán 1979).

From this homogeneity, the goddess insists that "[what] is" must also be indivisible. In one sense this follows quite easily: if there are no variations across it, then it is not possible to pick out any one part or section as being distinct from any other. This is one kind of indivisibility: what we might call "conceptual indivisibility". But there are other kinds of divisibility, including perhaps the most obvious: "physical divisibility". Does the goddess mean that "[what] is" cannot be broken up or split apart? Perhaps, but it is not obvious that the goddess has been thinking exclusively, or perhaps at all, about "[what] is" in physical terms. This is a question to which we shall return, but so far we have no reason to rule out a physical notion of divisibility nor any reason to insist that this must be the sole or even the principle notion in play. If we retain the idea that we are still engaged in a most general enquiry, one for which we can substitute any possible object of thought as a subject for the verb "is", then this will mean that the goddess's conclusions will apply to physical objects as well as anything else we might try to think of. There is, in any case, an argument that would rule out physical divisibility. If we imagine a cake, all of which "is", then any cut we make that physically separates one part of the cake from another will have to introduce "[what] is not" (there will have to be some "not cake" separating the now distinct pieces). The problem, however, is that this indivisibility does not seem to follow directly from the idea of homogeneity. The best way to make that link is to think the goddess believes that division can occur only if there is some reason for a division to occur in one place rather than another. In other words, if something is divisible there must be some sufficient reason why that thing should be divisible at some point rather than another. Now, if "[what] is" is homogeneous, then there is no reason for it to be divisible at one point rather than another. The goddess concludes that it is divisible at no point; it is indivisible.

This line of thought is important for a number of reasons. First, we might ask why the goddess concluded that "[what] is" must be divisible nowhere, and not that it must be divisible everywhere. Homogeneity, we might complain, can show only that what is true at one point must be true at every other; it does not by itself show whether the object is everywhere divisible or everywhere indivisible. We shall return to this question: some of Zeno's paradoxes show what difficulties result from thinking that magnitudes are divisible everywhere, so perhaps we might supplement the goddess's thinking with arguments along those lines. Also, this argument about divisibility seems to have impressed some later Greek cosmologists, the atomists, who insisted that the universe could be explained as the product of the interactions between enormous numbers of indivisible physical things (see pp. 105–7, 159–62).

Before moving on, notice that at the beginning of her deduction, the goddess closely related the idea that "[what] is" is all together and continuous with its being "one" (B8.6). In what sense the goddess insists that "[what] is" must be one has been the subject of considerable debate. It is not clear, for example, that she has shown that there can be only one thing at all: what we call a radical "eliminativist" monism. That very strange view would hold that reality is single in the sense that there is indeed only one thing, which is perfect, unchanging and so on. Only one thing could satisfy all the various necessary requirements on "[what] is". In antiquity at least, Parmenides was generally taken to be a monist of this sort, and his admirer Melissus is certainly a monist of this sort. In any case, it is possible to construct an argument along the lines of what we have in the "Way of Truth" for this conclusion. If there were two things that "are", then there would have to be something between them, something that made them distinct and two. What could this be? It could not be "[what] is", since then there would be no distinction between our two imagined things; there would be in fact just one continuous thing that is. But the only other possibility is that the two are made distinct by "[what] is not", and this would contravene the "choice" back in B2. Or, perhaps if there were two things, each would have "not to be" the other, and this too contravenes B2.

An argument could be made along these lines, but it is not clear that the goddess has done so and nowhere in the "Way of Truth" is this kind of monism argued for directly. Perhaps, some have suggested, the goddess wants to leave open that there are many things each of which fulfils the characteristics she deduced for something that is: that is, it is homogeneous, ungenerated and so on. Anything we might think of that can fulfil these criteria can be said to be something that "is", but there is no reason in principle why there could not be more than one such thing.[10] If, however, the goddess does want to argue for the more disquieting thought that there is only one thing, then we are left with a series of difficult problems. If she is right, then since there is only one thing we "are not", nor – strictly speaking – can there be both a goddess and the mortal to whom she is speaking. (Indeed, if there is only one thing there cannot be both that one thing and some-one thinking of it, since then there would be at least three things: the thinker, the object of thought and the thought itself. The goddess may have anticipated and even welcomed this strange consequence. At least, in the short and puzzling DK 28 B3 she asserts that "it is the same thing to think and to be".)[11] Some of these odd consequences might lie behind Parmenides' decision to put his "Way of Truth" in the mouth of a divine authority. It is not, strictly speaking, something that we human beings can reason about ourselves. The goddess is per-haps, therefore, a mechanism for delivering a conclusion that cannot consistently be reached by human reasoning.

Leaving such speculations aside for now, let us get back to the "Way of Truth".

But unchanging in the limits of great bonds it is without
beginning, without end, since coming to be and destruction
have been pushed far off and persuasive truth has cast them
away. The same, in the same place, it remains and lies by
itself, and so stays rooted there. For strong Necessity holds
it in the bonds of a limit, which hold it all around.

(DK 28 B8.26–31)

"[What] is" turns out next to be unchanging. The goddess seems
to want to rule out change of any sort. Certainly, she talks in spatial
terms that suggest that "[what] is" undergoes no change of place. It
does not move. The exact argument here is rather obscure, but the
goddess is keen to stress the necessity of its changelessness, by talking
about the "bonds" that hold it in place. Yet again, there is considerable debate over the precise argument being offered. Is it, as some
have held, the argument that "[what] is" cannot move because in
order to move it would have to move into "[what] is not": the argument that void of some sort is a necessary condition of motion? If so,
then this would seem to rule out both "[what] is" moving as a whole
(since there is no "[what] is not" outside "[what] is") and also any
internal motion within "[what] is" (since there is no "[what] is not"
inside "[what] is") (see e.g. Sedley 1999: 118; also Malcolm 1991: 75
and n.1). However, others have noted no explicit reference to void
in these lines and also find it hard to believe that we should take
Parmenides to be talking about "[what] is" in literal spatial terms.[12]
After all, although it is cast in spatial terms and talks about bonds
and "staying in the same place", this argument also seems intended
to cover all change. "[What] is" will also not change colour or shape
since, when the goddess comes to recap her argument later, she says
that she has shown that "[what] is" alters neither its place nor its
"shining colour" (8.41). Change is conceived as a kind of coming
to be and is therefore banned along with every other coming to
be. So when a chameleon changes from blue to red, say, this is the
coming to be of a red chameleon and the perishing of a blue one.
Does that mean that "[what] is" can have some colour, provided it
does not change its colour and that its colour is homogeneous? Can

"[what] is" be a homogeneous and unchanging red, for example? It is not clear. Perhaps we would have to say something similar to the argument we offered for why there can be only one thing. If "[what] is" were red, then [it] would not be blue. (Here we might revive the objection about different senses of "to be". I can think of a "not-red" chameleon without failing to have a thought about anything.)

The "Way of Truth" ends with some more tricky lines. Some seem to revisit things already argued for, such as the homogeneity and perfection of "[what] is", but there are new points here too. Particularly striking is the likening of "[what] is" to "the bulk of a well-rounded sphere":

> But because there is a far-point of a limit, it is completed, on all sides like the bulk of a well-rounded sphere, equidistant from the centre in all directions. For it must neither be any more nor any less here or there. For nor is there what is not, which would prevent it from reaching to its like, nor is it possible that there is more of less of what is here and there, since it is all inviolable. For being equal in all directions it stays uniformly in its limits.   (DK 28 B8.42–9)

Now we can revive our questions about whether the goddess is thinking of "[what] is" as something physical, something with spatial extension, shape and size (cf. Owen 1960: 61–6, with Sedley 1999: 121–2). If so, then she has to face some annoying questions. How big is it? If it is a sphere then it has at least an outer surface and a centre. Are these not distinct parts and were we not told that [it] is indivisible? If it is a sphere, what is *outside* the sphere? Nothing? Then why is it limited? But if there is something outside the sphere this would have to be the dreaded "[what] is not". Although there have been attempts to defend the idea that the goddess is claiming that "[what] is" is literally spherical, it seems more likely to be a claim that "[what] is" is perfect. After all, she says only that [it] is "like" the bulk of a sphere. From whatever perspective you look on it, it is the same. However you conceive of it, it is the same. There are no differences, no parts discernible.

We can glance back now and consider our progress from the initial "choice". We might have set out along this route with some confidence, accepting only what looked like a minor restriction that whatever we thought about must "be"; that seemed quite innocuous at the time. But we are left with an odd and alienating picture of reality. Following consistently the ban on "[what] is not", it has turned out that we are left with an unfamiliar reality, which leaves no room for change, plurality, motion, difference, people, days or nights. The goddess has produced an ambitious and startling result from what looked like an unobjectionable starting-point.

The "Way of Opinion"

As if this startling conclusion were not enough, the goddess now turns and offers a very different sort of account. She had promised to tell us not only about the true nature of reality, but also about mortals' opinions:

> You must also know everything, both the unshakable heart of persuasive truth and also the opinions of mortals, in which there is no true conviction. But all the same, you will learn these too, how the things believed must assuredly be, pervading everything thoroughly.   (DK 28 B1.28–32)

Now she returns to that promise.

> For they made up their minds to name two forms, of which there must not be even one – that is their mistake – and separated them as opposites in body and set up signs separately from one another. Here, shining fire of light, gentle, very delicate, in all ways identical to itself but not the same as the other. There, also by itself, opposite, dark night, a dense and heavy body. I tell you this entire plausible ordering so that never will mortals' opinion outstrip you.   (DK 28 B8.53–61)

Why should she do this? Does it suggest a lack of confidence in the "Way of Truth"? Not at all. At no point does the goddess give the slightest indication that anything other than the conclusions of the "Way of Truth" ought to be accepted (see Owen 1960: 49–55). At the beginning of the "Way of Opinion" she stresses this by noting explicitly the end of the trustworthy account about truth and the beginning of a new account of mortal opinion, which is a "deceptive ordering of words" (B8.52; "ordering" here is a translation of the Greek *kosmos*: not only will the account be deceptive, but what it is about, the cosmos we are familiar with, is something deceptive. A few lines later at 8.60 the goddess uses the related word "arrangement", *diakosmos*, to describe the world she will go on to describe in the "Way of Opinion"). Nevertheless, there are at least two good reasons for her to press on and give not only an explanation of how people generally go wrong, but also an account of the world in terms familiar from other competing Greek cosmologies.

The first reason is that it is often not enough merely to know the correct account about something. It is often important also to know the reasons why alternative incorrect accounts are sometimes accepted instead. This can be educationally very useful. It will help the goddess's attempt to persuade us of the truth if she can also demonstrate what is wrong with alternative accounts. It can be part of her attempt to rid us of any residual doubts and any remaining commitment to a view of reality incompatible with the conclusions of the "Way of Truth". The goddess herself also offers a second reason. She has just begun her cosmology by setting out the two principles. She explains how important this account is, but also explains why: it is offered to us "so no mortal account will outstrip you". The best interpretation of this is that it is a further dialectical move. The goddess offers the best cosmology possible: no other cosmology can come close to competing with it. (Indeed, it is possible to think that it is a cosmology that perhaps deviates *as little as possible* from the "Way of Truth"; it begins with the thought that there are two things rather than one.) But even this, the very best possible cosmological account, is bogus and deceptive. If we are armed with the best cosmology possible and can see that even this is hopelessly misguided then we will not be tempted by any other cosmology someone might offer, now or in the future. We shall never be tempted to abandon the truth for some alternative since the very best on offer is still nonsense. The "Way of Opinion" can therefore act as a kind of prophylactic. The goddess knows that we might still be tempted to consider new and innovative cosmologies in the competitive marketplace of ideas. Still, not only can she – and, of course, Parmenides – demonstrate her prowess in producing such an account, she can inoculate us against ever being tempted to abandon the conclusions of the "Way of Truth" by offering the best such account and emphasizing that even it is hopeless. The entire project of this kind of cosmological speculation is doomed, no matter how sophisticated or how complex it becomes. It is doomed because it is subject to the very same failing of all mortal opinion: it thinks that "'[it] is' and '[it] is not' are the same and not the same" (see Reinhardt 1974; also suggestions in Mackenzie 1982).

More detailed conclusions about the specifics of the cosmology that the goddess offered are difficult to draw because this section of the poem clearly interested later ancient authors rather less than the earlier sections, such that only a few short fragments remain (see Granger 2002). From the end of B8 we can see that it is a cosmology built on two fundamental and opposite stuffs: bright, light, fire and dark, heavy, night. We have already suggested that the location of the goddess's revelation, beyond the gates of day and night, somehow relates to a desire to dissuade us from there being a basic and fundamental opposition between day and night and the various changes that the alternation between the two might bring. Here, the deceptive cosmology builds in that opposition at its foundations and the goddess makes clear even at the outset that although each of this pair may share some of the characteristics of "[what] is" from the "Way of Truth" (for example, it seems that neither fire nor night ever comes to be or passes away), in other ways this dualistic cosmology is quite incompatible with the strict denial of the possibility of "[what] is not": the goddess stresses that each of the pair is distinct, unlike, and *is not* the other. Starting from only these two basic components – the smallest possible deviation from the apparent monism of the "Way of Truth" – it is shown how an account might be constructed of the familiar world of mortals. From the other fragments that survive it seems that the goddess gave an account that covered many of the usual subjects: the nature and workings of the heavenly bodies, the mechanisms of growth and reproduction and the workings of perception. It is also possible to see echoes in the cosmological account of things we have learned in the "Way of Truth". This in no way serves to support the content of the cosmology, but rather shows how easy it might be to fall from consistently following the correct path. The very slightest deviation from that route can lead to all kinds of misconceived notions.

Let us take as an example DK 28 B10, in which the goddess gives a programmatic statement of what her account will include:

> You shall also know the nature of aither and all the signs in the aither and the destructive effects of the shining sun's pure torch and from where they came to be. You shall learn the wandering accomplishments of the round moon and its nature. And you shall learn about the surrounding heaven, from where it grew, and how Necessity, leading it, constrained it to hold the limits of the stars.   (DK 28 B10)

Note the echoes of motifs from the "Way of Truth". Once again we have a set of signs, but now they are the moving perceptible heavenly bodies rather than the guiding characteristics of "[what] is". In these few lines the goddess works in references to things coming to be, changing and moving: all things banned by the "Way of Truth". And she describes these cosmological processes of change and motion as led by necessity, in similar terms to those she had used to describe the necessary changelessness of "[what] is". Now we are armed with the *Truth* we can diagnose the errors, the mixing of being and not-being in all this, and we can spot the many reminiscences of phrases or ideas in the "Way of Truth", now subtly perverted.[13] And we are similarly armed against any other cosmology that might be proposed. We are also able to see how deceptively similar these cosmological accounts are: the same words, almost, deployed in a different order can produce such different and misleading results. Each time we recognize what is wrong in the "Way of Opinion" or in any similar cosmological account, we recall and remember the original and authoritative account of the "Way of Truth".

SIX

Reactions to Parmenides

However influential or powerful we imagine the arguments of Parmenides to have been, they were certainly not successful in discouraging entirely the practice of cosmological speculation. Indeed, if Parmenides had intended to put an end to all such accounts of the origin and composition of the cosmos, then he would surely have been very disappointed by the response to his arguments. The period after Parmenides saw no diminution in attempts to explain the universe and the processes of change and generation within it, although perhaps Parmenides would have been pleased to see that those attempts tended to be more self-conscious and precise in their claims about which things "are", which things are fundamental to the universe and how these fundamental things compose everything else. It is also worth noticing that Parmenides had himself, arguably, already led the way by producing the first post-Parmenidean cosmology in his own "Way of Opinion".

Parmenides' supporters: Zeno and Melissus

Before we turn to those philosophers who seem to have been influenced by Parmenides and tried to find a way to return to cosmological system-building, we can look briefly at two philosophers who were inspired by Parmenides to write in support of his general project. The three together – Parmenides, Zeno and Melissus – are sometimes described as the "Eleatic" school, although Melissus was not in fact from Elea but from Samos, an island at the opposite end of the Greek world. That Melissus, a prominent Samian citizen and general, was evidently so influenced by Parmenides is a good example of the circulation of ideas and, presumably, texts across the Mediterranean at this period (see pp. 10ff.).

Melissus and Zeno each deserve serious consideration of their own, and Zeno's paradoxes in particular have continued to fascinate and frustrate philosophers since his own time. My principal interest in them here, however, is to point out the diverse ways in which these two philosophers are "Eleatic". Zeno, the more famous of the two, composed a number of paradoxical arguments designed to show the difficulties involved in maintaining a number of intuitive beliefs about space, time, plurality and motion.[1] Most of his work is lost, so we have to reconstruct his arguments from reports in later critical writers such as Aristotle. In one of the few likely quotations from Zeno, an argument against pluralism runs as follows:

> If there are many things, then there must be as many of them as there are, no more and no less. If there are many things then they must be limited.
>
> If there are many things then there are infinite things that are. For there are always other things between the things that are, and again other things between these too. And thus the things that are are infinite. (DK 29 B3)

The argument is obscure in its details but clear in its structure and destructive purpose. It challenges a believer in the existence of a plurality of things (again, note how Zeno is careful to remain neutral about what these things are; it does not matter at all to his argument whether we think of atoms, or elements, or people) to show how this does not commit him to holding two contradictory thoughts: that the things that are are both finite and infinite in number. Any belief, it is implied, that necessarily leads to such contradictory consequences must be rejected.

Perhaps the most famous of Zeno's arguments are his paradoxes of motion. For evidence of what these paradoxes were, we have to rely on reports by Aristotle, who is keen to dismiss them and often provides only a very cursory account of what they were. A certain amount of reconstruction is therefore needed. There are two major paradoxes: the Stadium (sometimes known as the Dichotomy or the Achilles) and the Arrow.[2]

The Stadium

> The first argument says that there is no motion, because it is necessary for something moving to arrive at the mid-point before the end-point.
>
> (Aristotle *Phys.* 239b11–13 [DK 29 A25])

> The second is called the "Achilles" and says that the slowest runner will never be caught by the fastest, because it is necessary for the pursuer first to arrive at the point from which the pursued set off, so it is necessary that the slower will always be a little ahead.
>
> (Aristotle *Phys.* 239b14–18 [DK 29 A26])

As Aristotle himself notes, the philosophical puzzle is the same in both cases, although the Achilles version is rather more fun. We shall have to expand the first argument since Aristotle's report is extremely concise. Imagine Achilles trying to cross a room. Before he gets to the end of the room, he must get half-way across. But before he gets half-way across he must get a quarter of the way, and so on. In short, before completing any part of the journey it will be necessary to complete a journey half-way. If that is right, then any journey, however small, will seem to require the completion of an unending series of prior journeys, since any distance can be further divided to generate more and more smaller distances, each of which will in turn have some mid-point that will have to be crossed first. Now it looks as if in order to do anything so mundane as just crossing a room, Achilles will have to complete an infinite series of prior tasks. But surely it is impossible to complete such an unending series? However many he completes, there are still more and more to do. So Achilles cannot cross the room.

The second version turns this into a problem about completing a race, but essentially the problem is the same. Imagine that Achilles races a tortoise but, sportingly, gives the tortoise a 100m head start. However fast Achilles runs, Zeno's argument suggests, still he cannot catch the tortoise because (assuming, just for ease, that the tortoise moves at 1/10 Achilles' speed) when Achilles gets to the point from which the tortoise started the tortoise will have moved on 10m. And when Achilles gets to that point, a further 10m on, the tortoise will still have progressed, this time just 1m. And when Achilles gets to this new point, the tortoise will still be a little ahead. Note here that the problem is *not* that Achilles would have to travel an infinite distance to catch the tortoise, since we can calculate he will have overtaken the tortoise if he can run just over 111.11 metres. Nor is the problem that it would take an infinite amount of time to catch the tortoise, since once we have specified the time it takes him to traverse the first 100m head start, we can easily calculate a time by which he would have overtaken the tortoise. Rather, the problem is once again that, just as in the first version, in order to reach the goal of a point just ahead of this slow-moving target Achilles seems first to have to perform an infinite series of actions since he needs to pass each one of an unending sequence of points where the tortoise once was.

The crux of the problem is that we want to believe these three claims:

(i)   In crossing a whole distance AB we cross all of the intervening points on the line AB.

(ii)   The line AB contains an infinite number of points. (This is true however long the line is, since a point itself has no magnitude and a line of any magnitude can be divided.)

(iii) It is impossible to complete an infinite series of tasks.

The combination of these three generates the paradox. In reacting to the paradox, ancient readers of Zeno took differing approaches. Aristotle himself questions (i) by invoking one of his favourite contrasts: between something's being "potentially" and its being "actually". The line AB, for example, only *potentially* contains this infinite series of points. It *could be* divided anywhere, should we wish. But it does not *actually* contain them. A point is made actual only when we in fact make some kind of division of the line, whether physically or in thought. After all, says Aristotle, lines are not composed of points: how could they be if points are themselves without any magnitude? So Achilles does not have to touch each one of an infinite number of actual points in getting from A to B and, says Aristotle, the problem is dissolved. The problem is that once we begin thinking through Zeno's paradox we do begin to make these divisions, thinking of each point that comes in the never-ending sequence.

Alternatively, some philosophers denied (ii). The atomists, for example, claim that after a certain level of division you reach units that, while they are of some magnitude, cannot themselves be divided: *atoms*. While they seem primarily to have been interested in physical units of matter, the same idea could be held also about units of spatial distance: after a certain level of division we reach spatial magnitudes that, while they have some size, are not in fact further divisible. The upshot of this would be that the line AB is composed of a large – but not infinitely large – number of atomic units. And Achilles can certainly manage a finite number of tiny tasks. This approach has its own consequences, however, since now all motion threatens to become a sequence of "jerks", as a moving item can never be half-way along an atomic spatial unit; it must either not yet have begun moving across or else be at the end.[3]

The Arrow

The dimension of time has not yet played a serious role in these puzzles, but in the next paradox Zeno puts it at centre stage.[4] "The third argument is the one just mentioned, that the moving arrow is at rest. This follows from thinking that time is composed of 'nows'. For if that is not granted the argument will not follow" (Aristotle *Phys.* 239b30–33 [DK 29 A27]). Aristotle refers back to an earlier, but also very brief, discussion of this argument:

> Zeno argues wrongly. If, he says, everything is at rest or in motion, but (i) something is not in motion whenever it is against what is equal, and (ii) everything moves in the "now", then the moving arrow is motionless. But this is false, because time is not composed of indivisible "nows".
>
> (Aristotle *Phys.* 238b5–9 [DK 29 A27])

Once again the argument needs some reconstruction. One plausible version runs as follows. Imagine an arrow in flight. At some point in its flight, I take a freeze-frame photograph of it. Is it moving in the photograph? No, the photograph shows a static image of an arrow occupying a particular region of space equal in size and shape to its own dimensions. (This is probably what Aristotle means by saying that something is not in motion whenever it is "against what is equal".) But I could take a similar photograph at any and every instant of the arrow's flight. So, in fact, it is true at any and every instant during the flight that the arrow is not moving. We can set out the argument in the following steps:

1. At any "now" an arrow is not moving.
2. This is the case for any and every "now" in the arrow's flight.
3. So throughout an arrow's flight an arrow is in fact not moving.
4. What is not moving is at rest.
5. So an arrow in flight is always at rest.

We need to clarify what is meant by a "now": as used here it means an instant – a durationless point in time, the temporal analogue of a geometrical point. Aristotle objects that the argument makes an invalid inference from 2 to 3. What is true *at every instant* is not necessarily true of the whole duration since a duration of time is not composed of instants (just as a geometrical line is not composed of points). So although it is true that an arrow is not moving at every instant, this does not mean that it does not move over a period. The concern now, however, is that it is unclear how a "now" is related to a stretch of time. What is time made of if not of "nows"?

It is also possible to object that step 1 trades on an ambiguity. In the sense that it is true that the arrow is not moving at any instant, it is also true that the arrow is not at rest at any instant. (So we can also claim that step 4 is in this sense false.) This is because the properties of being at rest and being at motion are true only of things over periods of time. Perhaps it would be helpful to distinguish between what is true "in" and "at" an instant. Nothing can properly be said to be at rest "in" an instant, just as nothing can move "in" an instant. If an instant is a durationless point of time, then of course there can be no motion or rest in it. But we can say that something can be at rest or in motion "at" an instant just as we can say that the arrow in the freeze frame photo is in motion "at" that instant (not "in" it) because it is in motion over the period within which this instant occurs.

The problem with this response is that it appears to beg the question. In order to evade the paradox it confidently assumes that the arrow is in motion. Certainly, once we are agreed that the arrow does move then we can go on to say something about what we should think about its motion or rest at an instant during its flight. But whether the arrow moves at all is precisely what Zeno wants to question. Further, this response yields an important point to Zeno. It accepts that, strictly speaking, nothing is "now" moving (nor, it turns out, is anything "now" at rest), if by "now" we mean a durationless instant. But if nothing is ever "now" moving, then when *is* it moving? This seems to be quite a concession and it might carry some important consequences. While we might begin with the reasonable thought that if motion occurs, it occurs in the present, the response to the arrow paradox has led instead to the thought that motion and rest are not properties we ought to ascribe to things on the basis of how they are in this strict sense of "now". Instead, motion and rest turn out to be things that we attribute to things in virtue of their having been in different locations in the past from those they are in now.

Another line of response is to offer an atomic account of time, the analogue of the spatial atomism canvassed in reply to the Stadium. If, contrary to Aristotle, it is suggested that time is composed of indivisible "nows", but "nows" each of some temporal duration, then we can avoid Zeno's conclusion. At the points between one now and the next it is true that the arrow is not moving, but since each now is not further divisible then it is not the case that the arrow is not moving throughout the period of its flight. Of course, atomic time – like atomic space – is not without its own consequences, which would have to be explored fully if this were offered as a serious reply to Zeno.

In both the arguments about plurality and those about motion, Zeno shows that some of our very basic starting assumptions are not free from complexity and perhaps even internal inconsistency. In his *Parmenides* (128bff. [DK 29 A11–12]), Plato makes Zeno admit that his philosophical purpose was to offer a defence of Parmenides (see above, pp. 15ff.). That defence must be of an indirect sort. Zeno imagines that many people will react to Parmenides' "Way of Truth" simply by asserting the reality of plurality, motion, change and the like. They might claim that Parmenides' arguments can be ruled out of hand immediately, without having to point to any particular logical fault they might display, since they conclude by denying what we ought to take as the starting-points of any enquiry; namely, the reality of all these various categories. Zeno responds by asking such objectors to try to make sense of these categories of plurality, change and the like. His paradoxes put pressure on these "common-sense" notions and show that, in fact, they are either entirely ill-conceived and internally inconsistent or else certainly have no better claim to be commonsensical or unquestionable starting-points for any account of the world. Aristotle apparently hailed Zeno as the first "dialectician" since, like Socrates after him, he works by taking someone else's preconceptions or beliefs and working within them to uncover inconsistencies and shaky foundations (see the report in Diog. Laert. 8.57 [DK 29 A10]).

Melissus' defence of Parmenides is of a very different kind. He chooses to write a work that sets out a recognizably Parmenidean picture of an everlasting and changeless reality, but in a prose form. He writes directly, without the elaborate mythological framework of Parmenides' goddess and her initiation of the young traveller, and in other ways seems to have been concerned to offer a clear and unambiguous statement of his form of Eleaticism. For example, there has been some discussion over whether Parmenides intends "[what] is" to be everlasting or whether he is trying to express the different thought that it is timeless (see Owen 1966; Schofield 1970; Tarán 1979). Melissus, in contrast, very clearly opts for the former alternative: "Whatever is always was and always will be. For if it came to be then necessarily, before it came to be, there was nothing. If, then, there was nothing, never would anything come to be from nothing" (DK 30 B1).

A similar pattern emerges elsewhere. Although in Parmenides there is some doubt over whether "[what] is" is spatially extended or, indeed, has a shape, there is little room for doubt that in Melissus "[what] is" is spatially infinite in extent, just as it is temporally infinite. Again, Melissus' reality is definitely one in number. Fragment B6 states: "If it is to be infinite then it would be one; for if there were two then they could not be infinite but they would have boundaries with one another". Evidently it is not enough to be infinite by being boundless in at least one direction (as two lines might be infinite, one in one direction and one in another, although they meet at a shared point). "[What] is" must be absolutely boundless.

Earlier (p. 97), we noted some uncertainty over whether Parmenides himself denied motion to "[what] is" on the grounds that there can be no void. Again, there is no similar uncertainty over Melissus' position: locomotion both within and without "[what] is" is ruled out since if "[what] is" were to move, [it] would need somewhere to move to. It must therefore find some unoccupied place where "[it] is not". But there cannot be unoccupied place without there being "[what] is not".

> Nor is there any void (*keneon*). For the void is nothing and what is nothing could not be. Nor is there motion: for it is unable to move aside at any point, but, rather, it is full. If

> there were void, then it could move aside into the void. But,
> as there is no void, then there is nowhere for it move aside
> into. (DK 30 B7.7)

We can extract from the argument the following conditional statement, which lies at the heart of much subsequent debate about the
nature and possibility of motion:

> If X moves, it moves into what is not/the void.

This can be understood to mean that space is necessary for motion,
and perhaps even that some absolutely empty space (void) is necessary for motion: if everything were packed tight and full there
would be no room for anything to move at all. The clarity of Melissus' expression would no doubt have encouraged later thinkers to
focus on the argument in this form. The Eleatics deny the possibility
of motion by ruling out what would be necessary for it to happen:
the void. Others, however, the atomists among them, agree that the
conditional is true (you *do* need void for motion to occur) but argue
that since, evidently, things do move there must be unoccupied space
(void). Others still, Anaxagoras, Empedocles, and Aristotle among
them, say the conditional is false: you do not need empty space for
motion to happen. Indeed, Aristotle tries to argue that motion would
be impossible if there were any void.

In all, it would be wrong to think of Melissus' philosophy as simply
a more straightforward version of Parmenides' poem, because the
differences between him and Parmenides are not cases of simplifi-
cation or mere clarification but of an application of Parmenidean
modes of thinking in a new context. It is worth pausing, first, to
ask why he should have chosen to write such a work in prose. This
may represent a decision on Melissus' part to return to the prose
medium used by Anaximander and strip away Parmenides' Homeric
allusions, or perhaps it shows a growth in the popularity of written
texts of a technical and broadly scientific nature in contrast to the
oral performances that suited the verse form.[5] It is also helpful to
think of his work as a brand of Eleaticism offered in the tradition of

more familiar cosmological accounts, since his interest is focused more acutely on questions of change and qualitative variation rather than on Parmenides' own interest in the logic of the verb "to be" and its relationship to possible objects of thought and speech. Melissus begins not with the argument that it is impossible to think or speak of "[what] is not" but with the physicist's premise that "[what] is not" cannot be the source of any coming to be. If that is the correct view of his preferred focus, then it is possible that Melissus is the important first step in the story of the reception of Parmenides by those who still liked to think of themselves as offering accounts of the physical world. They could look to Melissus as an application of Parmenidean principles to physical questions of the extent of the universe or of the possibility of change, and react accordingly. (Indeed, it is Melissus who is named in Chapter 1 by the author of the Hippocratic treatise *On the Nature of Man* as an example of misguided thinking and misplaced use of argument.)[6] As we shall see, many of them react by accepting the impossibility of coming to be from what is not and of passing away into what is not. But more specifically, Melissus also challenges any view that wishes to save the appearances of plurality and change as follows:

> For if there were many things, they would have to be the sort of things as I say the one is. For if there is earth, and water, and air, and fire, and iron, and gold, and what is alive, and what is dead, and black, and white, and all the other things that men say are real, if there are these things and we see and hear rightly, then each of these would have to be such as first we decided, and not change or become different, but each would be always what it is.   (DK 30 B8.2)

This demands that any account of the world has to answer Melissus' concerns about the existence of plurality and the existence of various perceptible properties and common substances. We should note that Melissus includes himself among those who see and hear change. Unlike Parmenides, who hands his account over to be delivered by a goddess who can look down on and criticize the misguided mortals, Melissus' argument is being delivered by one of us, a mortal who is faced with a perceptible world but driven by force of argument to question its truth. Melissus, of course, goes on to argue that since we perceive all the various items on his list changing and coming to be then we must necessarily be perceiving wrongly. And once more, his challenge has to be answered by any later theorist who wants to posit some underlying unchanging things in the world: if that is indeed the case, then why do we perceive things so differently? Can the evidence of our senses be given any weight in our thinking about the basic elements and processes at work in the world? Parmenides and Melissus therefore not only set the scene for much of the metaphysics of the next century or more but also open up all manner of epistemological difficulties for later accounts of the world to negotiate.

Chronological concerns

At this point, however, we should recognize that our apparently satisfying story of the transmission of Eleatic thought, via Melissus to later cosmologists, runs into some significant chronological difficulties. It would be neat to suppose that Anaxagoras and Empedocles, both of whom – as we shall see – clearly react in some ways to Eleatic thought, were aware of both Parmenides and Melissus' work. Unfortunately, the relative chronologies of Zeno, Melissus, Anaxagoras and Empedocles are not certain and it is likely that they were all more or less contemporaries. This matters if we want to assert particular lines of influence between them, and means that we need to be very careful before asserting any particular relationship between their works. Let us take, for example, the question of whether motion requires the presence of "[what] is not", or void. Clearly, by the time of the atomists, a generation after these philosophers, it was a clear and agreed matter of debate. But remember that there is good reason to be wary of thinking that Parmenides himself asserted that void is a necessary condition of motion (see p. 97; cf. Malcolm 1991). Many interpreters (e.g. Barnes 1982: 217–22) think that Melissus was the first to articulate such a view. There is also reason to think that Empedocles and Anaxagoras rejected the principle (see Empedocles DK 31 A35, cf. Barnes 1982: 397–402). Further, if – as some think – Melissus post-dates Empedocles and Anaxagoras then it seems that Melissus is answering them rather than vice versa, and their most likely Eleatic opponent is Parmenides himself. This would be an interesting result, since on this view Melissus is giving an Eleatic response to post-Parmenidean cosmology, and is part of an ongoing set of debates about the proper way to react to Parmenides' challenge.

Once again, we need to tread very carefully. I can see no definitive proof from the internal evidence of their respective surviving works of any sure lines of influence.[7] Not only are the respective dates of these thinkers themselves subject to a great deal of uncertainty due to the state of our evidence, but even if we could be more sure, there is good reason to be cautious about placing too much weight on them.[8] We have no guarantee that they each produced their works at the same stage of their respective lives and, as I noted earlier (pp. 9ff.), the context and nature of the production and circulation of philosophical works at this period is such that a philosopher's ideas might well be known about and subject to discussion well before the publication or circulation of a text of his work, let alone the text that is the source of our surviving quotations and reports. It would be neater if we could be more definite about the course of philosophical events at this period, but we simply cannot; we are left instead with the non-historical business of seeing how the ideas and arguments in the texts we have relate to one another, observing that the fifth century was clearly a period of deep and serious philosophical debate provoked originally by Parmenides and stoked by his various supporters and detractors.[9]

Cosmology after Parmenides

Cosmology after Parmenides still shows the variety and ingenuity we might expect, but there are some important new common traits present in the different systems. We shall examine each in detail later, but now let us notice what they all share. The Eleatic arguments had demanded that two significant questions be addressed. Any cosmology attempting to account for the world we perceive has to give an account of variety and change. It has to account for the fact that at any given moment there seem to be various different items in the world, items that display a wide variety of different characteristics and properties. It also had to account for how these different items change over time, taking on and losing different characters and properties, growing, moving and so on. In short, a cosmology should account for differences both at a time and over time and for our common perception of the diverse and changing world.[10]

One Eleatic precept adopted by all these differing cosmologies is a ban on any "absolute" coming to be or destruction. Nothing comes to be from what is not and nothing passes away into what is not. For example:

> The Greeks do not think about coming to be and passing away correctly. For nothing comes to be or perishes, but is formed by combination from existing things and dissolved [into them]. And so they would correctly say that coming to be is combination and perishing is dissolution.
> (Anaxagoras DK 59 B17)

> For it is impossible for there to be coming to be from what is not and it is impossible and unthinkable for what is to be destroyed. For it will always be there, wherever one might ever put it. (Empedocles DK 31 B12; see also Empedocles DK 31 B8, 9 and 11)

Other cosmologists show a similar acceptance of the principle.[11] We should note that what is new, after Parmenides, is not a sudden refusal to countenance generation from nothing. Thales and the other Ionians do not assert that there is any generation from nothing, but instead point to an already existent stuff out of which the cosmos forms. What is new, rather, is the self-conscious denial of generation from nothing based on some form of *a priori* reasoning, for which Parmenides can surely be credited as the source.[12]

It is not easy, however, to combine the principle of conservation with a continued interest in explaining change and difference. A common approach was to assert that the principle of conservation applies only to a limited set of things and that these things (whatever they are) are therefore to be identified as the fundamental constituents of the cosmos. If these things cannot be created and destroyed, they might nevertheless be used to explain the cases of change and difference we experience in different ways: they combine and recombine in various ways, never being created or destroyed themselves, but allowing various products to come to be and pass away. It should be clear that such a model requires a sophisticated approach to metaphysics because it now requires an account that recognizes two kinds of things: the unchanging fundamental things and the changing products of the fundamental things. It needs to say something about how they are related. It also needs to say something about how the fundamental things produce what they do. How do they, for example, "combine and recombine"?

Various decisions therefore have to be made and we shall be able to track the decisions made by each philosopher as we look at them individually. For now, let us note a general pattern. There is a certain pressure felt by these philosophers to abide by what we might call ontological economy, by which I mean that there is a tendency to try to posit as few fundamental things as possible. Parmenides' "Way of Opinion" had used only two: light and night. Empedocles, we shall go on to see, uses six: earth, air, fire, water and two principles of a different kind, Love and Strife. The atomists posit only two general kinds: atoms and void. But this ontological economy is in tension with the variety and plurality of what the fundamental things are then required to explain; namely, the diverse items and processes in the cosmos. A trade-off is needed: the more economical the starting fundamental ontology, the more work has to be done in bridging the gap between a small set of fundamental things and the wide variety of the world we experience. The gap has to be bridged by a satisfying account of how these few fundamental items produce variety and allow change.[13]

The gap between the fundamentals that obey the principle of conservation and the many and various items and changes we perceive shows that this cosmological project also owes us an epistemological account. Cosmologists after Parmenides must allow that the senses have at least some claim to provide truth, since it is presumably through our senses that we come to have the conviction that there is a cosmos, that there are many things and that there are instances of change. But once this is coupled with an ontology that distinguishes between fundamental and permanent entities and the many various changing items we perceive, then it becomes extremely difficult to hold that all information provided by the senses is to be accepted as true. We certainly do not perceive atoms, for example, although Democritus and Leucippus will tell us that the nature of atomic interactions is the best explanation for the plurality and change we do perceive. It is a common trend, therefore, in these cosmologists, for there to be some account of the extent to which the senses can be trusted. Empedocles, for example, notes the limited powers of the senses but also insists that proper attention should be paid to the information they can provide (DK 31 B2 and 3). Similarly, Anaxagoras famously said that the way the world appears to us offers a "glimpse" of the unseen, presumably meaning that our senses receive information that, while not wholly misleading, must be used with caution to provide evidence for generating an account of the true nature of things (DK 59 B21a; see below pp. 128–30).

While cosmological speculation continued unabated after the challenge set by Parmenides, the influence of his startling conclusions is evident, not only in particular aspects of the different cosmological theories that were produced but also in the evident awareness on the part of these later philosophers of the need for a more sophisticated and self-conscious approach to questions of existence and to addressing the relationship between appearance and reality. While both Heraclitus and Xenophanes before him had also raised questions about the uncritical acceptance of our own particular perspective on the world, Parmenides firmly tied these concerns to the most basic questions of ontology and in doing so set a clear agenda for much of the subsequent ancient tradition.

SEVEN

Anaxagoras

At some point relatively early in his life, Anaxagoras moved from his home town of Clazomenae, just North of Colophon in Asia Minor, to Athens. That he should have chosen to leave Ionia and head west indicates Athens' growing power and influence in the Aegean. It also shows its growth as a major philosophical centre as its cultural and intellectual attractions increased along with its political power. There is good reason to think that Anaxagoras was quite a prominent intellectual in his time and moved in important circles. He was associated with the leading Athenian statesman Pericles, and might even have attracted unwelcome attention and litigation from Pericles' enemies, who seized on Anaxagoras' views as an expression of unusual and potentially damaging religious opinions. Significant continuous stretches of his work survive, mainly as quotations by the Aristotelian commentator Simplicius. He wrote prose in a dogmatic and solemn style and is rightly famous for an unusual conception of matter and the introduction of *nous*, or mind, as some kind of causal principle.[1]

Coming to be

We can begin our exploration of Anaxagoras' physical system by considering his response to a surprising question, one that he may have posed himself. Fragment DK 59 B10 is sometimes considered to be inauthentic, but most agree that even if it does not preserve a genuine piece of Anaxagoras' work, it nevertheless encapsulates a genuine Anaxagorean thought: "For how could hair come to be from not hair and flesh from not flesh?"[2] We should note the Eleatic echoes. Not only does Anaxagoras apparently endorse the notion that nothing comes from what is not, but he also now seems to have expanded this thought to endorse the view that no X can come to be from what is not X. Instead of a ban on coming to be from nothingness, Anaxagoras' rhetorical question comes close to denying that there can be any coming to be of any sort whatsoever. Hair certainly does *seem* to come to be; at least, I have to go and have my hair cut every so often. So we must conclude either that this is a misleading appearance, and hair simply does not come to be (which would seem to be Parmenides' view), or else we have to conclude that hair always comes to be from hair. This latter is Anaxagoras' view, but, as we shall see, he has an interesting conception of the nature and structure of all matter that he thinks allows such claims to be compatible with our general experience of natural changes.

Let us begin to trace his views by looking at the opening of his work:

> All things (*chrēmata*) were together, infinite both in number and in smallness, for the small too was infinite. And, with all things being together, nothing was evident because of smallness. For air and aither enveloped everything, both being infinite. For these were the greatest things in everything, both in number and in size. (DK 59 B1)

Here we have the beginnings of a cosmogony. It describes an unusual state. Like most of his contemporaries, Anaxagoras refers to a precosmic state in order to explain and illustrate the mechanisms of change and composition that have resulted in the way things are now. For readers interested in possible reactions to the Eleatics, Anaxagoras' opening statements are defiant. In the face of Parmenides' and, perhaps, Melissus' distaste for plurality and change, Anaxagoras immediately asserts an indefinitely large number of existents and furthermore asserts that they used to be arranged differently. But there is still a faint echo of Eleaticism in the claim that in this original state all things were together, somehow mixed homogeneously. We soon learn that this homogeneity was merely apparent; the plurality was not evident because of the smallness of each of the original components of this mixture. Two sorts of bodies, air and aither, masked everything.

In this brief account Anaxagoras introduces us to his cosmos, and also to some important principles that he will make great use of as his theory unfolds. In particular, the idea of some characteristics being evident and predominant while others are masked and latent is something that will play a prominent role. But before we make any further headway in understanding his theory we run into some serious difficulties. What are the "things" that were together but masked by the air and aither? Anaxagoras is careful to use what seems to be a deliberately neutral and non-committal word, "things" (*chrēmata*), here and throughout the fragments. Whatever they are, they are important because they are constituents of the original state of the cosmos and seem to have been hidden and, we expect, were later revealed. But what are they? Anyone delving into recent discussions of Anaxagoras' physics will very rapidly realize that there is a wide range of different interpretations. There are two distinct areas of debate, although they are often interrelated. First, there is the question of Anaxagoras' ontology, of what he identifies as the fundamental constituents of the cosmos. Secondly, there is the question of what conception he has of the structure of matter and therefore of how the various fundamental constituents compose all other things.

Fundamentals of matter

Look at DK 59 B4b:[3]

> Before these things were separated off, when all things were together, no colour was evident. For the mingling of

all things (*chrēmata*) prevented it – of the wet and the dry, and the hot and the cold, and the bright and the dark – and there was much earth in there and seeds infinite in number and not at all like one another. For not one resembled any other. These things being so, we must believe that all things (*chrēmata*) were in the whole.

There are two broad approaches to the question of the nature of the "things" (*chrēmata*) in Anaxagoras: one more austere and the other more expansive.[4] The most austere conception of Anaxagoras' ontology holds that he considers only what we might call "the opposites" to be fundamental. These opposites would be things such as "the hot", "the cold", "the wet", "the dry", "the light", "the dark" and so on, as listed in the middle of this fragment (see Cornford 1975; Vlastos 1950; Schofield 1980: 100–144; and Sedley, forthcoming). It might seem odd to class these as stuffs, that is, as physical constituents of the world, but such a view is not uncommon in ancient Greek texts, particularly in medical writers, where these opposites are often credited with certain characters and powers. "The hot" for example, on this sort of view, is conceived as a kind of stuff. It is itself hot and its presence is what causes other things to be hot. The austere view of Anaxagoras' ontology holds that only these are fundamental and that all other things, including the various other items mentioned in the fragments, such as the seeds and the various things identified by other ancient sources as parts of Anaxagoras' ontology such as the "homoiomeries", are not themselves fundamental but rather are composites of the opposites. It is certainly true that these opposites appear prominently in the fragments and also, so far as we can tell, played a prominent role in Anaxagoras' theory of sense perception. Theophrastus tells us that Anaxagoras explained sense perception through the interaction of these opposites, so we experience and notice heat, for example, through the interaction of the hot in the object and the cold in us (Theoph. *De sensibus* 27–8 [DK 59 A92]). If this view is correct, however, it would also need to explain how these opposites in combination can produce all other things in the world. It also has to account for the presence of ancient reports that attribute to Anaxagoras a wider class of fundamental things.

More generous accounts of Anaxagoras' ontology add to the list other items that appear in the fragments. In particular, they tend to see the "seeds" that Anaxagoras mentions in both B4a and 4b as somehow fundamental. DK 59 B4a begins as follows:

> These things being so we must believe that there were present, in the things mixed together, many seeds of all kinds, of all things, having all sorts of forms and colours and flavours. And we must also believe that humans too were put together and all the other animals which have soul.

Clearly, these seeds play an important role, but once again accounts of that role differ. Some wish to retain the idea that these seeds account only for biological items, perhaps adding that they must be an indication that Anaxagoras noted the complexity of biological organisms and thought that this complexity could not adequately be accounted for simply through a combination of simple items such as the opposites (see Sider 2005: 171–2). (Here the "opposites camp" can respond by accepting that the seeds account for biological items but denying that they are fundamental members of Anaxagoras' ontology. They might be present in the original mixture but themselves composed of opposites. See, e.g. Schofield 1980: 121–33.) Others see the seeds as standing for a more general range of things. So, in addition to seeds of biological items, there are also seeds of gold, rock and the like. By calling these things seeds, Anaxagoras is wanting to assert that they are the building blocks out of which all things in the cosmos are constituted. At this point we can complicate things further by also considering the question of the "homoiomeries", which various ancient testimonia assert were what Anaxagoras identified as basic entities (see Mann 1980; Graham 1994; cf. Furley 1989c). The adjective "homoiomerous" is first used in Aristotle, where it describes items whose parts are similar in kind to the whole. So a piece of gold is homoiomerous because its parts are also pieces of gold. A bicycle is not homoiomerous since its parts are wheels, a chain and so on, none of which is itself a bicycle. Some commentators think that Anaxagoras' seeds are homoiomerous substances, so there are seeds of gold, flesh and so on.

For now, let us simply note these different interpretations. We can then see how they fare in explaining the various claims made in the fragments. First, let us recall the question about hair. It seemed to be claiming that, if hair comes to be at all (and that certainly appears to happen – my hair does grow), it must come from other hair. The most obvious source for the hair that comes to be on my head is the food that I ingest. If, therefore, when I eat my hair grows, then the obvious conclusion is that there must be hair in my food. My food must contain or partly be composed of hair. And it must also contain or partly be composed of bone, blood and the like, since these also seem to be generated when I eat and grow. All of this, however, gives us no definite answer to the question of what Anaxagoras' fundamental stuffs are, since everything now depends on different conceptions of what it means to say that there is hair, for example, "in" the sandwich I ate for lunch. That might mean that there are, somehow, "seeds" of hair in my sandwich. But even if there are such "seeds" present, what does it mean, precisely, to say that the sandwich contains such "seeds"? Are there tiny little pieces of hair in there? Or is there hair present, but thoroughly intermingled with all the other things that are in there too? Or is there hair present only in the sense that all of the opposites that compose my sandwich are also present in hair, but in different proportions to account for the differences between the properties of the bread, ham and so on and the hair that eventually grows on my head? The claim that hair does not come to be from what is not hair does not settle the question about the fundamental items in Anaxagoras' ontology. Hair might be one of them, but equally it might not; it might be composed out of some more fundamental things, such as the opposites.

We also ought to note that a related but distinct interpretative dispute concerns the way we are to imagine the structure of Anaxagorean matter. In addition to the discussion of what the "things" are, we can also wonder how those "things" are arranged to produce familiar items such as hair. One view, the particulate or "pointilliste" view, holds that Anaxagoras thinks that there are distinct portions or particles or – perhaps – "seeds" of all things in everything. A strand of hair, in that case, sufficiently magnified, would diplay various distinct portions of all the different "things" that there are. Alternatively, the view that has been more popular recently is the "continuum" view. This holds that Anaxagoras does not think that there are distinct portions of, for example, the hot and the cold in all things, but rather that all ingredients are thoroughly intermingled. When Anaxagoras claims that "the hot", for example, is never entirely separated from "the cold", he means that everything has some temperature between two indefinitely extendible extremes: nothing, however hot, could not be hotter.[5] In outlining this issue, however, we have already begun to move to consider the nature of Anaxagorean mixture, which was introduced even in the very first word of B1: "together".

Mixture and change

At the risk of even further complication, we should add to our discussion Anaxagoras' most famous pronouncement: "all things share a portion of everything", a refrain that appears in slightly different forms at a number of points in the fragments. Perhaps the best known formulation comes as fragment DK 59 B11:[6] "In everything there is a portion (*moira*) of everything except mind (*nous*), but there are some things in which mind too is present". Let us call this the thesis of universal mixture. Note that this is supposed also to hold at present when there are apparently various distinct and different things in the world; it is not just a description of how things were in the homogeneous state that we were told existed at the beginning. On the face of it, Anaxagoras has now added an even more surprising and outrageous claim to his already disconcerting thought that my sandwich contains hair, bone and so on. It now, apparently, contains a portion of *everything*. Well, nearly everything. Note the prominent exception: mind (*nous*) is not in everything, but only in some things. We shall come back to *nous* later since it occupies a very special role in the system as a whole.

We can now return to the question of the structure of Anaxagorean matter. In what way are there "all things" in, for example, my food? What are the "portions" mentioned in B11? To answer this question we need two further Anaxagorean principles. The first we have already met in B1: the notion that there can be latent elements that are not manifest in the character of the whole of which they are apart. The apparent character of something is determined by the character of those things that predominate in it. We can call this the principle of predominance. Secondly, we should add Anaxagoras' claims about divisibility and addition. There are two of these. The first is a general claim that of any given quantity, however small, there is a smaller quantity and of any given quantity, however large, there is a larger quantity (in fragment B3). This claim has sparked some speculation over a possible reaction to Zeno's paradoxes, many of which turn on the notion of the infinite divisibility of any extension (cf. Furley 1989c). Anaxagoras certainly asserts the possibility of infinite division but does not seem to think that anything problematic follows from this. Either he is simply unaware of the worries that Zeno had generated about such a possibility, or he is aware and thinks they can be avoided somehow. Perhaps he thought he could refute Zeno (in which case it is a real shame we do not know how) or perhaps for some other reason he simply did not consider Zeno's paradox worth answering. The second claim is one of the inseparability of things. In DK 59 B8 he tells us that "the things in the universe" can never be separated from one another, giving the example that the hot is inseparable from the cold and vice versa.

We have now assembled enough to put together an Anaxagorean account of change and also an explanation of the idea that there is a portion of everything in everything. In what follows, I shall proceed on the basis that the fundamental items in Anaxagoras' ontology are indeed the opposites, although I think that nothing crucial in the exposition depends on that choice.

Let us say that everything has a recipe: to make some X you need so much of ingredient A, so much of ingredient B and so on. A, B and so on must be present in the right *proportions*. (This is a thought also present in Empedocles; see p. 139.) If A, B and so on are the opposites then we might take the idea to be that blood, for example, must be composed so that it contains the correct relative proportion of hot and cold (it must be of the right sort of temperature), light and dark (it must be of a certain colour), rare and dense (it must be of a certain viscosity) and so on. Most important of all, the thesis of universal mixture tells us that blood contains at least some of every possible ingredient. In fact, there is at least some of every ingredient in everything.[7] If that is so, then it follows that blood can theoretically be generated from anything else, since there are always all the required ingredients. All that is required is for their relative proportions to be altered, and Anaxagoras consistently tells us that we should conceive of coming to be and passing away as processes governed by "combination and separation" (DK 59 B17; see p. 116). Of course, this combination and separation is only ever partial. We cannot, for example, ever separate out entirely the hot from the cold. But we can separate the hot from the cold such that there is only a very small portion of cold in a new mixture.

Perhaps an illustration of Anaxagorean alteration might help at this point. Bread can turn into hair because there is some hair in bread. (For how could hair come from not hair?) Let us give an account of the proportion of the ingredients involved in the two items, imagining just for the sake of simplicity that there are only three basic things, labelled A, B and C. In that case we can also imagine that there are particular proportional recipes for each of bread and hair. For example, bread = 2 parts A, to 3 parts B to 5 parts C; hair = 5 parts A, to 2 parts B to 3 parts C. Hair can be generated from bread because in bread we have all the ingredients we need for hair. Our digestive system and metabolism does the clever work of combination and separation. Note also that in theory, if not in practice, hair can also be transformed into bread. The principle that there is no smallest limit to any quantity allows that even the tiniest amount of bread contains at least some of all the required ingredients and could produce a very tiny amount of hair. Never will the possibility of such a change be ruled out simply because of the size of the amount in question. Nor will we ever be faced by a situation in which one of the required ingredients is missing because they can never be entirely separated out.

The explanation is certainly ingenious, but is it at all plausible? We might be concerned that Anaxagoras has helped himself to an outrageously extravagant set of principles that are far too strong for the rather modest work of explaining perceived processes of change. Perhaps we do want to know how bread, say, can become hair. But Anaxagoras' theory offers an explanation that would also suffice to show that bread can become rock, plastic or metal. If *everything* is composed from the same ingredients then there is no limit in principle on what can turn into what. Yet surely there are some transformations that are not merely practically impossible. Anaxagoras is certainly extravagant in this one respect, even though, if he holds that only a limited range of things such as the opposites are fundamental, he is not guilty of intolerably gross ontological extravagance. But on the other hand, he has produced a single explanation that is sufficient to cover every possible change: those we can currently observe and produce and those we might go on to discover later. It is a complete and relatively simple explanation of all change.

We should also notice that Anaxagorean physics leaves us with a curious account of the identity of the things we perceive around us. Lead and gold, chalk and cheese, are composed of entirely the same ingredients. Indeed everything is related to everything else in being composed of the same ingredients. Any distinctions between kinds of object cannot therefore be the result of differences in the kinds of constituents present, but rather must be entirely due to differences of a different sort, namely, of the proportions of the various ingredients. So if we have a piece of lead in our hands rather than a piece of gold, that is because what makes it lead predominates. All other things are in there latently. (Here, of course, the various different accounts of Anaxagorean ontology will differ. The "opposites camp" will say that this is lead because the proportions of the opposites are thus and so and different from those that would be the case were it a piece of gold. Those others who say that lead is itself one of the "things" that are fundamental will say that this is a piece of lead because it contains more lead than it does any other stuff.)[8]

These curious consequences might make us reticent to accept Anaxagoras' picture. But he did, it seems, recognize the possibility of such reticence and attempted to offer some more support for his claims. Sextus Empiricus offers a description of an Anaxagorean argument that includes Anaxagoras DK 59 B21:

> Anaxagoras, the greatest natural philosopher, in order to show how weak the senses are, says, "we are unable to distinguish the truth because of their lack of strength" (B21). And he offers as evidence of their lack of reliability the gradual change between two colours. For if we take two colours, black and white, and then pour out one into the other drop by drop, sight will be unable to distinguish the gradual changes, although they underlie the nature of things.
>
> (SE *M* 7.90)

Sextus is interested in offering evidence of early and widespread philosophical distrust of the senses as criteria of truth, and therefore focuses on the apparent scepticism expressed in B21 (cf. Cic. *Acad.* 1.44 [DK 59 A95]; Barnes 1982: 540–41). But the evidence that Anaxagoras goes on to offer shows a more nuanced view of the role of the senses in guiding us to the truth about nature, quite in keeping with his other famous pronouncement that what appears to us is a "glimpse of what is not evident".[9] The illustration of the gradual but imperceptible change from white to black as black pigment is introduced drop by drop is not only evidence for the weakness of the senses, but also evidence for Anaxagoras' contention that "in everything there is a portion of everything". Two related but distinct points might be made about the senses' inability to discern the true nature of things. Early on in the mixing process, what appears to be a perfectly good pot of white paint, for example, must be agreed to contain at least some black paint since some black has been seen being introduced. This is some support for the thesis of universal mixture. But also, each drop of black mixed in will make an imperceptible difference to the overall colour. What began as white will eventually be a grey, although at no particular stage will it have been possible to detect a perceptible change. This is some support for the principle of predominance.[10]

These observations are clearly intended as some kind of support for Anaxagoras' thesis of universal mixture and the idea that we generally perceive only the properties of the predominant elements in any given object. The substances we perceive contain not only evident but also latent elements. What looks like a perfectly pure white substance contains portions of black, undetectable because of their being a relatively small proportion of the whole. There are two ways in which we could understand this claim. Perhaps Anaxagoras means to say that if only our eyesight were more acute then we would be able to detect the change in colour if even just one tiny drop of black were added to a large pot of white paint. In this case, the small addition has made a difference to the colour of the whole that is in principle perceptible, but not such that our human eyesight is able to register it.[11] However he explained the differences in perceptual ability, this clearly leaves room for him to claim that certain things are imperceptible by human beings but perceptible by other animals. Alternatively, he could mean that at the very early stage of the colour-change process there is no difference in colour at all. Even the most powerful and acute visual apparatus would be unable to detect a change since no change in the colour of the whole has yet occurred. Only when the proportion of black within the whole has reached a certain level will there be any change in the colour of the whole.[12]

Mind

The one remaining crucial feature of Anaxagoras' physical system is the one item exempt from the universal mixture. Mind, *nous*, we were told, is present only in some things, presumably explaining the fact that some items in the world are alive while others are not or, perhaps more restrictively, the fact that some items in the world can think and perceive while others cannot. But *nous* also plays an important cosmological role since it provides the mechanism for moving from the relatively homogeneous state at the very beginning of the cosmos in which, so B1 told us, air and aither covered and masked all other things to the current state of variegation in which the "things" are present throughout all items in the world but in differing proportions here and there. *Nous* is responsible for that change. The mixture itself, we might remark, seems therefore to have no internal principle or cause of change. This principle is provided by *nous*, as we learn in the long fragment B12:

> The other things share a portion of everything, but mind (*nous*) is infinite and self-ruling and mixed with nothing. But it alone is itself for itself. For if it were not for itself but were mixed with another, then it would share in all things if it were mixed with any. (For, as I said earlier, in everything there is a portion of everything.) And the things it was combined with would impede it such that it could not rule any thing and be alone itself for itself. For it is the lightest of all things and the most pure and it holds all understanding about everything and the greatest power. And all things greater and smaller which have soul, mind rules them all. And mind ruled the whole rotation so that the rotation began. And first it began to rotate from a small area and then it rotated more and it will rotate even more. And the things combined and separated and distinguished, mind knew them all. And what things were going to be, and what things were, what things now are not and what now are and what will be, mind arranged them all and this rotation in which now revolve the stars and sun and the moon and the separated air and the aither. And the dense separates from the light, the hot from the cold and the bright from the dark and the dry from the wet. (There are many portions of many things.) But nothing separates or is distinguished entirely one from another, except mind. All mind is alike, both the greater and the smaller. But no other thing is like any other, but each single thing is and was most manifestly whatever things are most numerous in it.

The fragment begins by outlining the way in which *nous* is very distinct from everything else. It is unmixed and alone, unlike the mixed and inseparable elements. It also is described in terms that make it authoritative in some way over everything else. It "rules itself" and is aloof and removed from all that it rules. Indeed, its ruling over everything else seems to demand that it be pure and unsullied by mixture. It is still, however, somehow physical. At least, it is the lightest and purest of all things, which suggests that it is nevertheless comparable in these terms to the other elements. Its role in the development of the cosmos is here explained as a kind of motor force. *Nous* begins a revolution within the homogeneous mixture, which, perhaps on the model of some kind of centrifuge, begins to distribute the items in the mixture in a variegated fashion (a process also mentioned in DK 59 B13). Gradually things begin to separate such that distinct areas exhibit distinctive characteristics by the principle of predominance.

This is evidently a very early stage in the development of the cosmos. The major items picked out are the heavenly bodies: the sun, stars and moon. Other fragments show that the earth is a product generated by the centrifuge and not a part of the original mixture. DK 59 B15 tells us that the earth currently occupies a place in the cosmos that at one point was occupied by "the moist", "the cold" and "the dark". Earth is predominantly all these characteristics, so this is good evidence that it is the product of the predominance of certain of the opposites. "The rare", "the warm" and "the dry", on the other hand, were sent outwards, to form what we know as the atmosphere. In this way the most basic elemental masses were generated and *nous* began to produce something on the way to being recognizably our cosmos.

Further details about the finer points of cosmology and particular natural phenomena are not well described in the surviving fragments, although some of the reports of Anaxagoras' views in other writers show that he was prepared to talk at some length about such things. The role of *nous* in this process, however, and the range of its activities, invite more comment. As I mentioned in the Introduction, a passage in Plato's *Phaedo* (97b–9d) relates how Socrates was disappointed by Anaxagoras. He had heard a little of his theory, enough to find out that Anaxagoras had given a prominent role in his cosmology to *nous*. Thinking that this would provide his desired explanation of the world in terms of a designing intelligence, Socrates purchased Anaxagoras' work only to find that Anaxagoras did nothing of the sort. This Platonic picture has been extremely influential in the interpretation of Anaxagoras' conception of *nous*, encouraging readers to think of *nous* as merely some kind of motor force that generates a centrifuge but does little else. And we certainly ought to give Plato's description due weight in our considerations. But there are undeniable signs in the fragments that *nous* has been assigned a wider set of abilities. DK 59 B12 is concerned to demonstrate the power and influence of *nous*, especially over living things. The relationship between "soul" and *nous* is very unclear, however. Anaxagoras may mean nothing more than that living things (which he described as "things that have a soul or *psychē*" without implying the existence of any particular distinct entities to be called "souls") have or are governed by *nous* only in the sense that they are in some ways autonomous. One of the defining characteristics of *nous* at the beginning of the process of cosmos-formation is its self-governance. It would make good sense to attribute the degree of autonomy enjoyed by at least certain living things once the cosmos has been formed to the presence of *nous* and DK 59 B11, which is evidently describing a state once the cosmos has been formed, does indeed say that *nous* is present "in" some things (cf. Sider 2005: 132–3). More telling, however, are the comments in B12 that *nous* (i) "knew" everything that was mixing, separating and dissolving and (ii) "arranged" everything that was, is and will be. If we take these claims seriously, it seems that the role of *nous* extends beyond merely kick-starting a process of cosmogony and leaving things to turn out in whatever way they should happen to. The extent of this enlarged role is less clear. Perhaps *nous* takes an active causal role in the entire history of the cosmos. It continues to generate the force and motion required to maintain the processes of separation and recombination, which are involved in every change since the constant application of force is needed to maintain the degree of variegation and the continual processes of alteration we see around us. (Certainly, the *nous* that is said even now to govern "all things that have soul" is easily linked to the ability of living things to initiate motion and change.) On the other hand, perhaps *nous* understood the workings of the cosmos well enough to be able to impart the initial motion in such a way as to produce the desired ongoing effects we still see around us without the need for constant further intervention. On either view, it has been suggested that, in his reading of Anaxagoras, Socrates may have overlooked some kind of deliberate ordering of the cosmos by *nous* for a purpose. After all, the claim that it "arranged" everything does sound as though it had some kind of plan to enact and, as it turns out, *nous* did produce a cosmos conducive to the production of organic life.[13]

Perhaps as a further comment on these questions, it is important to note that Anaxagoras is regularly mentioned, particularly by Aristotle, as holding a particular view about what would constitute the good human life. For Anaxagoras, it seems, a good human life is one dedicated to the acquisition and contemplation of cosmological truths (see Aristot. *EE* 1216a1ff.; cf. *NE* 1179a13ff. [DK 59 A30]; also cf. Diog. Laert. 2.7, 10 [DK 59 A1]). This need not mean, of course, that there is some intrinsic value to the cosmos itself, although it might be easier to see why cosmology should be so praised if its object of study is itself something good and beautiful. But perhaps he claims only that there is value in human intellectual endeavour and, in particular, in attempting to understand our universe as a whole. It is more than likely that such intellectual endeavour is to be conceived as the use of the *nous* "in" us and it is unlikely to be a coincidence that the best use of our *nous* is in coming to understand the products of *nous*; namely, the cosmos itself. The precise nature of any link between cosmology and ethics in Anaxagoras must remain a matter for speculation, given the thin evidence. Even so, Anaxagoras was clearly interested in drawing links between his own chosen philosophical enquiry and what it means to live a good human life.[14]

EIGHT

Empedocles

Empedocles is one of the most colourful and fascinating personalities in this period of early Greek philosophy. Clearly a charismatic figure, a whole range of stories and legends grew up about him and his life, perhaps the most famous of which is that he died by leaping into the crater of Mount Etna on his native Sicily in order to prove that he had become a god (see Diog. Laert. 8.69, cf. Kingsley 1995: 233ff.). The truth of these various stories is subject to considerable doubt, but they testify to the interest and mystery generated in antiquity by Empedocles' work and his apparently ostentatious self-promotion.

Empedocles is one of the great philosophical poets and continues to provoke fascination, reignited recently by the publication of new sections of Empedocles' work rediscovered on a papyrus held in Strasbourg.[1] It is fair to say, however, that the new interest has led in the main to many new questions and reopened various already long-running disputes; very little of the content and nature of Empedocles' philosophy can be said to be generally agreed among modern interpreters.

One poem? One philosophy?

Diogenes Laërtius, in his *Life of Empedocles*, mentions two titles for Empedocles' work: *On Nature* and *Katharmoi* (translated as

"*Purifications*") (Diog. Laert. 8.54, 56, 77). Diels and Kranz take these to refer to different works, and use this to divide the surviving fragments – all of which are composed in the same hexameter verse – according to what they perceive to be different topics or areas of thought. Some of the surviving fragments, to be sure, seem to offer what we might call a familiar type of cosmology; Diels and Kranz assign these to *On Nature* (B1–111). Other fragments, however, seem to describe a cycle of reincarnation and offer instructions in ritual purification for some kind of moral error made in a previous incarnation; these are assigned to *Purifications* (B112–53). Further, the fragments contain addresses to at least two different audiences. DK 31 B112, which Diogenes introduces as the opening of *Purifications*, addresses the citizens of Acragas. DK 31 B1, which Diogenes assigns to *On Nature*, addresses a single person, named Pausanias.

Even before the publication of the new papyrus material, this division had been challenged. Some commentators are convinced that there is no reason why the surviving fragments should not all come from a single work, perhaps referred to in antiquity by two different titles (cf. Osborne 1987a; Trépanier 2004: 1–30). The papyrus material offered some support for this view, since some of the pieces preserved on the papyrus (named by the editors "ensemble a") supplement and continue one of the fragments (DK 31 B17) transmitted by various ancient sources. B17, which we shall come to consider below, is itself difficult to interpret, but all commentators agree that it contains material best thought of as part of Empedocles' cosmological theory, perhaps even the introduction to the cosmology. Ensemble a, however, although it continues the themes of B17, also provided some unexpected information. Not only does it contain some tantalizing suggestions of a religious or ethical aspect to this cosmological theme, but at the side of one of its lines was found a Greek capital letter gamma, standing for the numeral 300.[2] This is a scribe's mark, noting the number of lines copied and therefore the amount he was due to be paid. It tells us, therefore, that by the beginning of B17, we are already 232 lines into the poem, certainly enough to allow B112 to stand as the opening of the whole work, perhaps also an invocation to the Muse, and then a turn to address Pausanias in particular.[3]

Not all commentators are convinced that there was only one Empedoclean work and even within the "two works" camp there is a division between those who would prefer to see *Purifications* as a strictly religious work, detailing certain ritual commands, and others who think of it as a more detailed philosophical work to stand alongside *On Nature*.[4] But what is important for our purposes is that all sides now tend to agree that, even if there were two works, there is an onus on any interpretation of Empedocles' thought to try if at all possible to retain a unity and coherence between all of the preserved evidence. In other words, the division of material into different works should not allow us to ignore certain pieces of evidence as not pertinent to Empedocles' philosophy as a whole. Empedocles is therefore an excellent case in which we have to think carefully about what we assume to be the nature of early Greek philosophy; it is certainly not possible to ignore what we might initially take to be "un-philosophical" or "religious" aspects of his work and concentrate on the cosmological sections without the risk that we might thereby seriously misconceive the overall tenor of his thought. Precisely how we go about reconciling the various pieces of evidence we have, however, is quite another matter.

The cosmos

Some aspects of Empedocles' cosmological view are, we might note with some relief, relatively uncontroversial. DK 31 B12, as we saw above (p. 116), accepts Parmenides' ban on absolute coming to be and passing away; B8 continues by identifying growth and death of composite mortal things as, in fact, the mixture and re-mixture of something else.[5] We learn about the principal and fundamental constituents of the universe – what Empedocles terms the "roots" – in B6: "First, hear the four roots of all things: shining Zeus, life-bringing Hera, Aidoneus and Nestis – who touches the mortal spring with tears". Empedocles' colourful verse is a far cry from the grammatically simple, plain and repetitive prose of Anaxagoras. Here, for example, he uses the names of various traditional Greek gods to refer to his four roots. Other fragments, however, suggest that these are also identified as, probably in respective order, fire, air, earth and water.[6] These four roots, in various combinations and ratios, produce the variety and differences in the cosmos we inhabit. This much is reminiscent in general terms of Anaxagoras' view, although Anaxagoras has – on any interpretation – a much more generous starting ontology that Empedocles' four roots. Empedocles then supplements his ontology with two further items: Love (or Aphrodite) and Strife. These two act on the roots and in opposition to one another. From time to time, one or other of these two becomes dominant, even to the point of exercising total control over the roots. We can be fairly sure about the state of things at a time of complete Love: the four roots are thoroughly intermingled and held together in harmony forming a cosmic sphere (DK 31 B27, 30, 31). No doubt, it is no coincidence that such a state is reminiscent both of Anaxagoras' original homogeneous mixture before the working of *nous* and also of Parmenides' description of the perfect spherical nature of "[what] is".

The state of complete domination by Strife is less clearly described in the fragments. It might be a state of utter chaos. More likely, however, is that it is a state in which the four roots are completely separated one from the other: all earth clings together, all water and so on. Strife, on this view, is something of a factionalist, making like items band together and have nothing to do with anything different from themselves (see Graham 2005: 236–40). This makes a sharp contrast with Love, whose intention seems to be to unite disparate elements and provide a complete harmonious mixture. The ethical and political overtones of this ostensibly cosmological theory should not be cast aside; not only is it likely that Empedocles is deliberately borrowing from contemporary political discussions about the unification or separation of classes within a polis, but it is also likely that his choice of Love and Strife builds an ethical aspect into the basic workings of the cosmos. There is good reason to think, at least for the moment, that we might assign a positive value to Love and its work and a corresponding negative value to Strife. We shall return to this question when we consider his other religious and ethical pronouncements.

There appear to be set periods of the alternating dominance of Love and Strife, although the chronology of this overall cosmic cycle is obscure.[7] But we can see how the basic ontological toolkit of the four roots and Love and Strife can be used to account for the cosmos we inhabit. All things in the cosmos are composed of the four roots in some combination or other. The ratio of this combination can be used to account for the different properties of various kinds of thing. Indeed, Empedocles goes so far as to offer recipes for certain kinds: bone is apparently two parts earth, two parts water and four parts fire (DK 31 B96); flesh and blood is apparently equal parts fire, water and air (DK 31 B98). The ratios are undoubtedly crude and, with only four basics elements, Empedocles cannot account in a plausible manner for all the various kinds of item found in the cosmos. He limits himself to four basic stuffs, and is therefore perhaps hampered in the explanatory power of this more economical ontology, but he is not – it seems – committed to finding some of every one of the roots in every item: bone seems to contain no air, for example. It is not hard to imagine someone (both someone like Anaxagoras and also someone with no particular cosmological theory of his own) objecting to Empedocles' theory on the grounds that it is simply unbelievable that we could reduce all the items in the cosmos to combinations (albeit in different ratios) of only four basic roots.[8] But Empedocles offers a response in the form of an analogy:

> For just as when two painters decorate offerings, men well-gifted by cunning in the craft, when they take in their hands many-coloured substances, mixing in harmony some more, others less, they produce from them images which resemble all things. They fashion trees and men and women and beasts and birds and water-bred fish and long-lived gods, best in honour. Just so, let no deception seize your mind that there is any other source of all the countless mortal things you see. But know this clearly; you heard this account from a god.
>
> (DK 31 B23)

The general outline of the analogy is clear. Just as only a few pigments can be mixed together in different amounts and used to create a vast variety of colours, so too we should accept that only a small number of basic stuffs can be mixed together in different amounts to generate a similar variety of things. This is a very clever point: Empedocles might reasonably expect his audience to be familiar with the possibilities created by blending pigments. Why should we not similarly be happy with the possibilities of blending only a few basic roots? Of course, the analogy will be able to persuade us only of the possibility of this general kind of theory; it goes nowhere in persuading us of the truth of Empedocles' own particular choice of these four roots.

The analogy also has deeper connotations. The painters are creating votive tablets – offerings for a god or goddess asking for favours or aid – depicting gods, fish, beasts, men and women, birds and so on.[9] In short, they are painting a depiction of the cosmos. The analogy is not therefore limited to making a structural point about the possibilities of mixing a small starting range of components. The ultimate products of the painters' efforts are depictions of the very products about which we are principally concerned in cosmology; namely, the animals, plants and so on that inhabit the cosmos. (Compare the list of what is depicted here in B23.6–8 with the almost identical list in B21.10–12.) If we can paint a picture of the cosmos using only a few colours, surely we could similarly imagine the cosmos itself being constructed from only a few basic roots?

Also, we might wonder if this fragment suggests that for Empedocles there is an element of deliberation and teleology in his view of the world. The painters are creating their picture for some purpose. In order to paint a bird, for example, they will mix colours in different ways to paint the plumage, the beak and so on. Each brush stroke and choice of colour will be dictated by the ultimate goal of generating a picture of a bird. Are they, therefore, intended to be correlated with similarly deliberative agents in nature who set out similarly to combine the roots in a certain form in order to generate a cosmos? Notice that there are two painters. (Empedocles uses a special "dual" form of the verbs, reserved for when there are two subjects.) In that case, perhaps it is plausible to take this as an analogy for the cosmic pair of Love and Strife. But at this point it becomes more difficult to press the analogy much further. Are Love and Strife deliberative forces? Perhaps. They are certainly often described in terms that attribute to them desires, concerns and plans. Love, in particular, is sometimes described as a kind of craftsman, fashioning natural objects such as an eye as an artisan constructs, for example, a lamp (see DK 31 B86, B87; cf. B73). Do they cooperate, as the painters appear to do? That sounds very unlikely. As we have already seen, their ultimate aims are quite opposed. And in any case, it is not true for either Love or Strife that their ultimate goal is the state of a cosmos such as we now are in. Whatever the precise overall balance of power between Love and Strife in the present state of the cosmos, it is obvious that the four roots are at present neither entirely separated nor entirely intermingled. Our cosmos must now be at some intermediate stage. In that case, the analogy must be limited: while it is the goal of the painters to depict a cosmos like ours, it is the goal of neither Love nor Strife to generate a cosmos filled with trees, birds and the like. If they are like painters, then perhaps we should imagine two squabbling painters, one intent on smudging together all the paints across the whole canvas while another intends to paint discrete stripes of each pure pigment. Any picture that emerges is the fortunate result of their antagonistic competition. Nevertheless, it must certainly be agreed that for a cosmos such as ours to exist, which exhibits partial mixture and partial separation, the powers of both Love and Strife must be manifested to some degree.

Cosmic cycles and the generation of life

Beyond these general observations about the four roots, Love and Strife, we begin to find a great deal of controversy concerning the overall workings of the Empedoclean cosmos. In particular, much discussion has centred on the question of the cyclical nature of the relationship between Love and Strife and the related question of whether a cosmos such as the one we inhabit is generated both as Love gradually brings harmony to the factionalized world of total Strife and also as Strife gradually breaks up the completely harmonized sphere of Love. One fragment in particular has been used by both sides in the dispute. It opens as follows:

> I shall tell a two-fold tale: at one time they grew to be one
> single thing from many, at another again they grew apart to
> be many from one. Double is the birth of mortals, double
> the passing-away. For the coming together generates and
> destroys one, (5) and the other of them, as they grow apart
> once more, was nourished and flew away. And these never
> cease from forever changing, at one time all coming together
> into one by Love, at another time they each move apart by
> the hostility of Strife. <So they have learned to grow into
> many from one>[10] (10) and end again as many as the one
> grows apart. In one way they come to be and they have no
> lasting life; in another they never cease from forever chang-
> ing and thus are always unchanging in a cycle.
>
> (DK 31 B17, lines 1–13)

A later line (18) specifies that the "they" in these lines are the four
roots, so this section, with its constant structuring form of alternating lines balancing one another, describes the roots coming together
and then moving apart under the influence of Love and Strife. These
combinations and separations create a "double birth" for mortal
things since, on one plausible interpretation of the obscure lines
3–5, the coming to be of any given composite item in the universe
is created by a recombination of roots that must be separated and
moved from something else and somewhere else. For example, the
growth of an animal requires the combination of various roots that
must be taken from and separated from other composites: the animal's food, for example. There is in each coming to be of a composite
item therefore both a generation and a destruction. And every time
such a composite item passes away, the roots that formerly composed
it must go somewhere else and result in a new case of generation.

Discussion of what this fragment might tell us about the history
of the cosmos as a whole has focused on trying to pin down the
precise nature of the promised "two-fold" tale. There are, generally
speaking, two rival interpretations. On one account, the "symmetrical view", there are two occasions on which a cosmos such as ours
is created: (i) as the disparate elements factionalized by Strife begin

to come together as Love gradually increases in power; and (ii) as the homogenized elements of the sphere of Love are gradually separated by Strife. In both processes there are generated composites that manifest both a degree of mixture and also a degree of separation of the roots. This view preserves a pleasing symmetry in Empedocles' theory overall and can emphasize the reference to a "cycle" at the end of the section quoted above.[11]

The alternative, "asymmetrical", view holds that a cosmos such as ours is generated only in periods of increasing Love. This view can be supported, as we shall see, by the fact that the vast majority of our detailed information about the generation of life seems to refer to the powers of increasing Love. Strife has no cosmogonical function on this view; instead its gradually increasing power shatters the sphere of Love and produces a factionalized state with no recognizable cosmos being generated in the process. This too, of course, can claim to be compatible with there being a regular cycle of cosmic change.[12]

Both views encounter difficulties in incorporating all the available evidence. For example, Aristotle (*Gen. et. corr.* 334a5–7 [DK 31 A42]) says that Empedocles saw the present state of the cosmos as being now "under" Strife, just as it was previously "under" Love.[13] Does this mean that in the present cosmos Strife in on the increase? What of the description in DK 31 B128 of a previous "golden age" of harmony among men, surely when Love was more ascendant than now? It would certainly seem odd if, having given a detailed account of how Love's increase can lead to the production of life such as we see around us now, it should then turn out that our cosmos is in fact one produced by increasing Strife.

Further, our most important piece of external evidence about the generation of living things, Aëtius 5.19.5 (DK 31 A72) identifies four stages in the generation of living things. These are:

1. separate distinct limbs
2. combinations of these limbs
3. "whole-natured" forms
4. individuals not born from earth as before but from one another.

It is not clear from the outset that this can be a set of four stages of increasing dominance by Love or by Strife. The first two stages, at least, look like they describe a theory of zoogony ascribed to Empedocles by other ancient sources and that can be supported by other surviving fragments (see DK 31 B57, 59–61). These two stages are most probably the work of increasingly dominant Love. First, in stage 1, separate limbs are created as Love begins to join unlike roots together, mixing them to produce bone, flesh and blood, by blending roots in the various ratios we saw described in B96 and 98. This generation of separate limbs is described in B57. Then, as Love becomes more influential, these limbs and organs are combined, but in a haphazard fashion. B59–61 describe various random combinations of limbs and organs, often producing nightmarish forms that were unable to survive as functioning individuals. Aristotle complains bitterly about the theory, convinced that Empedocles has concocted an implausible fairy tale in order somehow to account for the fact that the various species we see around us appear well constructed and adapted to successful living in their various environments (see, in particular, Aristot. *Phys.* 198b10ff.). This offends Aristotle, who instead insists on seeing a genuine teleology in natural developments. According to Aristotle, a dog, for example, grows and develops as it does because its various characteristics best suit its canine life; this purpose is a genuine causal factor involved in the dog's development. We, on the other hand, might well applaud Empedocles for anticipating some important aspects of a Darwinian-style theory of natural selection; species are subject to random variation and generation and only the well- or best-adapted survive and flourish. Incidentally, this could be good evidence against inferring intentional design of the cosmos by Love and Strife from the painter analogy of B23: even if Love is responsible for the combinations that eventually result in the production of birds, trees and so on, there is little reason to think that Love is actively engaged in trying to produce well-adapted members of certain species. They seem rather to be a (temporary) by-product of a global process of increasing combination and mixture.

Thus far, Aëtius' four stages seem to be telling a story of increasing Love. But stages 3 and 4 are harder to fit neatly into such a picture.

Stage 3 relates the birth from the earth of whole individuals and stage 4 outlines the move to sexual reproduction rather than the combination of previously disparate parts. Stage 3 seems to be described in fragment DK 31 B62, which links the generation of these "autochthonous" individuals to the increasing separation of heat, which somehow forces them up out of the ground. Is this separation of heat more likely to be the result of increasing Strife than increasing Love? The fourth stage, of sexual reproduction, might at first glance seem to continue the theme of increasing Love since, after all, there is an obvious connection between Aphrodite and sexual union. But B62 describes the generation of the two sexes in less than positive terms: the men and women are "full of lamentation". And Greek literature often portrayed the division of the sexes as either a product of the gods' displeasure with previously asexual humanity (as in Aristophanes' speech in Plato's *Symp.* 189d–93b) or else, as in the myth of Pandora, as a punishment and cause of strife and discord (see Hesiod, *Works and Days* 42ff.).

In all, it is very difficult to say with any great certainty much about the details of Empedocles' cosmic cycle. There is no reason, in fact, to discount the idea that the powers of Love and Strife may wax and wane even within a cosmic cycle: although every so often Love and Strife may dominate entirely, there is no reason to think that their respective powers increase and decrease smoothly in the intervening periods. There may be times when Love grows in power before giving way to Strife, without either of them being able to make the decisive move to complete domination. In that case, our present cosmos may well show simultaneously the products generated since the last sphere both in periods of increasing Love and also in periods of Strife's ascendancy.[14] On any interpretation, however, it must be agreed that in some sense our cosmos is the product of the workings of both Love and Strife. It displays both the separation of the roots (the earth, the ocean, the air, the sun) and also their mingling. It would certainly be a mistake to think of only Love as a creative force, since in order for there to be a world such as ours it is essential that Love should not have everything her own way. Similarly, Strife's total dominance produces not a recognizable cosmos, but the absolute insulation of one root from another. Empedocles needs, at least for his natural philosophy, to stress both the antagonism and simultaneous presence of these two forces in our current cosmos, whatever the overarching conception of larger-scale cosmic cycles.

The daimōn

Empedocles himself claims a very special kind of position: a more than mortal position of authority and insight. The opening of *Purifications*, which – if there was only one poem – might be the opening of the entire work, casts Empedocles addressing the citizens of Acragas as a god delivering an important message to mortal human beings:

> O, friends who live in the great town of shining Acragas, dwelling in the heights of city, taking care to do good deeds, respectful harbours for guests, having no commerce with evil, hail! I come to you an immortal god, no longer mortal, honoured by all – it appears – decked in ribbons and festival garlands. The moment I come to the prosperous cities I am honoured by men and women. Thousands of them immediately follow me asking where to find the path to profit. Some want prophecies, others want to hear a healing spell for all sorts of illnesses ... (DK 31 B112)

No doubt, this is in part a claim to special authority on Empedocles' part and can usefully be compared with the stance of the goddess in Parmenides' poem. But the differences between the two are marked. While Parmenides' narrator looks to a further divine authority for the content of his message, Emepdocles' narrator simply is that divine authority. Here in B112, Empedocles himself is claiming a divine status and asserting a direct access to truth. Elsewhere, it is true, there is a more standard invocation of a Muse as a source of inspiration and guidance (B131), but there is clearly something unusual and special about Empedocles' *persona* in this opening address and his claims to fame and special powers.[15]

As we read other fragments, it becomes clear that Empedocles' cosmos is home to a hierarchy of beings. In addition to Love, Strife and the roots, which we have already seen referred to in the guise of familiar Greek divinities, Empedocles refers to mortal human beings, such as the citizens of Acragas, the gods and also the *daimones* (the plural of *daimōn*). Empedocles identifies himself at various points both as a god and as a *daimōn* and relates a story of how he has been punished for some act he committed under the influence of Strife. This condemned him to be subject to a series of reincarnations, moving around the various components of the cosmos:

> There is an oracle of necessity, an ancient decree of the gods, everlasting, sealed with broad oaths: whenever, in his misdeeds, he stains his dear limbs with blood … he swears an oath in error, one of the *daimones* who have enjoyed a long life must wander for 30,000 seasons away from the blessed, in time growing as every sort of mortal thing, exchanging the painful paths of life. For aither's power pursues him into the sea; the sea spits him onto the earthy land, earth into the beams of the shining sun which then tosses him into aither's whirls. Each receives him in turn from another and they all hate him. I too am now one of these, an exile from the gods and wanderer, trusting in mad Strife.   (DK 31 B115)

This material may indeed seem a surprising addition to a cosmological story of the four elements, Love and Strife, but it is no more surprising than the presence in, for example, the cosmological account in Plato's *Timaeus* of an extended discussion of the process by which souls are reincarnated in various forms of life (see *Tim.* 90a–92c). The real difficulty lies not in taking this material to be an integral part of Empedocles' philosophy, but in attempting to marry the details of the *daimōn's* story with the cosmological account we have already outlined. In what way does the process of reincarnation fit with the cosmic changes from the sphere of Love to the factionalized world of Strife and back again? How should we combine the cosmic roles of Love and Strife with their roles in the story of the *daimōn*? And who, precisely, are these *daimones*? Are all we human beings in fact *daimones*, some of us unaware of our true nature and needing Empedocles' advice in purifying ourselves? Or are there two races: mortal human beings and *daimones*? Are the gods and the *daimōnes* the same? It should come as no surprise that there is as much disagreement among commentators over these questions as over any other aspect of Empedocles' philosophy.

We can make some progress by considering in more detail the information we have about the *daimōn*'s exile. In DK 31 B115 the gods have decreed a fixed term of 30,000 seasons of banishment for the transgression of some sort of bloodshed. This banishment involves the *daimōn* wandering through the cosmos between the various elements. Other fragments that relate the story of Empedocles' own banishment add that he has been a boy, a girl, a bush, a bird and a fish (DK 31 B117).[16] The reference at the end of B115 to Empedocles' "trusting in raving Strife" has often been taken as a further explanation of the cause of the *daimōn*'s downfall: somehow, on Strife's prompting, the *daimōn* performed the act that led to his banishment. This would assign a significant ethical dimension to Love and Strife since Love would be associated with harmony and proper conduct and Strife with transgression and disorder. Certainly, there is evidence elsewhere that might support such a view (e.g. the golden age of B128) and it is likely that the influence of Love and Strife is felt in the human sphere as much in terms of social – and perhaps religious – concord or discord as in the physical blending or separation of the four roots. But it is also possible that "trusting in raving Strife" in B115 is a further comment on the constant movement between elements that here characterizes the banishment of the *daimōn*, rather than a comment on the cause of that banishment. The *daimōn* "trusts in Strife" in the sense that he is tossed between the separate elements and subject to the dissociation produced by Strife's influence in the cosmos, which is also reflected in the roots' hatred of the wanderer and the constant series of exchanges. The initial transgressive act, in that case, need not be at Strife's prompting.

We might still wonder about the initial bloodshed that is described as the cause of this banishment. There are two general sources of concern, both driven by doubt about precisely how the spilling of blood detailed in B115 fits in the overall cosmic cycle. First, we might ask: whose blood was spilt? Was it part of some sort of discord between *daimones*? Those who think that the banishment of the *daimōn* is part of the break-up of the perfect sphere of Love have some difficulty in accounting for any kind of misdeed. Whose blood is there to be shed?[17] On the other hand, if the *daimōn*'s banishment occurs at some point in an already partially differentiated cosmos there is less immediate difficulty. Either the influence of Strife generates conflict and murder between the *daimones* or, as we shall soon learn, any act of killing and meat-eating in fact is tantamount to murder and might result in the longlasting banishment.

Secondly, some commentators are concerned that the assignment of a strict period of banishment coupled with a notion of a strict period between cosmic cycles might lend an air of determinism to the *daimōn*'s error. If the *daimōn*'s goal is, for example, to return to the harmonized state of total Love then there seems to be no alternative course of action than simply waiting for the cycle to come around. Nothing the *daimōn* does will affect that, just as perhaps it was inevitable that as Strife exerted a cosmic influence, the *daimōn* might be led to transgress the gods' decree.[18] Here, once more, we are hampered by various indeterminacies in the evidence. B115 says only that the *daimōn* wishes to return to a place among the gods, a message repeated in B147. It is not certain that this is a description of the sphere under Love and, on the contrary, it might be difficult to see that there can be gods or *daimones* or, indeed, any distinguishable individuals at such a time. The *daimones*, so far as we can tell, are material beings and therefore must be somehow composed of the four roots that will become homogenized by the total dominance of Love. Empedocles is careful to refer to the *daimones* as "long lived" rather than "immortal" in the strict sense (cf. Curd 2005: 142–3). Some commentators might embrace this and recognize that the ideal state towards which the *daimōn* strives is, paradoxically, one in which all individuality is extinguished; the social harmony of the "golden age" of B128 would on such a view just be a step nearer to that ultimate goal. Alternatively, the *daimōn* is aiming for communion with the gods, which can occur at some stage of the cosmic cycle between total homogenization and total separation of the roots. (If the gods and *daimones* are the same then this would be a return to his peers.)[19]

It is, in any case, evident that Empedocles is implicitly committed to a curious account of the *daimōn*'s identity over time.[20] He identifies himself as a *daimōn* rather than a particular human individual, "Empedocles", and so is able to say that he has himself also been a bush, a fish and so on. The possibility of such transformations has plausibly been offered as the rationale for the apparent prohibition on eating meat, something paralleled in Pythagoreanism, which also shares a relevantly similar view of reincarnation (see p. 38). Empedocles not only rejects killing generally (e.g. B136, B139 supplemented by "ensemble d" of the papyrus) but also offers the following nightmarish description of a traditional Greek blood sacrifice:

> A father, lifting his beloved son – now changed in form
> – sacrifices him with a prayer, the great fool. They have no
> idea, sacrificing him as he begs. But the father cannot hear
> the shouts and, sacrificing in his home, prepared a terrible
> meal. In just this way a son takes his father, children take
> their mother and, stealing away their life, they scoff their
> own dear flesh.   (DK 31 B137)

The father in this case does not intend to kill his child. He is, we might imagine, sacrificing a sheep or cock in a traditional manner. But he does not realize that this animal is in fact his son "changed in form"; presumably his son had died and the *daimōn* that was his son is now the sacrificial animal. The possibility of a *daimōn* moving from one form of life to another now makes all meat-eating potentially cannibalistic: Empedocles uses the transitivity of identity to say that since the sheep, say, is the *daimōn* that was the son, so in eating the sheep we eat the son. Pythagoras, we remember, once prevented someone beating a dog since he recognized it as the soul of a friend (p. 38). Here, Empedocles uses a much more graphic example to make a similar point.

B137 might have further consequences. If it is intended to serve as a prohibition on animal sacrifice and meat-eating generally, then it suggests that there are sufficient *daimones* currently undergoing banishment and wandering through the cosmos that it is prudent to abstain from meat in order to avoid risking eating a family member. A similar lesson to that in B137 is provided by Empedocles' recommendation that we should avoid heterosexual reproduction.[21] Given the problems of identity generated by these wandering *daimones* then just as every act of eating meat risks being cannibalistic, so every act of heterosexual reproduction risks being incestuous: Empedocles himself has, we should note, been both a boy and a girl. These prohibitions lead us to consider one of the pressing questions about the *daimōn*'s story in general. Perhaps every living human is a *daimōn* engaged in such wandering. The recognition of this fact, coupled with the recognition of the nature of the cosmos as a whole, is a necessary part of achieving freedom from banishment.[22] Otherwise, if we are to distinguish the *daimones* and their various incarnations from a separate race of mortal human beings, perhaps making the former products of Love and the latter products of Strife, it is not clear why we should all avoid meat-eating; if I am not a *daimōn* then eating meat is not cannibalistic.[23] Certainly, Empedocles does occasionally draw attention to his status as a *daimōn* (e.g. B115.13) or distinguish himself from mortals (B113), but this is all compatible with a conviction that we should all identify ourselves as the *daimones* we truly are rather than the particular human individual we happen to be at the moment. Teaching us our true identity will be part of the didactic aim of the poem(s) as a whole.

Questions about the nature of human existence and questions of eschatology are never far away from questions of natural philosophy, in the early period of Greek philosophy as much as in its later, classical and Hellenistic periods. Plato's *Phaedo*, *Republic* and *Timaeus*, for example, all combine an interest in the basic structure of the universe with questions about the fate of a human soul after death. Empedocles is yet another example of this pervasive tendency and is himself following in a tradition including Pythagoras, whose interest in questions of identity between mortal lives we have already noted (p. 38).[24] The obvious similarities and equally clear differences between him and Anaxagoras should also alert us to the continuing diversity, both in form and in content, of philosophical output after Parmenides. It is not a mistake to consider the fifth-century pluralists as engaged in some kind of common response to Eleaticism, but we should not allow that to obscure the significant differences of approach and philosophical interest they continue to exhibit.

NINE

Democritus and Leucippus

Abdera, a town on the North coast of the Aegean, was not known for the intelligence of its inhabitants. The late antique joke-book the *Philogelos* ("*Laughter-lover*") contains a number of jokes aimed at this stereotype. For example: "Did you hear the one about the Abderan who heard that onions cause wind? He strapped a bunch to the back of his boat, thinking it would make it go faster!" But despite this reputation, the city was home not only to the great Sophist Protagoras, but also to two other important philosophers: Leucippus and Democritus.

These two are most famous for their description of an atomist cosmology. According to them, the universe is a limitless expanse containing two kinds of thing: the void (empty space) and atoms (everlasting and indivisible bits of matter). As the countless atoms move in the void they come together and disperse to create various worlds and all the things in them. We know next to nothing about Leucippus, and it is very difficult to determine which elements of the atomist cosmology we should assign to him or to Democritus. In fact, Leucippus' achievements seem to have been so overshadowed by Democritus that Epicurus, the Hellenistic atomist, even denied that there ever had been a philosopher by that name.[1] We know a bit more about Democritus. His dates are disputed and there are various competing ancient reports, but we can be confident that he outlived Socrates, perhaps by up to fifty years.[2] We also certainly know enough to be sure that he had an enormous range of philosophical interests, covering not only topics in cosmology but also various other fields of natural philosophy (including embryology and other specialist topics), mathematics, ethics, politics and aesthetics. We can say something about some of these areas of his thought, but the vast majority of our evidence, and the vast majority of scholarly discussion of his philosophy from antiquity on, has centred on his atomist cosmology.[3] Aristotle's obvious interest in Democritus – shown by the fact that he wrote a work *Against* (or, perhaps, *On*) *Democritus* (see Diog. Laert. 5.27; Simpl. *De caelo* 294,33), which is now lost – was centred on his physical theory and this interest is then replicated in other sources dependent on Aristotle. But there is no reason to assume that Democritus himself would similarly have privileged his atomism over various other areas of his thought.

It might seem churlish, after some of the difficulties with much early Greek philosophy, to complain because we have so much information about Democritus from so many different sources. But there are significant difficulties in assessing the reliability and consistency of the many various reports. The emphasis generated by the interest in atomism has had a curious effect on the transmission of information about Democritus. The vast majority of our sources are testimonia discussing his physical theories. But on the other hand, most of the more or less verbatim fragments of Democritus concern his ethical and political ideas. These latter have been transmitted principally as brief sayings in ancient collections of philosophical wisdom and were probably cited in antiquity by later writers such as the Cynics who were interested in Democritus' claims about self-sufficiency and related issues.[4] Our third strand of information about Democritus comes from various later sceptical writers who were attracted to his apparent reticence about the reliability of the senses. The question of how to marry these divergent sources of information about Democritus is critical to the assessment of many aspects of his thought. We need also to bear in mind that Democritus was subject to a great deal of criticism from the inheritors of his atomist physics, the Epicureans. No doubt encouraged by a desire to demonstrate their own originality, they were quick to criticize Democritus for various mistakes and omissions in his philosophy. It is not always clear that the Epicureans were entirely fair in their criticisms and they may generally have taken, for their own polemical purposes, an excessively uncharitable view of their atomist predecessor.[5]

Atoms and void, division and motion

For now, let us follow Aristotle's lead and concentrate on Democritus' physics and metaphysics. To explain the choice of an atomist cosmology we need to remember once again the Eleatic challenge. In particular, there are two Eleatic claims that figure prominently in the atomist picture.

- "[What] is" is homogeneous and indivisible.
- Motion is possible only if we accept that there is "[what] is not".

The first claim will be important when we come to consider the atom and why it is that a Democritean atom cannot be divided. (The Greek word *atomos* means "uncuttable", "indivisible".) We might note at the outset, however, that the indivisibility of the atom guarantees that it conforms to one half of the Eleatic ban on absolute coming to be and destruction: atoms cannot be destroyed. They also cannot be created and new atoms cannot be formed.

Before we turn to think about atoms in more detail, let us consider the other member of the atomists' ontology: the void. The void has received comparatively less attention than the atom, but in many ways the void is the more surprising member of the pairing.[6] Certainly, by positing that there is such a thing as void, Democritus and Leucippus took a radical step. Previous pluralist cosmologies, such as those of Anaxagoras and Empedocles, had reacted to the Eleatic challenge simply by asserting that motion could occur in their respective visions of the universe. From what we can tell, they simply thought that it was incorrect to assert that in order for motion to take place, the universe could not be a *plenum*, entirely full.[7] That was certainly a respectable ancient view: Aristotle himself reaffirms it (Aristot. *Phys.* 4.8–9; and see Furley 1976; Makin 1993: 105–15; Berryman 2002). Democritus and Leucippus, on the other hand, met the challenge head-on and accepted both the necessity of void for motion and also the existence of void.

Democritus and Leucippus think that in order to have any kind of cosmology that can account for the world we perceive then we must allow for two vital characteristics: plurality and motion. Once they have allowed those two, they can begin to construct an account of the universe while retaining other Eleatic elements such as the principles of conservation. The void will serve a dual purpose of separating the atoms and also giving them space in which to move, so its role is absolutely crucial.

Remember Melissus, DK 30 B7, which we considered briefly earlier (p. 111):

> Nor is there any void (*keneon*). For the void is nothing and what is nothing could not be. Nor is there motion: for it is unable to move aside at any point, but, rather, it is full. If there were void, then it could move aside into the void. But, as there is no void, then there is nowhere for it move aside into. (DK 30 B7.7)

For anything to move there must be somewhere for it to move to. This somewhere must be unoccupied, else it could not move into it. And, when it moves, it must leave behind some new unoccupied space. Consider those puzzle games made of a number of tiles arranged in a grid, leaving one empty space. By moving one tile at a time, it is possible to rearrange them all. If there is no space then there can be no movement. And, whenever motion occurs an empty space is created: as soon as a tile moves to occupy the one empty space, it leaves a new space behind. For an Eleatic such as Melissus, motion is easily dismissed. There is no void, because there can be no "[what] is not". However, the conditional "if there is motion then there is [what] is not" is a two-edged sword. Democritus and Leucippus turn it to their advantage as part of an argument for the existence of void, simply by adding the premise that "there is motion".

The claim that there is motion might seem uncontroversial, because we perceive motion all the time. But the Eleatics object that we have no reason to believe that our senses offer us any access to the true nature of things. Here, Democritus and Leucippus simply have to stand their ground and assert that they have confidence in some of what our senses tell us. As we shall see, there is reason to think that Democritus was, at least sometimes, not prepared to accept everything the senses tell us as true. But we can assume that, in offering a cosmological account, the atomists wanted to explain how there is a cosmos at all, and it is not too far-fetched to think that any cosmos must exhibit some sort of change and plurality. The atomists begin, therefore, with the idea that there is a cosmos and that there is motion, plurality and change. Some support for this view comes from Aristotle:

> Some of the ancients thought that "what is" is necessarily one and unmoving. For, there being no void, neither could it move (there being no separate void) nor could there be many things (there being nothing to separate them) ... But Leucippus thought he had arguments which were consistent with sense-perception and removed neither coming-to-be, nor passing away, nor motion and plurality from the existents. He agreed in these respects with what appears to be the case; he agreed with those who posit the "one" that there could be no motion without void, and he says that the void is not and that nothing that is is not (for what properly is is full). But what is of that latter kind is not one, but infinite in number and invisible because of the smallness of the masses. They move in the void (for there is void) and as they come together they generate coming-to-be; as they move apart they generate passing-away.
> (Aristot. *Gen et. Corr.* 325a2–6, 23–32 [DK 67 A7])

For now, note that Aristotle puts the atomist project in terms of an attempt to offer arguments in response to the monist Eleatics, but consistent with sense perception. More specifically, Leucippus is here said to want to give an account consistent with the reality of coming into being and passing away (of some sort), motion and plurality. Of course, this does not mean that Leucippus has to be committed to accepting everything that common sense might suppose. But he is committed to telling a story that accounts for some coming to be and change, and can explain how it is that things appear to us as they do if they are not in fact the real nature of things.

The void, therefore, stands not so much as a modification of Eleaticism as a sign of the atomists' complete opposition to Eleaticism's starting-point. Parmenides had insisted that we choose between two routes and that the route of "[it] is not" is entirely unthinkable. But Democritus and Leucippus proudly proclaim that their universe contains both atoms and void, both "[what] is" and "[what] is not". Democritus and Leucippus were themselves aware of how paradoxical it might have sounded to say that the void is. The evidence for this comes from a lost work of Aristotle, *On Democritus*, used by the commentator Simplicius:

> Democritus considers the nature of everlasting things to be small beings, infinite in number. He posits in addition to these space, infinite in extent. He calls this space by the following names: "the void", "the nothing" (*ouden*), "the infinite"; each of the beings he calls by the following names: "the hing" (*den*), "the full", "the existent".
>
> (*De caelo* 294, 33ff. [DK 68 A37])

We should note in particular one pair of the terms used for atoms and void. The void is "nothing" (*ouden*) and an atom is "hing" (*den*). *Den* is an unusual word used here by the atomists to make a particular point. Clearly, *den* is formed by taking *ouden* – the standard and common Greek word for "nothing" – and removing the *ou*, which is a standard Greek negative prefix. Take away the "not" from "nothing" and you get "hing". So, in choosing to emphasize this pair of expressions, Democritus and Leucippus are saying that we must accept that atoms and void come as a complementary pair. Without atoms we could have no void (since, without there being plural and separate things, there could be nothing to separate and divide them), but similarly without void there could be no atoms (since there would be nothing to separate and divide these atoms). Given this mutual interdependence, it is not at all significant which terms we use to describe them; we might as well construct a word for the atoms, for what is, out of the word we use to describe the void, nothingness (as *den* comes from *ouden*) as vice versa. As we are told elsewhere, they are fond of saying that the void exists "no less" than the atoms, the atoms "no more" than the void. We are left with the deliberately paradoxical claim that there is both "what is" and "what is not" and, moreover, that "what is not" is, no less than "what is" (see e.g. Aristot. *Met.* 985b7–9 [DK 67 A6]).

Now we can consider the atoms. As has been pointed out since antiquity, each atom displays many of the characteristics of the Eleatics' notion of "[what] is". Although there are many atoms, indeed infinitely many, and they vary in shape and size, every atom is everlasting and undergoes no change other than motion. Further, although the atoms have different shapes, every atom is otherwise homogeneous: it has no internal variations of composition. If we concentrate for the moment on the most immediately arresting characteristic of the atom, namely its indivisibility, we immediately face a problem. Why is an atom indivisible?

Once again, we need to see the Eleatic background. In particular, we might consider one of Zeno's paradoxes of divisibility, which could be paraphrased as follows.[8] Take something that is spatially extended. If it is spatially extended it has (spatial) parts that can be distinguished. It therefore seems possible to divide it, marking off these different spatial parts. Now, what of these new parts? Are they or are they not also spatially extended? Here we face a dilemma: if they are not spatially extended then how do we suppose they could have combined to form the original extension? It is impossible to construct a line, for example, from extension-less geometrical points. On the other hand, if they are extended then we can further divide them. At each stage, we must ask whether we have reached the endpoint of divisibility. If we are dealing with parts that themselves have some extension, however small, then division can continue. If the parts are without extension, then we seem – absurdly – to have divided the original extension away into nothingness. The atomists took the paradox as a challenge to any physical theory such as theirs that wishes to assert that there are extended, but indivisible, atoms. These must be extended if they are to combine to produce larger extended bodies. They must also be indivisible if they are to be fundamental everlasting components of the universe that persist through all other changes.

Once we have accepted an atomist cosmology then it is easy to see how we might counter Zeno's paradox as applied to physical divisions. A china cup, for example, might appear to be a unity but it can be broken. And each of the pieces of the broken cup can be further broken up. I could, if I wished, take all the pieces and grind them up further and further. But although I will generate a larger and larger number of pieces, they will each still have some size such that, in principle, they could recombine to produce the original cup. At no point can I grind the pieces away into nothingness. Eventually, atomist theory tells us, we shall come to a stage at which the pieces, although still with some magnitude, are not even in principle divisible. The most powerful crushing equipment could not break them. These are the atoms.

This is convincing only if Democritus and Leucippus can secure the central claim that there are extended yet indivisible things. They need to have some answer when someone, perhaps still impressed by Zeno, asks precisely why an atom cannot be divided. It is rather unclear, however, what their answer was and we are hampered by lacking their own explanation of the theory. In addition, the evidence we do have – above all, Aristotle and the Aristotelian commentators – does not itself offer a clear and satisfying account. Some charitable reconstruction is needed.[9]

It is very unlikely that Democritus thought that atoms are just too small to be further divided. On this view, atoms would have some magnitude, but either would be so tiny that they have no parts (an odd view, but not unparalleled in antiquity)[10] or simply would be too tiny to divide. But Democritus is elsewhere reported as saying that there is no upper limit to the size of an atom; there could well be atoms the size of our own cosmos somewhere in the universe. Also, the divisibility in question is not "practical"; our concern is not to find things that we cannot in practice divide, but some things that cannot even in principle be divided. Smallness does not seem an adequate justification.

Some sources speak as if atoms are too hard or dense to be divided. This is a more promising line of thought, but we need to be careful. Hardness or density is in one sense a property of compound bodies, and the atomists tell us that it depends on the proportion of atoms and void in a given item. A diamond, for example, is harder than a sponge because the arrangement of atoms in a diamond is different from that of the atoms in the sponge. A single atom cannot, of course, display hardness in this sense. We make better sense of the idea of atomic hardness by focusing on the related claim that atoms are indivisible because they are homogeneous and full or solid. An atom contains no internal void; it is absolutely solid. Even atoms whose shape involves thin parts or hooks contain no *internal* void. This is an important difference between atoms and items composed of a number of atoms arranged in a particular way. A diamond may be extremely hard and difficult to cut, but it still contains both atoms and void. A single atom, on the other hand, is homogeneous in a way even the diamond is not.

Given the homogeneity of the atom, Democritus and Leucippus might well have borrowed another Eleatic principle. Parmenides had insisted that "[what] is" "is no more at one point than at another" (DK 28 B8.22–5), asserting its homogeneity and lack of internal divisions. Melissus (DK 30 B7.2) makes a similarly close connection between "[what] is" being one and its being homogeneous. It might well be that the atomists used a similar kind of indifference argument: there is no more reason for an atom to be divided at a given point than at any other point (since there are no faults, or fissures, no internal void) and that is why it is indivisible. There certainly is a reason why a compound object, on the other hand, can be divided at certain points rather than others: because these are areas of void within it.

We might stop at this point to question the atomists' reasoning. There is no more reason for an atom to be divided at one point than another. We might think this means only that an atom is divisible either everywhere or nowhere. Why are the atomists entitled to conclude that the latter option is the case? Some commentators, interested in a difficult stretch of argument in Aristotle's *De Generatione et Corruptione* (*Gen et. corr.* 1.2 [DK 68 A48b]), are concerned that the atomists might illegitimately have confused the claim that "for every point, it is possible for an atom to be divided at that point" with the claim that "it is possible for an atom to be (simultaneously) divided at every point". The rejection of the second claim is then fallaciously meant to justify the rejection of the first and give an argument for atomism (for discussion see Makin 1993: 53–4; Hasper 1999; Sedley 2004; Betegh 2006: 266–8). Whether or not this argument's validity can be rescued, there is the further question of whether it is in fact Democritus' and Leucippus' own argument. Quite possibly they felt sufficiently confident in borrowing and relying on an Eleatic principle to deduce indivisibility directly from homogeneity without considering any further serious objections.[11]

Generating worlds

Democritus and Leucippus also set out to explain the apparent variety of what we perceive in our cosmos, once again using their relatively sparse ontology of atoms and void. The explanatory power of this ontology is first augmented by an argument to show that the atoms are not all alike. Rather, there are atoms of every imaginable shape and, perhaps, of every imaginable size. The argument form is once again a version of "indifference" reasoning: there is "no more reason" for there to be atoms of shape A than of shape B, and so on. So there must be atoms of both shape A and shape B (see Simpl. *In Phys.* 28.4ff. [DK 67 A8]).[12] Similar arguments augment the ontology not by adding to its variety but by increasing its scope. The atomists conclude that the universe is infinitely extended both spatially and temporally and that it contains an infinite number of atoms of these various shapes, since there is no more reason for the universe to be of any one given size than any other.[13] With those conclusions secured, the atomists are in a position to begin a positive explanation of the cosmos. But before we come to consider that account, it is worth reminding ourselves that thus far the atomists have relied only on the most general of empirical evidence from which they have derived the most general premises: that there is a cosmos, that there is a plurality of things, that things move. The generation of the atomic theory has used no additional empirical evidence.

Their sparse ontology leaves no room for additional fundamental entities. They cannot, therefore, look to things such as Anaxagoras' *nous* or Empedocles' Love and Strife to explain how the world came to be. Instead, they insist that the very infinity of the universe and the atoms within it is sufficient to account for the formation of a cosmos such as the one we inhabit and the generation of all the various things our cosmos contains. It has come to be without the input of any guiding intelligence or any other cosmic factors beyond the atoms and their incessant motion within the void. Our cosmos is just one within the infinite universe. Given the infinities of time, space and matter, there is "no more" reason for a single cosmos to be formed than for an infinite number to be formed. And we know that at least one has been formed, namely ours, so we have reason to think that there are countless others too.

The precise mechanics of cosmos formation are necessarily speculative. Our evidence suggests that Democritus and Leucippus believed that atoms in a certain region of the void begin to move in a kind of vortex, the motion of which sorts the atoms within it into groups of similar shape and size in a kind of centrifuge or, alternatively, in a process similar to that in which grain is "winnowed" to separate wheat from chaff (see Diog. Laert. 9.31–2 [DK 67 A1]; cf. Bailey 1928: 90–101, 138–55; Furley 1987: 140–46; Hankinson 1998: 207–9). Once a cosmos has been formed then the atoms within it begin to move and interact, coming together and moving apart, and – in the case of our cosmos – come to form earth and sky and eventually generate the various forms of life. Within the cosmic system atoms will tend to move in certain ways according to their shape and the surrounding atoms, so we can begin to describe certain natural tendencies or laws. Like other groupings of atoms, however, the cosmos is not permanent and eventually dissolves, its atoms leaving to continue their unceasing motion.

The process of cosmos formation is purely mechanical and follows directly from the behaviour of the atoms in a pre-cosmic state. No further explanatory factor is required. But the atomists also make the bold claim that they can adequately account not only for the fact that there is a cosmos at all, but also for all the complexity and apparent adaptation of the various species in our cosmos, including ourselves. The crucial point here is that there are an infinite number of cosmoses and that there has been an infinite amount of past time for cosmoses to form. Given this superabundance, it is no longer the case that our cosmos is something special whose existence and specific nature needs to be explained. Rather, it becomes inevitable that given the infinite universe at least one cosmos like ours must have come to be, since every possible cosmos must come to be. And what is the case for the cosmos itself also is the case for all the constituents of it. Given the infinite number of worlds, somewhere at some time there had to be a world in which there emerged animals like us, indeed individuals just like us. So we are not special and in need of explanation by some special kind of cause. We had to come to be. (Indeed, given the infinities of atoms and space, there must be innumerable worlds just like ours down to the smallest detail; cf. Warren 2004.)

Importantly, it is not "mere chance" that a cosmos just like ours should come to be. But, of course, there is equally no grand purpose served by our cosmos's existence and it was not designed or intended in any way; in that respect it might also be correct to say that it came to be "by chance" (cf. Aristot. *Phys.* 195b36–196a3 [DK 68 A 68], 196a24–b5 [DK 68 A69]). Leucippus encapsulates the atomist position with this famous remark: "Nothing comes to be at random, but everything is by reason and out of necessity" (DK 67 B2). Like Empedocles, the atomists accounted for the apparent adaptation of species in our world by suggesting that only the well-adapted varieties thrown up by the process of atomic motions have survived. And, like Empedocles, as a result they won Aristotle's disdain. They also came to be criticized heavily by the later atomists, the Epicureans, because it was felt that their conception of necessitated mechanistic atomic motions left no room for independent human agency. If human beings too are composed of atoms, the Epicureans worried, then their actions seem to be thoroughly determined. It is not clear whether Democritus and Leucippus were consciously determinist in this way, but we might certainly think that atomist cosmologies owe some explanation of human action and its relation to the underlying interactions of atoms (cf. Bailey 1928: 186–8).

Explaining difference and change

The passage from Aristotle's *De Generatione et Corruptione* we considered above (p. 156) already gives the beginnings of the atomists' explanation of change. Like the other pluralists, they distinguish between apparent and absolute coming to be and passing away. The various changes and alterations we perceive are to be explained as effects of the atoms coming together and dispersing as they move through the void. As a tree grows, for example, the atoms constituting the tree increase in number. When a lump of sugar dissolves in hot coffee, the atoms of the sugar disperse. At no point do any atoms come to be or pass away.

The atomists now have some reasonable resources for explaining how the atoms can combine to produce composite items as different from one another as, say, a tree, a dagger and a lake. Aristotle explains some of those methods, explaining as he does so some of the atomists' own terminology:

> And just as those who set out a single underlying existent and generate the other things by its affections, positing the rare and the dense as the principles of those properties, in the same way these [the atomists] too make differences the causes of all other things. But they say there are three differences: shape, arrangement, and position. For they say that what is differs in "rhythm", "touching", and "turning" ("rhythm" is shape; "touching" is arrangement; "turning" is position). For A differs from N in shape, AN from NA in arrangement and Z from N in position. (Aristot. *Met.* 985b10–19 [DK 67 A6])

Aristotle's use of an analogy between atoms and letters may well be inspired by the atomists themselves; it was certainly reused by the Hellenistic Epicureans (see Lucretius *DRN* 1.823–6, 907–14). The variety of atomic shapes, coupled with the possibility of their combination in a variety of series and in different alignments, generates an enormous variety of different possible ways in which atoms might combine. This variety can then be used to account for the various different properties of composite items in a reductive fashion by accounting for them in terms of the shapes and arrangements of their constituent atoms. For example, when Aristotle's pupil, Theophrastus, comes to describe Democritus' account of various perceptible properties, he explains that things are hard or soft according to the position and grouping of the interstices of void between the constituent atoms. The arrangement of these atoms can also, he says, be used to account for an object's weight. These two properties must have different explanations, however, because iron is harder but lighter than lead. Democritus, we are told, inferred that although iron must have, overall, more void per unit volume than lead, it must differ in another way, by its atoms being less uniformly arranged (Theoph. *De sensibus* 62 [DK 68 A135]). Of course, Democritus has no direct evidence for the atomic arrangement of lead. He is inferring from the perceptible properties of the macroscopic substance that there must be some relevant explanation in terms of its atomic arrangement, based on the premise that his atomist ontology is true; the weight of lead *must* be explicable in atomic terms and cannot be due to any further factors. It is not difficult, furthermore, to see how the atomists' theory can also be used to account for change. Items can change either through the introduction of new atoms (as in cases of growth) or the loss of atoms; they can also change by their atoms being rearranged or realigned (as, for example, the sea becomes white foam when disturbed).

Democritean metaphysics and epistemology

We can ask two important questions of Democritus' method of accounting for the various perceptible properties of items we encounter in the world. The first is: how plausible is this tactic? Does it offer satisfying accounts of the many various properties we come across in the world solely in terms of atoms and void? We might, for example, be relatively happy with accepting a reductive account of weight or hardness in terms of the atomic constituents. But what about colour? The atoms themselves are not coloured, so colour must be generated entirely as a result of arrangement and interaction between a perceiver and a perceived object. How plausible is Democritus' view, especially given that the details of his explanations (the particular shapes of atoms involved, for example) are entirely speculative?

The second question is: what is the precise metaphysical consequence of these explanations? There is considerable debate over what Democritus' explanations of such properties imply for the existence or reality of the properties being explained. Did he intend to explain them away, so to speak, by saying that colour, for example, is "nothing but" atoms in certain arrangements? (We might call this an "eliminativist" move: there are no colours really, just atoms arranged in the void.) Or did he mean to account for colour not so as to do away with it, but rather just to explain the causes of colour in atomic terms? (We might call this a "reductive" move: we are asked to understand what colour is in terms of something more fundamental.)

There is a particularly famous Democritean pronouncement that is often the starting-point for further discussion of this central issue. It is often cited in discussions of Democritus' epistemology and, in particular, in discussions about whether he is a sceptic of any sort. The case for him being a sceptic would seem to rest on his apparent downgrading of perceptible properties such as colour in comparison with what "truly" exists; namely, the atoms and the void. Since we cannot perceive atoms and void, but do perceive things such as colour, this would seem to show that our senses are extremely poor guides to the reality of things. "By convention sweet, by convention bitter, by convention hot, by convention cold, by convention coloured; in reality atoms and void" (DK 68 B9).[14]

There are various important sources that offer different perspectives on Democritus' view. (i) Aristotle links Democritus closely with Protagoras. Both Protagoras and Democritus argue, according to Aristotle, that we should say that of two conflicting perceptions (e.g. you think the wind is warm; I think it is cold) that there is "no more" reason for one to be correct than another. But whereas Protagoras concludes that both perceptions are true, Democritus concludes that neither is (Aristot. *Met.* 1009b7ff. [DK 68 A112]).[15] (ii) Aristotle's pupil, Theophrastus, devotes a long section (49–82) of his work *De sensibus* (*On the Senses*) to an exposition and criticism of Democritus' attempts to account for perceptible properties in terms of the atomic constitution of the perceived object and its interaction with the atomic constitution of the perceiver.[16] (iii) The Pyrrhonist sceptic Sextus Empiricus devotes a section of his work to outlining Democritus' view on the reliability of the senses as criteria of truth and cites small passages from Democritus' own work in support of his interpretation. For Sextus, Democritus denies that the senses have any access to the truth, being able to generate only "bastard" knowledge, but accepts that reason can attain "legitimate" or "genuine" knowledge (SE *M* 7.135–40 [DK 68 B9, 10, 11]).[17] (iv) Plutarch writes a work *Against Colotes* which attacks the Epicurean Colotes' work *That it is Impossible even to Live According to the Views of the Other Philosophers.* Colotes had attacked Democritus on the grounds that by making everything except atoms and void "by convention", he had denied the reality of all perceptible properties and even all compound bodies. If only atoms and void are real, Democritus himself – a mere conglomeration of atoms in the void – is not real (Plut. *Adv. Col.* 1108E–1111E).[18]

Making good sense of the distinction between things "in reality" and things "by convention" in the light of these different sources of information is absolutely crucial to our understanding of Democritus' original thought. However, the problem for anyone attempting to offer a comprehensive account of Democritus' epistemology and its associated metaphysics is that our ancient reports are, on the face of it, very divided. Some make Democritus out to be a staunch sceptic, denying that our senses give us any true information about the world. Others say that he was more generous, allowing that our senses do tell us about the world and, in fact, can be used as a good starting-point in investigating the world. Others still say that Democritus was like Plato in denying that the senses could give us access to what is real, but recommending that we should rely instead on our reason. Recent scholarly opinion is often similarly divided.

Some things are clear and uncontroversial. First, some kind of division is proposed between the fundamental things in the world (atoms and void) and other properties (for example, colour and temperature). Secondly, these other properties do not belong to atoms and void themselves (an atom does not have a colour). From this point on, however, the controversy begins. It might be helpful to set out the different camps.

Eliminativism

This reading says that, according to Democritus, colour, for example, is not real. We see things as coloured, but in reality they are not; they are just compounds of colourless atoms. Colour is therefore not part of the fabric of the world and we are mistaken to believe that things are coloured. On this reading (the reading promoted especially by the later atomists, the Epicureans, and reflected in works such as Colotes') Democritus was extremely sceptical about the evidence of the senses. When we say, for example, "the sky is blue", we are saying something false. Because we do not directly perceive the reality of atoms and void, our senses cannot give us access to the true nature of the world. This picture emphasizes the Eleatic strand in Democritus' thought since it makes him deny the reality of anything that is not unchanging and everlasting.[19]

Relativity

Another reading accepts that Democritus means to argue that colour is not a property of atoms and void themselves but takes the "in reality"–"by convention" distinction to mean not that colours are not real at all but rather that they arise only when a certain kind of sensory interaction takes place. Colours are "relative" or "by convention" in the sense that they depend on a certain relationship between an object and a perceiver. We are not mistaken when we say, for example, "the sky is blue", provided we understand the relative nature of colour.

For the atomists, perception works through the interaction of the atoms in the perceived object and the atoms of the perceiver's body. In contact senses (e.g. taste) this is simply by the atoms of the object coming into contact with the atoms of my tongue and this being registered in a particular way in the atoms of my soul. In distance senses such as sight, contact occurs between the sense organ and thin films of atoms, called *eidōla*, which are constantly being emitted by all composite bodies and fly off in all directions. So when I see the *Mona Lisa*, for example, my eyes receive the *eidōla* emitted by the painting and their impact on me causes the particular sense experience. Different people have different atomic arrangements, which is why people think something sometimes tastes bitter (perhaps they are licking an ice cream after brushing their teeth) and at other times does not and why sometimes two different people think that one and the same thing is sweet and bitter (perhaps one has just brushed her teeth and the other has not). The fact that this is how perceptible properties arise does not mean that they are not real, only that they are "conventional" in the sense that they depend on a particular kind of agreement between perceivers (e.g. to agree that in general ice cream tastes sweet) or perhaps even a kind of agreement between the perceiver and the perceived object.[20]

It is not at all easy to decide between these views, precisely because they can both be supported by some of our evidence. Often, commentators need to explain away a particular awkward piece of evidence as a misunderstanding or deliberate distortion on the part of the source. (Perhaps Sextus, for example, illegitimately emphasizes or cites out of context certain apparently sceptical pronouncements.) In part, our preferred conclusion will depend on whether we are happy with a picture of Democritus that would make him deny the reality of everything but the atoms and void but go on nevertheless to write treatises on natural philosophy, ethics, politics and the like that treat their respective subject matter as genuine objects of enquiry. Perhaps, on the other hand, critics such as the Epicureans were correct to diagnose a serious inconsistency in Democritus' views and to argue that, had he taken his ontology and his epistemology in all seriousness, he should not have pursued such topics. Perhaps his position was not clear and consistent. Perhaps he had not entirely worked through the consequences of the starting assertion that the basic things in the world are just the atoms and the void. After all, as we saw at the very outset of our exploration of atomism, Democritus did seem to offer the senses *some* role in enquiry: they tell us that there is plurality, change and motion. We are left, as is often the case with these early philosophers, weighing different reports and comparing competing views of the level of sophistication it is right to expect of philosophers such as Democritus. Furthermore, there is some reason to think that ancient interpreters were similarly unsure of what to make of claims such as B9. It is worth noting that certain successors of Democritus, characters such as Metrodorus of Chios, Anaxarchus and Pyrrho of Elis, each took the "reality/convention" slogan as an inspiration for their own differing philosophies; it is evidently a claim susceptible to many different interpretations.[21]

Ethics and politics

Of the nearly three hundred extant "fragments" of Democritus, the vast majority are concerned with ethical and political questions and usually take the form of, often fairly banal, observations and recommendations for living a good life. The philosophical interest of these has been the subject of some disagreement, and some commentators pass over them without much comment. That is unfortunate, because whether or not Democritus offered a fully theorized exposition of a "eudaemonist" ethical position of the sort familiar from Socrates, Plato, Aristotle and the Hellenistic philosophers, we ought to remember that his philosophical interests were far from exhausted by atomism.[22] The longest fragment usefully includes many of the themes of his ethical thought:

> Good cheer (*euthymia*) arises in men through a moderation
> of joy and a good balance in life. Deficiencies and excesses
> tend to change into one another and set up great motions

in the soul. Souls moved out of large intervals are neither well settled nor in good cheer. So you should pay attention to what is possible and be content with what is present, paying little heed to and not dwelling in thought on what is envied or marvelled at. But you should consider the lives of people in trouble, thinking about what they suffer so that what you have at present appears great and enviable, and it no longer happens that you suffer in the soul through desire for more. For he who wonders at those who are rich and are thought blessed by other men and constantly dwells on it in his memory is always forced to find new things and is driven by a desire to do something which cannot be put right and which the laws forbid. So some things you should not seek, but be happy with others, comparing your life with those who fare worse and consider yourself blessed when you consider what they suffer and by how much better your life is proceeding than theirs. Clinging to this thought you will live your life a more cheered person and will remove many troubles from your life, namely envy, jealousy and ill-will.   (DK 68 B191)

Democritus' account of how to attain the desired state of *euthymia* reflects a number of currents of ethical thought to be found also in contemporaries such as Socrates and the Sophists and continued in later philosophers, notably the Epicureans. He recommends a life of moderation, in which one studies one's desires and beliefs and rejects any that are unfounded or that will lead to discomfort and mental disturbance. He sees that there is a central role in a good life for certain pleasures, but rejects profligacy and unbridled hedonism. As we might expect given his atomist ontology, he rejects the notion of an immaterial soul and an afterlife. He also sees an important role for social and political harmony in the provision of a good life: the personal and political realms are interdependent in such a way that it is essential for the pursuit of one's own well-being that one should try to engineer the appropriate political context.[23] Interpersonal conflict, envy and spite are all detrimental to the social good and to the good of each individual.

It has sometimes been asked whether Democritus offered an ethical view fully integrated with his atomism. Of course, certain of his
views (e.g. about the absence of an afterlife) are derived from his
cosmology, but some commentators have wondered whether Democritus imagined that there was a certain physical disposition of
the atoms of a person, or perhaps just of a person's soul, that is to
be identified as the ideal state of well-being. Certainly, some of the
ethical fragments use terms reminiscent of the physical doctrines.
(For example, in describing the effects of teaching on a pupil, DK 68
B33 echoes the term "rhythm" that we saw [p. 165] Aristotle explain
as the atomists' term for atomic shape; B191 refers to "motions" in
the soul.) It is extremely difficult, however, to find any conclusive
evidence to support or reject such a view and it must, unfortunately,
be left unresolved.[24]

TEN

Epilogue

The last generation of "Presocratics" includes two further prominent philosophers: Philolaus and Diogenes of Apollonia. They both offer important lessons for any attempt to offer a general account of the development of early Greek philosophy.

Philolaus of Croton

Philolaus' philosophy brings us back, almost full circle, to the Ionian beginnings of our story and the Pythagoreans' interest in number, harmony and the nature of the soul. Perhaps the first self-proclaimed Pythagorean to compose a treatise, Philolaus combines Pythagorean interests evident from the earliest periods of the movement, some hundred years before, with a familiar form of cosmological account, no doubt influenced by the similar attempts of thinkers such as Empedocles and Anaxagoras a few years earlier.[1] It is possible that Philolaus' work is the principal source for Aristotle's account of Pythagoreanism in general.

Philolaus' cosmology begins as follows: "The nature in the cosmos was fitted together from unlimiteds (*apeira*) and limiters (*perainonta*), both the cosmos as a whole and everything in it" (DK 44 B1). DK 44 B2 then goes on to argue further for this dualist system, insisting on the necessity of both "unlimiteds" and "limiters" to generate the cosmos and the things in it. The obscure identity of these "unlimiteds" and "limiters" has been one of the principal puzzles in interpreting Philolaus' account and commentators have often made a link between this apparently abstract ontology and Pythagorean ideas about number and shape, identifying the "limiters" as numbers (or numbers of a certain kind) or abstract geometrical shapes that are then somehow imposed on the "unlimiteds", perhaps conceived as a kind of unformed matter. Perhaps the most plausible suggestion for the identity of the "unlimiteds" is that they are various continua (of pitch, heat, colour or mass). The "limiters" in that case would be particular points along those continua. Together they generate a particular temperature, shape or colour. Such a view would make good sense of the apparent co-dependency of the two classes and the necessity of them both for the composition of our cosmos.

Beyond these particular puzzles, there are some important general points to bear in mind about Philolaus' method. B6 gives an argument for the necessary pre-existence before our cosmos of the "limiters" and "unlimiteds" and also insists on the necessity of a further factor in addition to these two classes of things: *harmonia*. B1 introduces the notion of *harmonia*, by referring to the "fitting together" of the "limiters" and "unlimiteds", but B6 makes clear that this introduction is needed precisely because the "limiters" and the "unlimiteds" are so unlike one another. They cannot interact directly without the additional presence of this *harmonia*, and with it they interact so as to generate distinct items of definite character: the various things in the cosmos ranging from the heavenly bodies to the human body.

> Things are thus concerning nature and harmony (*harmonia*): the being of things, which is eternal, and nature itself admit divine and not human understanding except for the fact that it is not possible for any of the things that are and that we know to have come to be without the existence of the things from which the cosmos is composed, namely the limiters and the unlimiteds. Since these principles (*arkhai*) are unlike and not of the same kind as one another, then it

would have been impossible for them to have been formed into a cosmos,[2] had harmony not come to be in whatever way it did. Things which are alike and of the same kind as one another did not need harmony as well, but the sort of things which are unlike and not of the same kind as one another need to be brought together by harmony if they are to be held fast in a cosmos. (DK 44 B6)

It is worth dwelling on this argument, since it shows that in his cosmology Philolaus is dealing with a general metaphysical problem. He wants to account both for the variety and variability and also for the unity and order of the cosmos and feels it necessary to start with an ontology that includes more that one kind of basic existent. But having posited that basic distinction he needs also to give some account of how those basic items interact with one another and, more specifically, how they interact in such a way as to produce both the variety and the order we notice in the cosmos. *Harmonia* is therefore postulated as a means of ensuring their interaction and the coherence and unity of the cosmos. Considered in the light of the other Presocratic ideas we have encountered, there are plausible links to be drawn not only with the Pythagoreans but also with other cosmologies that involve the imposition of some kind of order or structure on distinct basic elements. We might think not only of Anaximander's unlimited *apeiron*, but also of the role of Anaxagoras' *nous* in generating distinguishable characters from an original homogeneous mass. What is perhaps most interesting about Philolaus, however, is that he explicitly draws attention to the general problem of guaranteeing the necessary interaction between his distinct basic cosmological components. Such explicit metaphysical concerns are also discernible in his near contemporary: Diogenes of Apollonia.

Diogenes of Apollonia

Theophrastus thought that Diogenes of Apollonia was "more or less the youngest of those who worked on these matters" (i.e. the natural philosophers) (Simpl. *In Phys.* 25,1–9 [DK 64 A5]). Although it is very likely that Diogenes was outlived by Democritus, it has become something of a convention to consider him as the last of the Presocratics.[3] His cosmological views also deserve consideration in their own right, of course, in particular his assertion of a thorough natural teleology that attributes much of the order and beauty of the cosmos to the working of intelligence (see DK 64 B3, B5, B8).[4] But here I want briefly to consider an argument that came at the opening of his work, just after the introduction:

> It seems to me, overall, that all things are alterations of the same things and are the same thing. And this is evident, for if any one of the things now in this cosmos (namely water, air, fire and all the other many things which are apparent in the cosmos), were different from another, that is being different and having a peculiar nature, and was not the same although it changed and altered again and again, then in no way would it be able to mingle with the other, nor benefit or harm another. Nor would a plant be able to grow from the earth, nor would any other living thing be able to come to be if it were not so composed as to be the same thing. But all these things, being alterations of the same thing, now and then become different and return to the same thing.
>
> (DK 64 B2)

The argument is hardly elegantly expressed, but it is important as a considered restatement of a kind of monism similar to the views of the Ionian philosophers with whom we began. It would be wrong to say, therefore, that early Greek philosophy displays a gradual move from monism to pluralism, because Diogenes is no less a monist than Thales. But it is also important that we recognize how different Diogenes is from the likes of Thales. Although they might agree that there is one single thing out of which all other things are generated, Diogenes is concerned not merely to assert that all things come from air, his preferred candidate for this privileged role. Rather, he first of all sets out what he takes to be a compelling argument for the need to assert a monist view as such and then goes on (in DK 64 B4 and B5 in particular) to give the case for seeing air as the particular stuff required and to identify air as the intelligent cause of the cosmic order. His initial argument for monism remains entirely neutral and rests on a general metaphysical claim about the need for interchangeable items to be somehow united. If *A* can *change* into *B*, then *A* and *B* must be ontologically alike. Otherwise, presumably, there is no reason to think that a change has occurred rather than the disappearance of *A* and the appearance of *B* in its place. This is then supplemented by an observation that all things (perhaps all natural things) can change into one another, which yields the desired result that all things must be composed from the same basic stuff. Similarly, the talk of benefit and harm might point to an argument that if *A* and *B* are to interact in any way, then they must be ontologically alike. The increased sophistication in Diogenes' account, therefore, is in terms of the level and nature of conceptual argument offered rather than in the complexity of his fundamental ontology. Like Philolaus, Diogenes draws attention to the metaphysical problems he faces in accounting for difference and change, and he too makes dealing with those problems an integral and explicit part of his cosmological account. Rather than any particular advance in the "scientific" content of their cosmologies, it is this increased sophistication and the rapid development of the tools of such abstract philosophical argument that ought to be recognized as the primary achievement of the early Greek philosophers.

Presocratic philosophy and classical philosophy

Both Philolaus and Diogenes of Apollonia display the hallmarks of a sophisticated and self-conscious approach to philosophy that had developed over the course of the fifth century. But equally, in other ways their respective philosophies, in their different ways, both point back to the very beginnings of Ionian enquiry: to Pythagorean interest in harmony and number and to Thales' or Anaximenes' interest in identifying a single substance or *arkhē* to stand as the origin and

fundamental constituent of the cosmos. And they also point forwards towards what is familiarly thought of as the great flowering
of Greek philosophy in the classical period. Even if we restrict our
consideration to Plato, there is no doubt that he is indebted in various important and complicated ways to a number of the Presocratics,
Philolaus and Diogenes included. The *Phaedo*, for example, explicitly
mentions Philolaus in its opening discussion of the predicament
of the incarnate soul and the *Philebus'* four-fold division of things
into the unlimited, the limit, the mixture and their cause is plausibly thought to owe something to Philolaus and other Pythagorean
cosmology.[5] In short, therefore, despite the temptation to consider
the Presocratics as a single group separate from Socrates and his
classical legacy and despite the temptation to agree with Aristotle's
account of Presocratic cosmological speculation in terms of a simple
narrative of progress, there are good reasons to be wary of both lines
of thought.

The same lesson might be drawn from considering philosophical
topics other than cosmology and metaphysics. Chapter 9 ended with
a glance at Democritus' ethical and political views. Such discussions
place him firmly in the mid-to-late-fifth century's increasing concern
with questions about the correct form of government, the role of
an individual in the *polis*, the relationship between the well-being
of an individual and that of the *polis* at large, the correct method of
ethical education and so on. These are the questions familiar from
the work of the Sophists, Socrates, Herodotus and Thucydides, and
the Athenian dramatists. In other words, Democritus shows that we
have already begun to move into the classical period and classical
philosophy. It also shows that the old claim that it was Socrates who
reoriented philosophy away from physics to ethics is, at best, an
exaggeration.[6] Our "Presocratics" were not averse to ethical thought
and even Socrates himself can be seen to engage from time to time
in a spot of natural philosophy of a sort (see Xen. *Mem.* 1.4, 4.3). The
crucial transition, if there was one, from "Presocratic" to "classical"
philosophy is not one of a radical shift in the philosophical questions
being addressed. After all, Plato and Aristotle show that they too are
happy to combine natural philosophy with other interests as part

of their philosophies. Rather, in many ways the important shift is geographical: at the end of the period of these early Greek philosophers, Athens has become a dominant economic and cultural centre. Some of our early philosophers had already began to make a mark there, if only to be considered a little dangerous in their innovative and potentially "atheist" ideas: Anaxagoras was thought to be part of Pericles' circle and Diogenes of Apollonia was known well enough to be parodied in Aristophanes' *Clouds*.[7] Democritus tells us that he went to Athens too, but complains, perhaps with disappointment, "nobody knew me" (see Diog. Laert. 9.36 and Cic. *Tusc.* 5.104 [DK 68 B116]). Towards the end of the fifth century, philosophy becomes focused increasingly on Athens and Athens becomes the place to make a philosophical reputation. There is also a change in the nature of the surviving evidence for philosophy: for the Presocratic phase we are often left only with much later sources, whereas for classical philosophy of the late-fifth and fourth centuries BCE we have at last some complete treatises and much more extensive evidence for surrounding Athenian social, political and religious concerns.

Even in its classical phase, Greek philosophy did not leave these earlier philosophers behind or refer to them only as subjects of historical interest. Much of the work of Plato and Aristotle can be read as an ongoing critical engagement with the likes of Heraclitus, Parmenides, Democritus and Leucippus. And after Aristotle, these early philosophers continued to play an important role in the development of the Hellenistic philosophies, from the Stoics' interest in Heraclitus to the Epicureans' difficult relationship with their atomist predecessors, to the sceptical schools' revisiting of the ideas of Xenophanes, Parmenides and others. The early Greek philosophers continued to influence ideas throughout antiquity and beyond.

Guide to further reading

The best next step for those interested in exploring the Presocratics further is a closer look at the primary source material. If we concentrate solely on books in English, there are two good general books that include translations of many of the sources together with interpretative commentary: G. Kirk, J. Raven and M. Schofield, *The Presocratics Philosophers*, 2nd edn (Cambridge: Cambridge University Press, 1983), which also includes the sources in the original language, and R. McKirahan, *Philosophy before Socrates* (Indianapolis, IN: Hackett, 1994), which does not. Other collections of translated sources, without extensive commentary, are available: for example, J. Barnes, *Early Greek Philosophy* (Harmondsworth: Penguin, 1987) and P. Curd, *A Presocratics Reader: Selected Fragments and Testimonia* (Indianapolis, IN: Hackett, 1996). It is always worth comparing two or more translations, since the differences will reveal the difficulties in working with these fragments and also point to important interpretative debates.

More extensive discussions of individual Presocratics can be found in the University of Toronto Press "Phoenix" series: T. Robinson's *Heraclitus* (1987), H. Lesher's *Xenophanes* (1992), D. Gallop's *Parmenides* (1984), B. Inwood's *Empedocles* (2nd edn, 2001) and P. Curd's *Anaxagoras* (forthcoming). Other important studies dedicated to individual philosophers include C. Kahn, *Anaximander and the Origins of Greek Cosmology*, 2nd edn (Indianapolis, IN: Hackett, 1994) and *The Art and Thought of Heraclitus* (Cambridge: Cambridge University Press, 1979) and C. Huffman, *Philolaus of Croton: Pythagorean and Presocratic* (Cambridge: Cambridge University Press, 1993).

For other discussions of these thinkers, readers might turn next to the essays in A. A. Long (ed.), *The Cambridge Companion to Early Greek Philosophy* (Cambridge: Cambridge University Press, 1999), which has chapters dedicated to individual philosophers and also to general philosophical themes and, at a less introductory level, two less recent collections: A. A. Mourelatos (ed.), *The Pre-Socratics* (Garden City, NY: Anchor, 1974) and R. E. Allen and D. J. Furley (eds), *Studies in Presocratic Philosophy* (London: Routledge & Kegan Paul: volume 1, 1970; volume 2, 1975).

J. Barnes, *The Presocratic Philosophers*, rev. edn (London: Routledge & Kegan Paul, 1982) is a lengthy and challenging discussion of the early Greek philosophical tradition. C. Osborne's *Presocratic Philosophy: A Very Short Introduction* (Oxford: Oxford University Press, 2004) is much briefer, but presents a lively and engaging thematic approach. Two recent books set out to present more revisionary histories of early Greek philosophy. P. Curd, *The Legacy of Parmenides* (Princeton, NJ: Princeton University Press, 1998) offers a new reading of Parmenides and, in its wake, a new interpretation of his successors. D. Graham, *Explaining the Cosmos: The Ionian Tradition of Scientific Philosophy* (Princeton, NJ: Princeton University Press, 2006) offers a new account of the Presocratic tradition, focusing in particular on cosmology.

Notes

1. Introduction: reading Presocratic philosophy

1. For concerns about the usefulness of the term "Presocratic" see A. Laks, "'Philosophes présocratiques': Remarques sur la construction d'une catégorie de l'historiographie philosophique", in *Qu'est-ce que la philosophie présocratique?*, A. Laks and C. Louguet (eds), 17–38 (Lille: Presses Universitaires du Septentrion, 2002) and A. A. Long, "The Scope of Early Greek Philosophy", in *The Cambridge Companion to Early Greek Philosophy*, A. A. Long (ed.), 1–21 (Cambridge: Cambridge University Press, 1999). Similar concerns might be voiced about the common distinction between "classical" and earlier "archaic" periods of Greek history, which would map relatively neatly on to the distinction between "Socratic and post-Socratic" or "classical" philosophy and earlier "Presocratic" philosophy. This might be taken to imply that the "archaic" period is both inferior and prefatory to the glory and achievements of the later classical period.

2. For a good and brief account of modern histories of Presocratic philosophy see C. Osborne, "Was There an Eleatic Revolution in Philosophy?", in *Rethinking Revolutions through Ancient Greece*, S. Goldhill and R. Osborne (eds), 218–45 (Cambridge: Cambridge University Press, 2006), esp. 220–24.

3. For accounts of Plato's reception of and engagement with earlier Greek philosophy see, for example, J. Palmer, *Plato's Reception of Parmenides* (Oxford: Oxford University Press, 1999), M. M. McCabe, *Plato and his Predecessors* (Cambridge: Cambridge University Press, 2000) and the essays in M. Dixsaut and A. Brancacci (eds), *Platon, Source des Présocratiques* (Paris: Vrin, 2002).

4. Plato makes the character "the Eleatic stranger" give a brief account of the history of philosophy in the *Sophist* (242c–243a).

5. See the classic studies by H. Cherniss, *Aristotle's Criticism of Presocratic Philosophy* (Baltimore, MD: Johns Hopkins Press, 1935) and W. K. C. Guthrie, "Aristotle as Historian", *Journal of Hellenic Studies* **77** (1957), 35–41. Recent work on Aristotelian or Peripatetic doxography, its aims and methods, is well exemplified by H. Baltussen, *Theophrastus Against the Presocratics and Plato: Peripatetic Doxography in the De Sensibus* (Leiden: Brill, 2000).

6. For ancient accounts of the role of Socrates see Aristot. *Met.* 987b1ff. and Diog. Laert. 1.18, 2.21 and 2.16.

7. Cf. the similar approach of J. Barnes, *The Presocratic Philosophers*, rev. edn (London: Routledge & Kegan Paul, 1982), xii–xiii.

8. DK includes these, but in a separate section: "C: Ältere Sophistik".

9. Separate volumes in this series will deal with Socrates and the Sophists.

10. "Classical Greece had two pasts, the actual past and the past it shaped for itself out of the pasts which successive generations had already shaped for themselves" (R. Osborne, *Greece in the Making, 1200–479BC* [London: Routledge, 1996], 355).

11. For discussion of Diels's methods in DK and in the 1879 work, *Doxographi graeci*, on which much of DK is based, see the essays in W. M. Calder and J. Mansfeld (eds), *Hermann Diels (1848–1922) et la science de l'antiquité* (Geneva: Fondation Hardt, 1999) and cf. Mansfeld & Runia, *Aetiana*. See also J. Mansfeld, "Sources", in *The Cambridge Companion*, Long (ed.), 22–44.

12. On this general issue see the important lessons in C. Osborne, *Rethinking Early Greek Philosophy: Hippolytus of Rome and the Presocratics* (London: Duckworth, 1987). Also see the essays in W. Burkert, L. Gemelli Marciano, E. Matelli and L. Orelli (eds), *Fragmentsammlungen Philosophischer Texte der Antike* (Göttingen: Vandenhoeck & Ruprecht, 1998) and, for a study of one writer's method of citation, H. Baltussen, "Philology or Philosophy? Simplicius and the Use of Quotations", in *Epea and Grammata: Oral and Written Communication in Ancient Greece*, I. Worthington and J. M. Foley (eds), 173–89 (Leiden: Brill, 2002).

13. For some interesting discussions of these issues see the essays in R. Rorty, J. Schneewind and Q. Skinner (eds), *Philosophy in History* (Cambridge: Cambridge University Press, 1984).

14. For further discussion of this tendency see J. Warren, "Diogenes Laërtius, Biographer of Philosophy", in *Ordering Knowledge in the Roman Empire*, J. König and T. Whitmarsh (eds), 133–49 (Cambridge: Cambridge University Press, 2007).

15. G. E. R. Lloyd, "Le pluralisme de la vie intellectuelle avant Platon", in *Qu'est-ce que la philosophie présocratique?*, Laks and Louguet (eds), 39–53 and A. Laks, "Remarks on the Differentiation of Early Greek Philosophy", in *Philosophy and the Sciences in Antiquity*, R. W. Sharples (ed.), 8–22 (Aldershot: Ashgate, 2005).

16. See the helpful remarks in Osborne, "Was There an Eleatic Revolution?", 243–5.

17. For more discussion see C. Osborne, "Was Verse the Default Form for Presocratic Philosophy?", in *Form and Content in Didactic Poetry*, C. Atherton (ed.), 23–35 (Bari: Levante, 1997); G. Most, "The Poetics of Early Greek philosophy", in *The Cambridge Companion*, Long (ed.), 332–62; and C. H. Kahn, "Writing Philosophy: Prose and Poetry from Thales to Plato", in *Written Texts and the Rise of Literate Culture in Ancient Greece*, H. Yunis (ed.), 139–61 (Cambridge: Cambridge University Press, 2003).

18. Cf. the comments by J. Barnes, *Early Greek Philosophy* (Harmondsworth: Penguin, 1987), 12, and G. E. R. Lloyd, "The Social Background of Early Greek Philosophy and Science", in his *Methods and Problems in Greek Science*, 121–40 (Cambridge: Cambridge University Press, 1991).

19. Although the same word is used for the public reading of the work and Socrates' own reading, there is no reason to assume that Socrates too had to read aloud. For a short discussion of theories of reading in the ancient world see W. A. Johnson, "Toward a Sociology of Reading in Antiquity", *American Journal of Philology* **121** (2000), 593–627.

20. The various stories about Anaxagoras' indictment by enemies of his friend, Pericles, fit with this dating whether or not they are accepted as true. See K. Dover, "The Freedom of the Intellectual in Greek Society", in his *The Greeks and their Legacy*, 135–58 (Oxford: Blackwell, 1988) and R. J. Wallace, "Private Lives and Public Enemies: Freedom of Thought in Classical Athens", in *Athenian Identity and Civic Ideology*, A. Boegehold and A. Scafuro (eds), 127–53 (Baltimore, MD: Johns Hopkins University Press, 1994). For Anaxagoras' dates see M. Schofield, *An Essay on Anaxagoras* (Cambridge: Cambridge University Press, 1980), 33–5; J. Mansfeld, "The Chronology of Anaxagoras' Athenian Period and the Date of his Trial", *Mnemosyne* **32** (1979), 39–69 and **33** (1980), 84–95; and D. Sider, *The Fragments of Anaxagoras: Introduction, Text, and Commentary*, 2nd edn (Sankt Augustin: Academia, 2005), 1–11.

21. J. Burnet, *Plato: Phaedo* (Oxford: Clarendon Press, 1911), suggests that this someone might be Archelaus. But the story of Socrates being a pupil of Archelaus is just as likely to have been concocted precisely on the basis of this passage in the *Phaedo*.

22. Barnes, *The Presocratic Philosophers*, 415, writes that Socrates got hold of a "second-hand copy". I can see no support for this in the text. On the book trade and the circulation of written texts in the classical period see W. V. Harris, *Ancient Literacy* (Cambridge, MA: Harvard University Press, 1989), 84–93. Xen. *Mem.* 1.6.14 tells us that Socrates and his friends would read the "thoughts of the wise men of long ago which they left in their books" looking to see if there was something good to be extracted from them.

23. For more on the Panathenaia see, for example, J. Neils (ed.), *Goddess and Polis: The Panathenaic Festival in Ancient Athens* (Princeton, NJ: Princeton University Press, 1992) and Osborne, *Greece in the Making*, 308–11. Also see G. Nagy, *Plato's Rhapsody and Homer's Music: The Poetics of the Panathenaic Festival in*

Classical Athens (Washington, DC: Center for Hellenic Studies, 2002), esp. 83–98. Other sources offer support for this picture. The rhapsode Cleomenes performed Empedocles' *Katharmoi* at the Olympic games. See Athenaeus 620d, Diog. Laert. 8.63 (DK 31 A12).

24. Other sources tell us that Pericles, for example, "heard" Zeno (Plut. *Per.* 4) but this may be nothing more than a later fiction linking Pericles to various unusual and subversive thinkers of the day.

25. On the symposium – a male, generally aristocratic after-dinner gathering that was often devoted to drinking, discussion and the performance of various forms of music and poetry – see, of course, the depiction in both Plato's and Xenophon's *Symposium* and also the essays in O. Murray (ed.), *Sympotica: A Symposium on the Symposium* (Oxford: Clarendon Press, 1990). The symposium seems to be the presumed context for some of Xenophanes' work: see esp. DK 21 B1.

26. On public performances see R. Thomas, *Herodotus in Context* (Cambridge: Cambridge University Press, 2000), 249–69.

27. Cf. H. Fränkel, *Early Greek Poetry and Philosophy* (Oxford: Blackwell, 1975), 257 n.9, and Schofield, *An Essay on Anaxagoras*, 28–32.

28. See V. B. Gorman, *Miletos: The Ornament of Ionia* (Ann Arbor, MI: University of Michigan Press, 2001) and A. Greaves, *Miletos: A History* (London: Routledge, 2002) for the history of Miletus.

29. The question of the levels and spread of literacy at this period is complex. For discussion see Harris, *Ancient Literacy*, 49–64, esp. 63–4 and cf. G. E. R. Lloyd, *The Revolutions of Wisdom* (Berkeley, CA: University of California Press, 1987), 70–78, and R. Thomas, *Literacy and Orality in Ancient Greece* (Cambridge: Cambridge University Press, 1992).

30. See Osborne, *Greece in the Making*, 243–91, for evidence of interrelations between states in the sixth century and cf. N. Purcell, "Mobility and the Polis", in *The Greek City from Homer to Alexander*, O. Murray and S. Price (eds), 29–58 (Oxford: Clarendon Press, 1990).

31. See Diog. Laert. 2.22; 9.5–6, 12, and cf. C. H. Kahn, *The Art and Thought of Heraclitus* (Cambridge: Cambridge University Press, 1979), 3–9. The Hippocratic *On Regimen* 1.5–24 is thought to reflect the influence of both Heraclitean ideas and prose-style. C. H. Kahn, *Anaximander and the Origins of Greek Cosmology* (Indianapolis, IN: Hackett [1960] 1994), 189 n.2, argues that this text predates Plato.

32. For a brief narrative see Osborne, *Greece in the Making*, 322–5, and Gorman, *Miletos*, 129–63. Herodotus, *The Histories* 6.18–21 has the story of the fate of Miletus.

2. Ionian beginnings

1. Later Russell qualifies this claim: "There is ample reason to feel respect for Thales, though perhaps rather as a man of science than as a philosopher in the

modern sense of the word" (*History of Western Philosophy*, 2nd edn [London: Allen & Unwin, 1961], 44).

2. On Pherecydes see M. L. West, *Early Greek Philosophy and the Orient* (Oxford: Clarendon Press, 1971), 1–75, and H. S. Schibli, *Pherecydes of Syros* (Oxford: Clarendon Press, 1990). On Hesiod's cosmos see J. Strauss-Clay, *Hesiod's Cosmos* (Cambridge: Cambridge University Press, 2003). For a recent discussion of Orphism and possible links to early Greek philosophy see A. Bernabé, "Orphisme et Présocratiques: bilan et perspectives d'un dialogue complexe", in *Qu'est-ce que la philosophie présocratique?*, Laks & Louget (eds), 205–47.

3. For a text, translation, and commentary on the papyrus see G. Betegh, *The Derveni Papyrus: Cosmology, Theology and Interpretation* (Cambridge: Cambridge University Press, 2004).

4. See Kahn, *Anaximander and the Origins*; West, *Early Greek Philosophy*; and G. E. R. Lloyd, "The Debt of Greek Philosophy and Science to the Ancient Near East", in his *Methods and Problems in Greek Science*, 278–98 (Cambridge: Cambridge University Press, 1991). There was even a healthy ancient disagreement over whether Greek philosophy did indeed owe anything to the "barbarians", which eventually became concerned with the question of whether Greek philosophy owed anything to earlier Hebrew thought. See, for example, Diog. Laert. 1.3 and cf. D. Ridings, *The Attic Moses: The Dependency Theme in some Early Christian Writers* (Göteborg: Acta Universitatis Gothoburgensis, 1995) and G. R. Boys-Stones, *Post-Hellenistic Philosophy: A Study of its Development from the Stoics to Origen* (Oxford: Oxford University Press, 2001), 176–202.

5. The relationship between "mythical" and "philosophical" accounts is contested and complex. For an introduction to the debate see G. Vlastos, "Theology and Philosophy in Early Greek Thought", *Philosophical Quarterly* 2 (1952), 97–123; W. Jordan, *Ancient Concepts of Philosophy* (London: Routledge, 1990), 8–18; the essays in R. Buxton (ed.), *From Myth to Reason?* (Oxford: Oxford University Press, 1999); K. Algra, "The Beginnings of Cosmology", in *The Cambridge Companion*, Long (ed.), 45–65, esp. 45–9; and K. Morgan, *Myth and Philosophy from the Presocratics to Plato* (Cambridge: Cambridge University Press, 2000), esp. 15–45.

6. For discussion see M. C. Stokes, *One and Many in Presocratic Philosophy* (Washington, DC: Center for Hellenic Studies, 1971), 31–6.

7. When a Milesian says that all things are "from" ("*ek*"), say, water, is the claim that they *originate* in water or that they are *constituted* by water? For some discussion of the problem see Stokes, *One and Many*, 37–8, 56–62; Barnes, *The Presocratic Philosophers*, 38–40; and D. W. Graham, "Heraclitus' Criticism of Ionian Philosophy", *Oxford Studies in Ancient Philosophy* 15 (1997), 1–50, esp. 13–17. D. W. Graham, *Explaining the Cosmos: The Ionian Tradition of Scientific Philosophy* (Princeton, NJ: Princeton University Press, 2006) offers an extended criticism of the view that the Ionians were material monists and instead proposes that they generally held a "generating substance theory": all things are generated "*ek*" some originating stuff, whether water or air or the *apeiron*.

8. On these see also the reconstructions in Barnes, *The Presocratic Philosophers*, 5–13.

9. Arist. *De caelo* 294a28ff.; Simpl. *De caelo* 522, 14 (DK 11 A14). G. S. Kirk, J. Raven and M. Schofield, *The Presocratic Philosophers*, 2nd edn (Cambridge: Cambridge University Press, 1983), 90, offer some thoughts in defence of Thales' view against Aristotle's attack.

10. Diog. Laert. 1.24 (DK 11 A1) also refers to the ability of amber to induce similar motions.

11. Cf. Aristot. *Gen. an.* 762a21ff.

12. For the eclipse see: Herodotus 1.74 (DK 11 A5); Diog. Laert. 1.23 (DK 11 A1). For the olive presses see: Aristot. *Pol.* 1259a6–17 (DK 11 A10); Diog. Laert. 1.26 (DK 11 A1). Also see Kahn, *Anaximander and the Origins*, 76 n.2.

13. On Thales and astronomy see S. White, "Thales and the Stars", in *Presocratic Philosophy: Essays in Honour of Alexander Mourelatos*, V. Caston and D. W. Graham (eds), 3–18 (Aldershot: Ashgate, 2002).

14. Thales is also said to have been able to calculate the size of the pyramids by noting the length of their shadow at the time of day when the length of a person's shadow is equal to his height (Diog. Laert. 1.27 [DK 11 A1]).

15. There were various different lists of the wise men of early Greece (see Diog. Laert. 1.13), but the inclusion of Thales is uncontroversial.

16. For a full discussion of the fragment and the rest of Anaximander's thought see Kahn, *Anaximander and the Origins*, and cf. G. Vlastos, "Equality and Justice in early Greek Cosmologies", *Classical Philology* **41** (1947), 156–78, esp. 167–73; G. Freudenthal, "The Theory of the Opposites and an Ordered Universe: Physics and Metaphysics in Anaximander", *Phronesis* **31** (1986), 197–228.

17. See DK 12 A9 for Simplicius' surrounding discussion of the "fragment". For an extensive discussion of elements and opposites in Anaximander see Kahn, *Anaximander and the Origins*, 119–65 and cf. J. Engman, "Cosmic Justice in Anaximander", *Phronesis* **36** (1991), 1–25, and M. Schofield, "The Ionians", in *Routledge History of Philosophy 1: From the Beginnings to Plato*, C. C. W. Taylor (ed.), 47–87 (London: Routledge, 1997), 63.

18. See, for example, Aristot. *Phys.* 187a20ff. (DK 12 A9) and Ps. Plut. *Strom.* 2 (DK 12 A10).

19. Cf. the account of elemental changes in Aristot. *Meteor.* 353b6ff. and cf. DK 12 A27.

20. See Schofield, "The Ionians", 60–63, which argues that only if each cosmos does not come to an end is there a need for the *apeiron* to be infinitely inexhaustible. Kahn, *Anaximander and the Origins*, 46–53, is reluctant to attribute multiple worlds to Anaximander, suggesting that the "many heavens" is a reference to the various celestial rings that compose the visible heaven. Cf. D. J. Furley, *The Greek Cosmologists, Volume 1* (Cambridge: Cambridge University Press, 1987), 29–30; R. D. McKirahan, "Anaximander's Infinite Worlds", in *Before Plato: Essays in Ancient Greek Philosophy VI*, A. Preus (ed.), 49–65 (Albany, NY: SUNY Press, 2001).

21. Cf. the argument for monism by Diogenes of Apollonia, p. 178.

22. For Anaximander's explanation of cosmogony see Ps. Plut. *Strom.* 2 (DK 12 A10).
23. This also provided him with a mechanism for explaining eclipses (Hippol. *Ref.* 1.6.4 [DK 12 A11]).
24. See Hippol. *Ref.* 1.6.6–7 and Aet. 4.3.23, 5.19.4 (DK 12 A11, 29, 30).
25. For its application by Parmenides see p. 91; for its use by the atomists see pp. 161ff. For an alternative account of Anaximander's argument making it an assertion that the earth is equally supported on all sides see Furley, *The Greek Cosmologists*, 24–6 and "The Dynamics of the Earth: Anaximander, Plato, and the Centrifocal Theory", in his *Cosmic Problems*, 14–26 (Cambridge: Cambridge University Press, 1989), where he writes: "It is not that the earth has no reason to move, but that although there is reason for it to fall, it is prevented from doing so by the equal support of the air all around" (*ibid.*: 22).
26. For further discussion see S. Makin, *Indifference Arguments* (Oxford: Blackwell, 1993), 101–5; Schofield, "The Ionians", 51–5; and R. J. Hankinson, *Cause and Explanation in Ancient Greek Thought* (Oxford: Oxford University Press, 1998), 14–16.
27. For a defence of Anaximenes see Barnes, *The Presocratic Philosophers*, 38–56.
28. Anaximenes' conception of *aēr* is certainly echoed in Diogenes of Apollonia's much later but similar view. See Aet. 1.3.26 (DK 64 A7), Simpl. *In Phys.* 25,1–9 (DK 64 A5) and cf. A. Laks, *Diogène d'Apollonie, la dernière cosmologie présocratique* (Lille: Presses Universitaires de Lille, 1983), 83–94, and this volume pp. 177–9.
29. Again, cf. Diogenes of Apollonia (DK 64 B5).
30. For an excellent and detailed discussion of the evidence and the problems it produces see W. Burkert, *Lore and Science in Ancient Pythagoreanism* (Cambridge, MA: Harvard University Press, 1972). See also C. A. Huffman, *Philolaus of Croton: Pythagorean and Presocratic* (Cambridge: Cambridge University Press, 1993), 17–26 and "The Pythagorean Tradition", in *The Cambridge Companion*, Long (ed.), 66–87, esp. 66–9. There is a brief account of early Pythagoreanism in C. H. Kahn, *Pythagoras and the Pythagoreans: A Brief History* (Indianapolis, IN: Hackett, 2001).
31. Plato's *Phaedo* also displays some clear Pythagorean influences. See P. Kingsley, *Ancient Philosophy, Mystery and Magic: Empedocles and Pythagorean Tradition* (Oxford: Oxford University Press, 1995), 88–95, and D. N. Sedley, "The Dramatis Personae of Plato's *Phaedo*", in *Philosophical Dialogues*, T. J. Smiley (ed.), 3–26 (Oxford: Clarendon Press, 1995).
32. There are some speculations in Barnes, *The Presocratic Philosophers*, 103–120. Cf. Burkert, *Lore and Science*, 120–65, who links *metempsychosis* with the various tales that attribute magical or divine powers to Pythagoras as a kind of shaman. Cf. Empedocles' presentation of himself as a *daimōn* (this volume pp. 146ff.) and cf. Kingsley, *Ancient Philosophy*, 292–6, and Huffman, "The Pythagorean Tradition", 75–8.
33. For some useful thoughts on what it means to be called and to call oneself a "Pythagorean" see Huffman, *Philolaus of Croton*, 9–12.

3. Xenophanes

1. For an edition of the fragments and commentary see J. Lesher, *Xenophanes of Colophon: Fragments* (Toronto: University of Toronto Press, 1992). There are useful discussions of aspects of Xenophanes' thought in Fränkel, *Early Greek Poetry*, 325–37; Barnes, *The Presocratic Philosophers*, 82–99, 137–43; S. Broadie, "Rational Theology", in *The Cambridge Companion*, Long (ed.), 205–24, esp. 209–12; J. Lesher, "Early Interest in Knowledge", in *The Cambridge Companion*, Long (ed.), 225–49, esp. 228–31; and E. Mogyoródi, "Xenophanes as a Philosopher: Theology and Theodicy", in *Qu'est-ce que la philosophie présocratique?*, Laks & Louguet (eds), 253–86. Also see K. Popper, "The Unknown Xenophanes: An Attempt to Establish his Greatness", in his *The World of Parmenides: Essays on the Presocratic Enlightenment* (London: Routledge, 1998).

2. Note that this fragment is a verse reconstructed by Diels from Clement of Alexandria's prose paraphrase. Clement describes this as an observation about how these people depict or paint their gods. (Xenophanes probably did not speak Egyptian but he might have known about Egyptian art.)

3. R. Geuss, "On the Usefulness and Uselessness of Religious Illusions", in his *Outside Ethics*, 131–52 (Princeton, NJ: Princeton University Press, 2005), 131–3, offers an alternative construction of Xenophanes' argument in which the fact that animals would not conceive of the gods anthropomorphically is designed to cast doubt on the cross-cultural human consensus of anthropomorphism.

4. See J. Annas and J. Barnes, *The Modes of Scepticism* (Cambridge: Cambridge University Press, 1985), esp. 161–2, and cf. the "Modes of Agrippa" explored in J. Barnes, *The Toils of Scepticism* (Cambridge: Cambridge University Press, 1990).

5. Cf. DK 21 B12 for a similar thought and cf. DK 21 B1.19ff. for Xenophanes' recommendations for the sorts of stories it is proper and useful to tell.

6. Such interpretations are linked to claims about Xenophanes' influence over Parmenides, whose "[what] is" is, in some sense, like a sphere. See J. Palmer, "Xenophanes' Ouranian God in the Fourth Century", *Oxford Studies in Ancient Philosophy* **16** (1998), 1–34.

7. Barnes, *The Presocratic Philosophers*, 89–92, finds in the first line of DK 21 B23 a (very) compressed argument for monotheism: "There is one god since (by definition) a god is greater than anything else, whether god or man". He does not comment here on DK 21 B18 or B36, which both seem to refer to a plurality of gods.

8. Barnes, *The Presocratic Philosophers*, 85, claims that "'it is not fitting' is Xenophanes' archaic and poetical notion of 'it is not logically possible'". I see no reason to remove the ethical and aesthetic connotations of the term.

9. We might note the story told twice by Aristotle and three times by Plutarch (DK 21 A12, 13) that Xenophanes insisted that different attitudes should be adopted towards dead mortals and gods. The former should be mourned but the latter should be honoured. The problem is compounded by the regular

practice in Greek religion of honouring a mortal who was later made into a god (as was Leucothea, about whose cult the Eleans question Xenophanes in Aristot. *Rhet.* 1400b5ff. [DK 21 A13]).

10. For an introduction to the various interpretations of Xenophanes' epistemology see Lesher, *Xenophanes of Colophon*, 159–69.

11. This last phrase might also be translated as "belief covers everyone".

12. For a brief account of this distinction in modern epistemology see J. Dancy, *Introduction to Contemporary Epistemology* (Oxford: Blackwell, 1985), 46–8.

13. D. Scott, *Plato's Meno* (Cambridge: Cambridge University Press, 2006), 83–4, dubs this "the problem of discovery".

14. The idea that Xenophanes is emphasizing the lack of *empirical* confirmation is strengthened if the verb translated here as "know" retains a close link to its etymological roots in the verb "to see". See H. Fränkel, "Xenophanes' Empiricism and his Critique of Knowledge (B34)", in *The Presocratics*, A. Mourelatos (ed.), 118–31 (Princeton, NJ: Princeton University Press, 1974) and *Early Greek Poetry*, 335–6; Barnes, *The Presocratic Philosophers*, 138; and Lesher, *Xenophanes of Colophon*, 162–3. Also see Popper, "The Unknown Xenophanes".

15. Note also: "Mortals *believe* (*dokeousi*) that gods are born and have clothing, voice, and body like theirs" (DK 21 B14; emphasis added). Cf. Xenophanes DK 21 B34 with Alcmaeon DK 24 B1, which contrasts human conjecture with divine understanding.

16. Morgan, *Myth and Philosophy*, 51, contrasts this with the Muses' promise at Hesiod *Theog.* 27 to tell many falsehoods that are "likenesses of the truth".

17. "In caves too water drips down" (DK 21 B37), might be another part of an extended discussion of the interaction of earth and water to form the current and changing landscape.

18. For Timon's use of Xenophanes see DK 21 A35 and Timon frr. 59 and 60. Cf. A. A. Long, "Timon of Phlius: Pyrrhonist and Satirist", *Proceedings of the Cambridge Philological Society* **24** (1978), 68–91.

19. See SE *PH* 1.20 and 1.213, and cf. Diog. Laert. 9.105 for Timon's pronouncement.

4. The oracles of Heraclitus

1. See M. Adoménas, "The Fluctuating Fortunes of Heraclitus in Plato", in, *Qu'est-ce que la philosophie présocratique?*, Laks & Louguet (eds), 419–47, and, for a Heraclitean reading of the *Symposium*, R. B. B. Wardy, "The Unity of Opposites in Plato's *Symposium*", *Oxford Studies in Ancient Philosophy* **23** (2002), 1–61. The relative chronology of Parmenides and Heraclitus is unclear. See D. W. Graham, "Heraclitus and Parmenides", in *Presocratic Philosophy*, Caston & Graham (eds), 27–44; A. Nehamas, "Parmenidean Being/Heraclitean Fire", in *Presocratic Philosophy*, 45–64; and Osborne, "Was There an Eleatic Revolution?", 230–37.

2. There is an excellent discussion of Heraclitus' method of composition and of strategies for reading Heraclitus in Kahn, *The Art and Thought of Heraclitus*, 87–95. For more discussion of the form of Heraclitus' work and the related question of whether it can be said to contain any "arguments", see: Barnes, *The Presocratic Philosophers*, 63–4, and "Aphorism and Argument", in *Language and Thought in Early Greek Philosophy*, K. Robb (ed.), 91–109 (La Salle, IL: Hegeler Institute, 1983); U. Hölscher, "Paradox, Simile, and Gnomic Utterance in Heraclitus", in *The Pre-Socratics*, Mourelatos (ed.), 219–38; M. M. Mackenzie, "Heraclitus and the Art of Paradox", *Oxford Studies in Ancient Philosophy* 6 (1988), 1–39; and H. Granger, "Argumentation and Heraclitus' Book", *Oxford Studies in Ancient Philosophy* 26 (2004), 1–17.

3. For the story see Herodotus, *The Histories* 1.53.

4. For other Delphic references cf. the sayings concerning Apollo's major attributes: the bow (DK 22 B48) and the lyre (B51), and see this volume, p. 70, on *harmoniē*.

5. Heraclitus earned the nickname "the obscure".

6. "Many do not think about things just as they come upon them, nor do they recognise what they have learned. But they believe they do" (DK 22 B17). Cf. M. Schofield, "Heraclitus' Theory of Soul and its Antecedents", in *Psychology*, S. Everson (ed.), 13–34 (Cambridge: Cambridge University Press, 1991), 32.

7. Cf. R. Dilcher, *Studies in Heraclitus* (Hildesheim: Olms, 1995), 11–26, for a similar exploration.

8. Noted by Aristotle at *Rhet.* 1407b13 (DK 22 A4); cf. Dilcher, *Studies in Heraclitus*, 27–52.

9. See also, and note the pun: "Those who speak with understanding (*xun noōi*) must hold on to what is common (*xunōi*) to all things ..." (DK 22 B114).

10. See esp. DK 22 B40, 42, 56, 81, 108, 129 for Heraclitean criticism of his predecessors and commonly accepted authorities.

11. On sleeping and waking as a repeated motif see also B21, B88 and especially B26. Also see this volume, p. 61.

12. See the reference to the Furies as ministers of Justice making sure that the sun sticks to its course: DK 22 B94. But note also the paradoxical equation in B80 of conflict and justice, discussed in this volume, p. 70.

13. For more discussion see Kahn, *The Art and Thought of Heraclitus*, 145–59.

14. Also note: "The wise, one, alone, both wishes and does not wish to be called by the name of Zeus" (DK 22 B32).

15. See Graham, "Heraclitus' Criticism of Ionian Philosophy", and *Explaining the Cosmos*, 113–47, for an interpretation of Heraclitus' cosmology as a criticism of his predecessors, particularly their concern to find a single "Generating Substance". Fire, on this view, is chosen because it is the most changeable, least substantial, kind of substance. Cf. Vlastos, *Studies in Greek Philosophy*, 353–65; David Wiggins, "Heraclites' Conceptions of Flux, Fire and Material Persistence", in *Language and Logos: Studies in Ancient Philosophy Presented*

to G. E. L. Owen, M. Schofield and M. C. Nussbaum (eds), 1–32 (Cambridge: Cambridge University Press, 1982).

16. See Mackenzie, "Heraclitus and the Art of Paradox", for a discussion of Heraclitus' deliberate use of paradox.

17. For possible religious connotations of the "purity" involved here and for religious themes throughout the fragments see M. Adoménas, "Heraclitus on Religion", *Phronesis* **44** (1999), 87–113.

18. For example, "The path of the carding-wheel is straight and crooked" (DK 22 B59).

19. Kahn, *The Art and Thought of Heraclitus*, prints this together with DK 22 B110 as his fragment LXVII.

20. "They do not understand how in disagreeing it is in concord (*homologeei*) with itself: back-turning arrangement (*harmoniē*), as of a bow and lyre" (DK 22 B51).

21. The text here is debatable. See also DK 22 B53.

22. For a brief discussion of the evidence for Cratylus' philosophy see D. N. Sedley, *Plato's Cratylus* (Cambridge: Cambridge University Press, 2003), 16–21.

23. For a similar *reductio* of extreme Heracliteanism by Plato in the *Theaetetus* and elsewhere cf. McCabe, *Plato and his Predecessors*, 93–138.

24. For discussion see: Vlastos, *Studies in Greek Philosophy*, 337–43; G. S. Kirk, *Heraclitus: The Cosmic Fragments*, corrected edn (Cambridge: Cambridge University Press, 1962), 366–84; Kahn, *The Art and Thought of Heraclitus*, 166–9; Mackenzie, "Heraclitus and the Art of Paradox", 1–4; Graham, "Heraclitus' Criticism of Ionian Philosophy", 5 n.20; and L. Tarán, "Heraclitus: The River-Fragments and their Implications", *Elenchos* **20** (1999), 9–52.

25. Of the three fragments, B49a is the most likely to be inauthentic.

26. Cf. the Heraclitean-sounding claims in Plato *Symp.* 207d–8b.

27. For further discussion see Kahn, *The Art and Thought of Heraclitus*, 216–27; Schofield, "Heraclitus' Theory of Soul", 27–32; and Broadie, "Rational Theology", 212–14.

28. For cosmic justice see DK 59 B94: the Furies, ministers of Justice, will prevent the sun from transgressing his course. (B94 is cited in column 4 of the Derveni papyrus immediately after B3, perhaps indicating that they were originally part of the same Heraclitean statement. The Derveni author cites Heraclitus in support of his own cosmological and eschatological interests, but may have been encouraged by a similar link in Heraclitus himself. See Betegh, *The Derveni Papyrus*, 325–48.) For other Heraclitean invocations of law and justice cf. B23, B28b, B33 and B44.

5. Parmenides

1. See, for example, G. E. L. Owen, "Eleatic Questions", *Classical Quarterly* **10** (1960), 84–102. For a discussion of scholarship on Parmenides in the 1960s

and 1970s see A. Mourelatos, "Some Alternatives in Interpreting Parmenides", *Monist* **62** (1979), 3–14.

2. A. Coxon, *The Fragments of Parmenides*, *Phronesis* supp. vol. 3 (1986) is a large-scale edition of the poem with commentary. D. Gallop, *Parmenides: Fragments* (Toronto: University of Toronto Press, 1984) is a useful, less extensive, edition.

3. The text here is debated. Some translations read "carry me over all cities".

4. For discussions of Parmenides' proem see A. Mourelatos, *The Route of Parmenides* (New Haven, CT: Yale University Press, 1970); H. Fränkel, "Studies in Parmenides", in *Studies in Presocratic Philosophy* 2, Allen & Furley (eds), 1–47, esp. 1–6; D. J. Furley, "Notes on Parmenides", in his *Cosmic Problems*, 27–37, esp. 27–30; Morgan, *Myth and Philosophy*, 67–81; and C. H. Kahn, "Parmenides and Plato", in *Presocratic Philosophy*, Caston & Graham (eds), 81–93, esp. 90–92. The first thirty lines of the poem survive in a quotation by Sextus Empiricus (*M* 7.111). Sextus goes on to provide his own interpretation of the proem as an allegory in which the mares are the non-rational impulses of the soul, the divine escort the soul's reason.

5. The obscure fragment B3 is often translated as "For the same thing is there to think of and to be", as if emphasizing the claim that it is possible to think only of "[what] is". For an alternative reading, translating B3 as "For thinking and being are the same" see A. A. Long, "Parmenides on Thinking Being", *Proceedings of the Boston Area Colloquium in Ancient Philosophy* **12** (1996), 125–51, who argues that the resulting picture of an identification of thinking/mind and being is not inconsistent either with Parmenides' radical monism nor with contemporary Greek thought, which was comfortable with attributing such psychological capacities to reality. Cf. "[what] is" feels no pain (Melissus DK 30 B7.4).

6. For this kind of account see also M. Furth, "Elements of Eleatic Ontology", in *The Presocratics*, Mourelatos (ed.), 241–70.

7. For a brief introduction to the use of "to be" in Greek philosophy see L. Brown, "The Verb 'To Be' in Greek Philosophy: Some Remarks", in *Language*, S. Everson (ed.), 212–36 (Cambridge: Cambridge University Press, 1994). C. H. Kahn, "Parmenides and Being", in *Frühgriechisches Denken*, Rechenauer (ed.), 217–26, gives a brief account of his preferred interpretation of "to be" in Parmenides. Cf. D. N. Sedley, "Parmenides and Melissus", in *The Cambridge Companion*, Long (ed.), 113–33, esp. 115–6.

8. Cf. the Anaxagorean question: "For how could hair come to be from not hair and flesh from not flesh?" (DK 59 B10), and this volume, p. 120.

9. The story of Plato's thinking about "what is not" is long and complicated, comprising his acceptance in the *Republic* that it is possible to know only "what is" (here being the Forms, perfect and everlasting simple intelligible entities, each being a paradigm of some quality or other such as "justice" or "beauty"), through his grappling with the paradox that if it is impossible to think or say "what is not" it seems impossible to think or say something false in the *Theaetetus* and *Euthydemus*, to his sophisticated and challenging account

of Being and Not-being in the *Sophist*. For some helpful discussions of this material see J. McDowell, "Falsehood and not being in Plato's *Sophist*", in *Language and Logos*, M. Schofield and M. Nussbaum (eds), 115–34 (Cambridge: Cambridge University Press, 1983); G. E. L. Owen, "Plato on not Being", in his *Logic, Science and Dialectic*, 104–37; N. C. Denyer, *Language, Thought, and Falsehood in Greek Philosophy* (London: Routledge & Kegan Paul, 1991); M. Frede, "Plato's Sophist on False Statements", in *The Cambridge Companion to Plato*, R. Kraut (ed.), 397–424 (Cambridge: Cambridge University Press, 1992); Palmer, *Plato's Reception of Parmenides*; and Kahn, "Parmenides and Plato".

10. See, for example, P. Curd, *The Legacy of Parmenides* (Princeton, NJ: Princeton University Press, 1998), 64–97, which also provides a useful guide to other interpretations.

11. See Long, "Parmenides on Thinking Being", and this volume p. 196, n.5.

12. See J. Malcolm, "On Avoiding the Void", *Oxford Studies in Ancient Philosophy* **9** (1991), 75–94, esp. 75 n.2, for references to those who see no mention of a denial of the void in these lines. Malcolm himself argues that Parmenides does deny motion, but not via a denial of the void. For more ramifications of different interpretations of this point see this volume, pp. 111–12.

13. For a good account of this see Mourelatos, *The Route of Parmenides*, and "'The Deceptive Words of Parmenides' '*Doxa*'", in *The Presocratics*, Mourelatos (ed.), 312–49.

6. Reactions to Parmenides

1. For stimulating discussions of Zenonian paradoxes see G. E. L. Owen, "Zeno and the Mathematicians", *Proceedings of the Aristotelian Society* **58** (1957–58), 199–222; G. Vlastos, "Zeno's Race-Course", *Journal of the History of Philosophy* **4** (1966), 95–108; D. J. Furley, *Two Studies in the Greek Atomists* (Princeton, NJ: Princeton University Press, 1967), 63–78; R. R. K. Sorabji, *Time, Creation and the Continuum* (London: Duckworth, 1983), 321–35; Makin, *Indifference Arguments*, 18–28; R. M. Sainsbury, *Paradoxes*, 2nd edn (Cambridge: Cambridge University Press, 1995); J. Faris, *The Paradoxes of Zeno* (Aldershot: Ashgate, 1996); R. D. McKirahan, "Zeno", in *The Cambridge Companion*, Long (ed.), 134–58; P. S. Hasper, "Zeno Unlimited", *Oxford Studies in Ancient Philosophy* **30** (2006), 49–85; and the essays in W. C. Salmon (ed.) *Zeno's Paradoxes* (Indianapolis, IN: Hackett, 1970).

2. There is also the curious paradox of the moving rows. See Arist. *Phys.* 239b33–240a18 (DK 29 A28). For the interesting claim that with this paradox Zeno aimed to block the postulation of atomic units see Owen, "Zeno and the Mathematicians", 151. Cf. Furley, *Two Studies in the Greek Atomists*, 72–7.

3. For various kinds of atomism as a response to Zeno see Furley, *Two Studies in the Greek Atomists*, study 1; Sorabji, *Time, Creation and the Continuum*, 336–83; and this volume on Democritus and Leucippus, pp. 159–60.

4. On Zeno's arrow paradox see G. Vlastos, "A Note on Zeno's Arrow", *Phronesis* **11** (1966), 3–18; J. Lear, "A Note on Zeno's Arrow", *Phronesis* **26** (1981), 91–104; and R. Le Poidevin, "Zeno's Arrow and the Significance of the Present", in *Time, Reality and Experience*, C. Callender (ed.), 57–72 (Cambridge: Cambridge University Press, 2002).

5. But note the judgement of Simplicius *De caelo* 558.17ff., who, having just cited Parmenides DK 28 B8.50–52 and B19, introduces Melissus DK30 B8 as follows: "But Melissus, as he is writing in prose, throughout his work and in these lines most of all makes his own thinking about these matters [the evidence of the senses] clearer". Cf. J. Palmer, "Melissus and Parmenides", *Oxford Studies in Ancient Philosophy* **26** (2004), 19–54, and, on Melissus B8, see S. Makin, "Melissus and his Opponents: The Argument of DK 30 B8", *Phronesis* **50** (2005), 263–88.

6. On the dating of this treatise to the late fifth century BCE see Kahn, *Anaximander and the Origins*, 126. Cf. Palmer, "Melissus and Parmenides", 43–4.

7. For example, Kirk *et al.*, *The Presocratic Philosophers*, 391–2, 400, suggest that Melissus B8 shows signs of a knowledge of Empedocles and Anaxagoras.

8. On dating these philosophers see W. K. C. Guthrie, *A History of Greek Philosophy Volume 2: The Presocratic Tradition from Parmenides to Democritus* (Cambridge: Cambridge University Press, 1965), 115–18; Mansfeld, "The Chronology of Anaxagoras' Athenian Period"; D. O'Brien, "The Relation of Anaxagoras and Empedocles", *Journal of Hellenic Studies* **88** (1968), 93–114; Curd, *The Legacy of Parmenides*, 17–18; Sider, *The Fragments of Anaxagoras*, 1–11.

9. See the useful remarks in Barnes, *The Presocratic Philosophers*, 305–8 (cf. his own practice at 397–402).

10. Generally, on these cosmologists' reaction to Parmenides see *ibid.*, 427–47; D. J. Furley, "Anaxagoras in Response to Parmenides", in his *Cosmic Problems*, 47–65; M. Furth, "A Philosophical Hero? Anaxagoras and the Eleatics", *Oxford Studies in Ancient Philosophy* **9** (1991), 95–130; Curd, *The Legacy of Parmenides*, 128–30; D. W. Graham, "Empedocles and Anaxagoras: Responses to Parmenides", in *The Cambridge Companion*, Long (ed.), 159–80; B. Inwood, *The Poem of Empedocles*, 2nd edn (Toronto: University of Toronto Press, 2001), 24–33. Some recent commentators (Graham, "Empedocles and Anaxagoras" and *Explaining the Cosmos*, esp. 186–95; Osborne, "Was There an Eleatic Revolution?") have raised important doubts about the "traditional" account of Anaxagoras, Empedocles and the rest reinvigorating cosmology by reacting to an Eleatic challenge. In part, the discussion will turn on what we take to be Parmenides' attitude to his own "Way of Opinion", but it is also worth emphasizing once again Melissus' role in making clear the Eleatic challenge to cosmology.

11. One notable exception is Xeniades of Corinth. We know little about him except that he declared that "everything is false", "everything that comes to be comes to be from what is not" and "everything that passes away passes away into what is

not". See Sextus Empiricus *M* 7.53 (DK 81) and cf. J. Brunschwig, "Democritus and Xeniades", in *Presocratic Philosophy*, Caston & Graham (eds), 159–67.

12. See, for example, Philolaus DK 44 B6, with the commentary in Huffman, *Philolaus of Croton*, and cf. pp. 176–7. Generally, on these cosmologists' reaction to Parmenides see Barnes, *The Presocratic Philosophers*, 427–47; Furley, "Anaxagoras in Response to Parmenides"; Furth, "A Philosophical Hero?"; Curd, *The Legacy of Parmenides*, 128–30; Graham, "Empedocles and Anaxagoras"; and Inwood, *The Poem of Empedocles*, 24–33.

13. This gap can be tackled in a number of ways, including the assertion of some kind of "emergence" of perceptible properties from fundamental properties; see, for example, A. Mourelatos, "Quality, Structure and Emergence in Later Pre-Socratic Philosophy", *Proceedings of the Boston Area Colloquium in Ancient Philosophy* 2 (1987), 127–94. Alternatively, the gap can be removed by denying the reality of the perceptible properties. See the discussion of different interpretations of Democritus' ontology in this volume, pp. 167ff.

7. Anaxagoras

1. For a text of the fragments see Sider, *The Fragments of Anaxagoras*. Schofield, *An Essay on Anaxagoras*, is the most recent monograph in English. For a discussion of an Anaxagorean influence on the cosmology of the Derveni papyrus see Betegh, *The Derveni Papyrus*, 278–305.

2. For discussion see Sider, *The Fragments of Anaxagoras*, 121–2, and Schofield, *An Essay on Anaxagoras*, 133–43.

3. For a discussion of whether B4a and 4b ought to be considered two halves of a continuous stretch of text see Sider, *The Fragments of Anaxagoras*, 90.

4. For a good discussion of the various interpretations of Anaxagorean matter see Curd, *The Legacy of Parmenides*, 131–54 and cf. P. Curd, "The Metaphysics of Physics: Mixture and Separation in Empedocles and Anaxagoras", in *Presocratic Philosophy*, Caston & Graham (eds), 139–58, esp. 140, 153–5.

5. For discussion see Barnes, *The Presocratic Philosophers*, 323–6, and Graham, "The Postulates of Anaxagoras", 101–12.

6. "all things would be in everything"; "all things share a portion of everything" (DK 59 B6); "other things share a portion of everything, but mind", "in everything there is a portion of everything, as I said earlier" (B12).

7. Note that this interpretation accepts that in the claim "In everything there is a portion of everything", Anaxagoras uses "everything" twice to refer to two different classes. In every object there is a portion of every ingredient. Some commentators object to this view and insist that all stuffs must contain portions of all other stuffs.

8. Here a regress threatens. The "ingredient" lead, which is "in" the piece of lead I am holding, is itself only lead because lead predominates in it, and so on. If this is the correct conception of Anaxagorean matter, I see no reason to think

that the regress is vicious. Anaxagoras embraces the idea of limitless division (B3) and the thesis of universal mixture asserts that there is nothing "pure" in the cosmos (except, perhaps, *nous*). The regress will seem vicious only if we still are wedded to the idea that we must at some level of division arrive at pure substances. Cf. Barnes, *The Presocratic Philosophers*, 327–39 and the account in Graham, "The Postulates of Anaxagoras", esp. 104–5 (and also see F. Cornford, "Anaxagoras' Theory of Matter", in *Studies in Presocratic Philosophy* 2, Allen & Furley (eds), 275–322, esp. 309–10; G. Vlastos, "The Physical Theory of Anaxagoras", *Philosophical Review* **59** (1950), 31–57, esp. 49–50; C. Strang, "The Physical Theory of Anaxagoras", in *Studies in Presocratic Philosophy* 2, 361–80, esp. 361–2; and Schofield, *An Essay on Anaxagoras*, 74–5). D. J. Furley, "Anaxagoras, Plato and Naming of Parts", in *Presocratic Philosophy*, Caston & Graham (eds), 119–26, suggests that such difficulties might have influenced Plato's causal account in the *Phaedo*.

9. "The phenomena: glimpse of what is not evident" (B21a [at SE *M* 7.140]). Some have questioned the authenticity of this fragment, arguing that it should instead be ascribed to Democritus (who is said to have approved of it) or perhaps the Diotimus also mentioned by Sextus. See G. E. R. Lloyd, *Polarity and Analogy* (Cambridge: Cambridge University Press, 1966), 338–41, and Sider, *The Fragments of Anaxagoras*, 165–6. Cf. also Democritus DK 68 B125.

10. Cf. Barnes, *The Presocratic Philosophers*, 538–40. Cf. the account in Mourelatos, "Quality, Structure and Emergence", 143–52.

11. Theophrastus (*De sensibus* 29–30) reports that Anaxagoras claims that the power of sense perception varies according to the size of an animal. Unfortunately, Anaxagoras' account apparently combines the claim that larger sense organs are able to detect all their proper objects to a greater degree and the claim that larger ears, for example, are better at detecting loud sounds and smaller ears are better at detecting delicate sounds. Theophrastus rightly objects (at 34–5).

12. The difficulty of deciding between the two understandings of "imperceptible" recurs throughout Anaxagoras' work. In B21a it is not clear whether the things that are "not evident" are merely unobservable "by us" or are things that are absolutely imperceptible. Similarly, when in B1 Anaxagoras describes all the various elements in the original homogeneous cosmic mixture as not evident because of their "smallness", we might wonder whether this is imagining some hypothetical observer who would have been unable to distinguish any elements or whether it is a claim that none of these elements were at all manifest in the intrinsic nature of the whole.

13. See D. N. Sedley, *Creationism and its Critics in Antiquity* (Berkeley, CA: University of California Press, forthcoming). The curious reference in the latter part of DK 59 B4a to other worlds elsewhere but just like ours has been taken by some as evidence that there is some model or design to which our cosmos conforms and that *nous* has devised for some good (perhaps in order to germinate the seeds present in the mixture). For a discussion of the various alternative views

see C. Louguet, "Note sur le fragment B4a d'Anaxagore: pourquoi les autres mondes doivent-ils être semblables au nôtre?", in *Qu'est-ce que la philosophie présocratique?*, Laks & Louguet (eds), 497–530, and cf. G. Vlastos, "One World or Many in Anaxagoras?", in *Studies in Presocratic Philosophy* 2, Allen & Furley (eds), 354–60; M. Schofield, "Anaxagoras' Other Worlds Revisited", in *Polyhistor: Studies in the History and Historiography of Ancient Philosophy*, K. A. Algra, P. Van der Horst & D. T. Runia (eds), 3–19 (Leiden: Brill, 1996); and Sedley, *Creationism and its Critics*. J. Mansfeld, "Anaxagoras' Other World", *Phronesis* **25** (1980), 1–3, takes B4a to refer to microscopic cosmoses within our own.

14. There are other traces of Anaxagorean sayings that might broadly be conceived as conveying an ethical message: the time before birth and sleep are both instructive of the nature of death (Stob. 4.52b.39 [DK 59 A34]); when Anaxagoras hears of the death of his son, he replies: "I knew I had fathered a mortal" (Galen *PHP* 4.7 [DK 59 A33] and Diog. Laert. 2.13 [DK 59 A1]).

8. Empedocles

1. Published in A. Martin and O. Primavesi, *L'Empédocle de Strasbourg (P.Strasb. gr. Inv. 1665-1666). Introduction, édition et commentaire* (Berlin: de Gruyter, 1999). Inwood, *The Poem of Empedocles*, is an edition with commentary and translation incorporating the new material, arranged according to Inwood's own conception of a single poem. For assessments of the impact of this material on Empedoclean scholarship see C. Osborne, "Rummaging in the Recycling Bins of Upper Egypt: A Discussion on A. Martin and O. Primavesi, *L'Empédocle de Strasbourg*", *Oxford Studies in Ancient Philosophy* **18** (2000), 329–56 and P. Curd, "A New Empedocles? Implications of the Strasburg Fragments for Presocratic Philosophy", *Proceedings of the Boston Area Colloquium in Ancient Philosophy* **17** (2001), 27–49.

2. For the "ethical" or "religious" themes, consider the curious references to what "we" do in coming together into a single cosmos in ensemble a. The papyrus also notes corrections of these first-person plural verbs, suggesting that an ancient reader found them difficult to understand and was probably comparing, for example, B26.5. For more discussion see Martin & Primavesi, *L'Empédocle de Strasbourg*, 90–5; Osborne, "Rummaging in the Recycling Bins", 344–52; A. Laks, "Reading the Readings: On the First Person Plurals in the Strasburg Empedocles", in *Presocratic Philosophy*, Caston & Graham (eds), 127–37; S. Trépanier, "Empedocles on the Ultimate Symmetry of the World", *Oxford Studies in Ancient Philosophy* **24** (2003), 1–57, esp. 1–4; D. N. Sedley, "Empedocles' Life Cycles", in *The Empedoclean Kosmos: Structure, Process and the Question of Cyclicity*, A. L. Pierris (ed.), 331–771 (Patras: Institute for Philosophical Research, 2005), esp. 356; and B. Inwood, "Who do We Think We Are?", in *The Virtuous Life in Greek Ethics*, B. Reis (ed.), 230–43 (Cambridge: Cambridge University Press, 2006), 240–43.

3. For a recent attempt at reconstructing the opening of the poem (assuming a single poem), and discussion of previous accounts, see S. Trépanier, *Empedocles: An Interpretation* (London: Routledge, 2004), 31–72.

4. Compare D. N. Sedley, *Lucretius and the Transformation of Greek Wisdom* (Cambridge: Cambridge University Press, 1998), 2–10, with D. O'Brien, "Empedocles: The Wandering Daimōn and the Two Proems", *Aevum antiquuum* new series 1 (2001), 79–179. D. O'Brien, "Empedocles: A Synopsis", in *Frühgriechisches Denken*, Rechenauer (ed.), 316–42, gives a useful synopsis of his overall interpretation of Empedocles.

5. On Empedocles and Parmenides see also Graham, "Empedocles and Anaxagoras", and R. D. McKirahan, "Assertion and Argument in Empedocles' Cosmology or, What did Empedocles Learn from Parmenides?", in *The Empedoclean Kosmos*, Pierris (ed.), 163–88.

6. For some concerns about these identifications see Kingsley, *Ancient Philosophy*, 13–68, 359–63.

7. For some attempts, using the evidence of a Byzantine scholiast on Aristotle, to pin down the periods of the cycle see M. Rashed, "La Chronographie du système d'Empédocle: document byzantins inédits", *Aevum Antiquum* new series 1 (2001), 237–59; O. Primavesi, "The Structure of Empedocles' Cosmic Cycle: Aristotle and the Byzantine Anonymous", in *The Empedoclean Kosmos*, Pierris (ed.), 245–64; and Sedley, "Empedocles' Life Cycles", 353–5. Sedley, for example, conjectures that the period between one sphere and another is 1.2 million years and that the sphere itself lasts for 2 million years.

8. For more discussion of the metaphysics of Empedoclean mixtures see Mourelatos, "Quality, Structure and Emergence"; and Curd, *The Legacy of Parmenides*, 155–71, and "The Metaphysics of Physics", 147–53.

9. Cf. B128. There, in the period when Love is dominant, she is worshipped with offerings of images or statues and "painted animals".

10. This line is missing from the source for this fragment but is restored here because it appears in B26.8 in a repetition of the surrounding lines.

11. See Trépanier, "Empedocles on the Ultimate Symmetry", for the use of symmetry as a motif in Empedocles' thought.

12. For the asymmetrical view and a review of previous interpretations see A. A. Long, "Empedocles Cosmic Cycle in the 'Sixties'", in *The Presocratics*, Mourelatos (ed.), 397–425, and cf. C. Osborne, "Empedocles Recycled", *Classical Quarterly* 37 (1987), 24–50. For a criticism of Long and restatement of the symmetrical view see D. W. Graham, "Symmetry in the Empedoclean Cycle", *Classical Quarterly* 38 (1988), 297–312, and, together with a review of more recent interpretations, Trépanier, "Empedocles on the Ultimate Symmetry".

13. Other reports describe a cosmogony in terms of fire, earth and so on being "separated out" (e.g. Aet. 2.6.3 [DK 31 A49]), which would most plausibly be the work of Strife.

14. See the suggestions in Sedley, "Empedocles' Life Cycles", that there are two

races of human beings: the products of Love's combinations and the products of sexual reproduction generated by Strife.

15. He promises to teach various special powers, including powers over the roots and the ability to revive the dead (B111). On Empedocles the magician, see Kingsley, *Ancient Philosophy*, 217–32, 296–316.

16. B146 suggest that becoming a human prophet, bard, doctor or leader is the final stage of the banishment, after which "they" (perhaps banished *daimones*) become gods (once again?)

17. Osborne, "Empedocles Recycled", 48, suggests that the reference is to the generation of blood from the perfect sphere as Strife begins to exert an influence. The one god (the sphere) sheds his own blood as a kind of archetypal sin.

18. For an interpretation responding to such concerns see C. Osborne, "Sin and Moral Responsibility in Empedocles' Cosmic Cycle", in *The Empedoclean Kosmos*, Pierris (ed.), 283–308, and cf. A. Laks, "Some Thoughts about Empedoclean Cosmic and Demonic Cycles", in *The Empedoclean Kosmos*, 265–82.

19. For the former alternative see Inwood, *The Poem of Empedocles*, 59–64. For the latter see Laks, "Some Thoughts", 277.

20. See Inwood, "Who do We Think We Are?", which emphasizes Empedocles' remarkable achievement in recognizing his identity between lives.

21. See Hippol. *Ref.* 7.29–30, printed in DK as one of the sources of B115. For an alternative interpretation see Inwood, *The Poem of Empedocles*, 64–8.

22. See the suggestions in P. Curd, "On the Question of Religion and Natural Philosophy in Empedocles", in *The Empedoclean Kosmos*, Pierris (ed.), 137–62.

23. For example, Sedley, "Empedocles' Life Cycles", 331–47, argues that not all human beings are *daimones* but some are instead the products of Strife's generation of sexually differentiated mortals.

24. Cf. Huffman, "The Pythagorean Tradition", 75–8. The ancient sources for Empedocles' DK 31 B129, the praise of an "exceptionally wise man", introduce it as being about Pythagoras.

9. Democritus and Leucippus

1. Diog. Laert. 10.13 (DK 67 A2). Bailey's 1928 account of ancient atomism is happy to distinguish between Leucippus' original theory and Democritus' modifications. The evidence to support such clear distinctions is not very strong.

2. For discussions of Democritus' dates see J. A. Davison, "Protagoras, Democritus, and Anaxagoras", *Classical Quarterly* 3 (1953), 33–45; Guthrie, *A History of Greek Philosophy Volume 2*, 386 n.2; D. O'Brien, "Démocrite d'Abdère", in *Dictionnaire des philosophes antiques*, R. Goulet (ed.), 649–75 (Paris: Éditions du Centre National de la Recherche Scientifique, 1994); and J. Salem, *Démocrite: Grains de poussière dans un rayon de soleil* (Paris: Vrin, 1996), 25–6.

3. For a list of Democritus' works see Diog. Laert. 9.45–9 (DK 68 A33).

4. The authenticity of these fragments is often disputed. See F. K. Voros, "The Ethical Fragments of Democritus: The Problem of Authenticity", *Hellenika* **26** (1973), 193–206; J. Warren, *Epicurus and Democritean Ethics: An Archaeology of Ataraxia* (Cambridge: Cambridge University Press, 2002), 30–32.

5. P.-M. Morel, *Démocrite et la recherche des causes* (Paris: Klincksieck, 1996) gives an account of Democritean philosophy that is particularly sensitive to the different sources and their own particular interpretative prejudices.

6. On the Democritean conception of the void, and possible contrasts with the later Epicurean version, see D. N. Sedley, "Two Conceptions of Vacuum", *Phronesis* **27** (1982), 175–93.

7. I noted above (p. 97) that there is some dispute over whether Parmenides himself denied motion via a denial of void. Certainly, Melissus offers such an argument and there is no chronological difficulty in seeing atomism as a response to Melissus.

8. The precise form of Zeno's argument is debatable. The evidence is collected in DK 29 A21–3. See Furley, *Two Studies in the Greek Atomists*, 63–9.

9. For discussions of the atomicity of the atom see especially *ibid.*, 57–103 (Furley emphasizes the Eleatic background); Makin, *Indifference Arguments*, 49–62; and C. C. W. Taylor, *The Atomists: Leucippus and Democritus* (Toronto: University of Toronto Press, 1999), 164–71.

10. The Epicureans developed atomism by saying that atoms are themselves composed of "minima", which are extended, but partless. See Epicurus *Letter to Herodotus* 58–9.

11. There is, however, an interesting problem that arises from this account. If two atoms touch, they would seem to generate a new, single, continuous body. (They need not touch only at a single point.) If this new body is continuous, how can it be divided? In other words, how can two touching atoms ever come apart? This disastrous consequence led some commentators in antiquity (notably Philoponus) to say that the atoms never in fact touch: they rebound from one another without ever coming into contact. This solution has been accepted in some modern interpretations (e.g. Taylor, *The Atomists*, 186) but seems implausible. See I. Bodnár, "Atomic Independence and Indivisibility", *Oxford Studies in Ancient Philosophy* **16** (1998), 35–61, esp. 44–56, and P. S. Hasper, "The Foundations of Presocratic Atomism", *Oxford Studies in Ancient Philosophy* 17 (1999), 1–14, esp. 6–11.

12. The evidence for enormous atoms (even as large as our cosmos) is in Diog. Laert. 9.44 (DK 68 A1), Dionys. *ap.* Eus. *PE* 14.23.2 (DK 68 A43) and Aet. 1.12.6 (DK 68 A47). See Makin, *Indifference Arguments*, 62–5.

13. See D. J. Furley, "The Cosmological Crisis in Classical Antiquity", in his *Cosmic Problems*, 223–35, for a brief account of the distinction between this view and the finite universe view of, for example, Plato and Aristotle.

14. This is the version cited by Sextus Empiricus at *M* 7.135. Galen *De medic. empir.* fr. (DK 68 B125) has a slightly different version. There is yet another at Plut. *Adv. Col.* 1110E.

15. Democritus attacked Protagoras' relativism: Plut. *Adv. Col.* 1109A (DK 68 B156), SE *M* 7.389 (DK 68 A114). For more on Democritus and Protagoras see Warren, *Epicurus and Democritean Ethics*, 14–18.

16. G. M. Stratton, *Theophrastus and the Greek Physiological Psychology before Aristotle* (London: Allen & Unwin, 1917) is still the only edition with translation into English of the whole treatise.

17. For more discussion of this passage see also D. N. Sedley, "Sextus Empiricus and the Atomist Criteria of Truth", *Elenchos* 13 (1992), 19–56.

18. It is very likely that Colotes' interpretation is polemical and distorts the Democritean account. Plutarch responds by claiming that the Epicureans are in no better a position than Democritus. For more discussion of the Epicurean reception of this aspect of Democritus' thought see Morel, *Démocrite et la recherche*, 11–12, 22–9, and Warren, *Epicurus and Democritean Ethics*, esp. 193–6. Cf. P. A. Vander Waerdt, "Colotes and the Epicurean Refutation of Scepticism", *Greek, Roman, and Byzantine Studies* 30 (1989), 225–67; D. J. Furley, "Democritus and Epicurus on Sensible Qualities", in *Passions and Perceptions*, J. Brunschwig & M. Nussbaum (eds), 72–94 (Cambridge: Cambridge University Press, 1993); and T. O'Keefe, "The Ontological Status of Sensible Qualities for Democritus and Epicurus", *Ancient Philosophy* 17 (1997), 119–34.

19. For this interpretation see, for example, SE *M* 7.135 (DK 68 B9). For an Eleatic reading of Democritus see R. B. B. Wardy, "Eleatic Pluralism", *Archiv für Geschichte der Philosophie* 70 (1988), 125–46. For various sceptical interpretations of Democritus see Barnes, *The Presocratic Philosophers*, 370–77, 559–64; Furley, "Democritus and Epicurus"; R. J. Hankinson, *The Sceptics* (London: Routledge, 1995), 47–9; and O'Keefe, "The Ontological Status".

20. For interpretations along these lines see P. Curd, "Why Democritus was not a Sceptic", in *Before Plato*, A. Preus (ed.), 149–69 (who also gives a good guide to previous accounts), and compare the account in M.-K. Lee, *Epistemology after Protagoras* (Oxford: Oxford University Press, 2005), 181–250, which includes a lengthy discussion of the problems of the various competing sources of evidence.

21. See Warren, *Epicurus and Democritean Ethics*, for some discussion of these "Democriteans".

22. J. Annas, "Democritus and Eudaimonism", in *Presocratic Philosophy*, Caston & Graham (eds), 169–81, argues for a "eudaemonist" Democritus. For an alternative view see C. H. Kahn, "Pre-Platonic Ethics", in *Ethics*, S. Everson (ed.), 27–48 (Cambridge: Cambridge University Press, 1998), 34–7, and Warren, *Epicurus and Democritean Ethics*, esp. 19–23, 32–44.

23. For acute interpretations of Democritus' social and political views see C. Farrar, *The Origins of Democratic Thinking* (Cambridge: Cambridge University Press, 1988) and J. Procopé, "Democritus on Politics and the Care of the Soul", *Classical Quarterly* 39 (1989), 307–31, and "Democritus on Politics and the Care of the Soul: Appendix", *Classical Quarterly* 40 (1990), 21–45. For other accounts of Democritus' ethical thought see C. Bailey, *The Greek Atomists and*

Epicurus (Oxford: Clarendon Press, 1928), 186–213; C. C. W. Taylor, "Pleasure, Knowledge, and Sensation in Democritus", *Phronesis* **12** (1967), 6–27, and *The Atomists*, 222–34; C. H. Kahn, "Democritus and the Origins of Moral Psychology", *American Journal of Philology* **106** (1985), 1–31; Annas, "Democritus and Eudaimonism"; and Warren, *Epicurus and Democritean Ethics*, 29–58 and J. Warren, "Democritus on Social and Psychological Harm", in *Democritus: Science, the Arts, and the Care of the Soul*, A. Brancacci & P.-M. Morel (eds), 87–104 (Leiden: Brill, 2006).

24. The most ardent supporter of such a link between ethics and physics is G. Vlastos, "Ethics and Physics in Democritus", *Philosophical Review* **54** (1945), 578–92 and **55** (1946), 53–64. For criticisms of Vlastos see Barnes, *The Presocratic Philosophers*, 530–34, and Taylor, "Pleasure, Knowledge, and Sensation" (but cf. Taylor, *The Atomists*, 232–4). Also see Warren, *Epicurus and Democritean Ethics*, 58–72.

10. Epilogue

1. For a discussion of Philolaus' dates see Huffman, *Philolaus of Croton*, 1–9. Huffman's monumental work is by far the best recent discussion of Philolaus. There is a shorter treatment in Huffman, "The Pythagorean Tradition", 78–84.

2. Alternatively, Philolaus may mean not the cosmos as a whole but any kind of order (*kosmos*).

3. Diogenes has received relatively little modern interest, but see Barnes, *The Presocratic Philosophers*, 567–83; Laks, *Diogène d'Apollonie*; Kirk et al., *The Presocratic Philosophers*, 434–52; and Graham, *Explaining the Cosmos*, 277–93.

4. For a discussion of Diogenes' possible influence on the author of the Derveni papyrus see Betegh, *The Derveni Papyrus*, 306–24.

5. See *Phaedo* 61d: Simmias and Cebes are said to be associates of Philolaus (see also Huffman, *Philolaus of Croton*, 406–10, and Sedley, "The *Dramatis Personae*"), and *Phileb.* 23c–27c

6. For this claim see Aristot. *Met.* 987b1–6; Diog. Laert. 1.18, 2.21. But at 2.26 Diogenes agrees that Archelaus, Socrates' supposed "teacher" also addressed some ethical questions.

7. For Anaxagoras, see, for example, Diog. Laert. 2.12–14 (DK 59 A1), Plato *Phaedr.* 269e–70a, Plut. *Per.* 4, 6, 32 (DK 59 A15–17). For Diogenes, see Aristophanes *Clouds* 225–36 (DK 64 C1) (first performed in 423 BCE) with commentary in K. Dover, *Aristophanes: Clouds* (Oxford: Clarendon Press, 1968) and cf. Laks, *Diogène d'Apollonie*, 77.

Bibliography

Adoménas, M. 1999. "Heraclitus on Religion". *Phronesis* **44**: 87–113.

Adoménas, M. 2002. "The Fluctuating Fortunes of Heraclitus in Plato". See A. Laks and C. Louguet (eds) (2002): 419–47.

Algra, K. 1999. "The Beginnings of Cosmology". See Long (1999): 45–65.

Allen, R. E. & D. J. Furley (eds) 1970. *Studies in Presocratic Philosophy*, vol. 1. London: Routledge & Kegan Paul.

Allen, R. E. & D. J. Furley (eds) 1975. *Studies in Presocratic Philosophy*, vol. 2. London: Routledge & Kegan Paul.

Annas, J. 2002. "Democritus and Eudaimonism". See Caston & Graham (2002): 169–81.

Annas, J. & J. Barnes 1985. *The Modes of Scepticism*. Cambridge: Cambridge University Press.

Bailey, C. 1928. *The Greek Atomists and Epicurus*. Oxford: Clarendon Press.

Baltussen, H. 2000. *Theophrastus Against the Presocratics and Plato: Peripatetic Doxography in the De Sensibus*. Leiden: Brill.

Baltussen, H. 2002. "Philology or Philosophy? Simplicius and the Use of Quotations". In *Epea and Grammata: Oral and Written Communication in Ancient Greece*, I. Worthington & J. M. Foley (eds), 173–89. Leiden: Brill.

Barnes, J. 1982. *The Presocratic Philosophers*, rev. edn. London: Routledge & Kegan Paul.

Barnes, J. 1983. "Aphorism and Argument". In *Language and Thought in Early Greek Philosophy*, K. Robb (ed.), 91–109. La Salle, IL: Hegeler Institute.

Barnes, J. 1987. *Early Greek Philosophy*. Harmondsworth: Penguin.

Barnes, J. 1990. *The Toils of Scepticism*. Cambridge: Cambridge University Press.

Benakis, L. G. (ed.) 1984. *Proceedings of the 1st International Congress on Democritus*, 2 vols. Xanthi.

Bernabé, A. 2002. "Orphisme et Présocratiques: bilan et perspectives d'un dialogue complexe". See Laks & Louget (2002), 205–47.

Berryman, S. 2002. "Democritus and the Explanatory Power of the Void". See Caston & Graham (2002), 183–91.

Betegh, G. 2004. *The Derveni Papyrus: Cosmology, Theology and Interpretation*. Cambridge: Cambridge University Press.

Betegh, G. 2006. "Epicurus' Argument for Atomism". *Oxford Studies in Ancient Philosophy* 30: 261–84.

Bodnár, I. 1998. "Atomic Independence and Indivisibility". *Oxford Studies in Ancient Philosophy* 16: 35–61.

Boys-Stones, G. R. 2001. *Post-Hellenistic Philosophy: A Study of its Development from the Stoics to Origen*. Oxford: Oxford University Press.

Broadie, S. 1999. "Rational Theology". See Long (1999a), 205–24.

Brown, L. 1994. "The Verb 'To Be' in Greek Philosophy: Some Remarks". In *Language*, S. Everson (ed.), 212–36. Cambridge: Cambridge University Press.

Brunschwig, J. 2002. "Democritus and Xeniades". See Caston & Graham (2002), 159–67.

Burkert, W. 1972. *Lore and Science in Ancient Pythagoreanism*. Cambridge, MA: Harvard University Press.

Burkert, W., L. Gemelli Marciano, E. Matelli & L. Orelli (eds) 1998. *Fragmentsammlungen Philosophischer Texte der Antike*. Göttingen: Vandenhoeck & Ruprecht.

Burnet, J. 1911. *Plato: Phaedo*. Oxford: Clarendon Press.

Buxton, R. (ed.) 1999. *From Myth to Reason?* Oxford: Oxford University Press.

Calder, W. M. & J. Mansfeld (eds) 1999. *Hermann Diels (1848–1922) et la science de l'antiquité*. Geneva: Fondation Hardt.

Caston, V. & D. W. Graham (eds) 2002. *Presocratic Philosophy: Essays in Honour of Alexander Mourelatos*. Aldershot: Ashgate.

Cherniss, H. 1935. *Aristotle's Criticism of Presocratic Philosophy*. Baltimore, MD: Johns Hopkins Press.

Cole, T. 1967. *Democritus and the Sources of Greek Anthropology*. Cleveland, OH: Press of Western Reserve University for the American Philological Association.

Cornford, F. 1975. "Anaxagoras' Theory of Matter". See Allen & Furley (1975), 275–322. First published in *Classical Quarterly* 24 (1930): 14–30, 83–95.

Coxon, A. 1986. *The Fragments of Parmenides. Phronesis* supp. vol. 3.

Curd, P. 1998. *The Legacy of Parmenides*. Princeton, NJ: Princeton University Press.

Curd, P. 2001a. "A New Empedocles? Implications of the Strasburg Fragments for Presocratic Philosophy". *Proceedings of the Boston Area Colloquium in Ancient Philosophy* 17: 27–49.

Curd, P. 2001b. "Why Democritus was not a Sceptic". See Preus (2001), 149–69.

Curd, P. 2002. "The Metaphysics of Physics: Mixture and Separation in Empedocles and Anaxagoras". See Caston & Graham (2002), 139–58.

Curd, P. 2005. "On the Question of Religion and Natural Philosophy in Empedocles". See Pierris (2005), 137–62.

Dancy, J. 1985. *Introduction to Contemporary Epistemology*. Oxford: Blackwell.

Davison, J. A. 1953. "Protagoras, Democritus, and Anaxagoras". *Classical Quarterly* 3: 33–45.

de Lacey, P. 1958. "*Ou mallon* and the Antecedents of Greek Scepticism". *Revue des études grecques* 82: 318–26.

Denyer, N. C. 1991. *Language, Thought, and Falsehood in Greek Philosophy*. London: Routledge & Kegan Paul.

Detienne, M. 1996. *The Masters of Truth in Archaic Greece*. New York: Zone Books.

Dilcher, R. 1995. *Studies in Heraclitus*. Hildesheim: Olms.

Dixsaut, M. & A. Brancacci (eds) 2002. *Platon, Source des Présocratiques*. Paris: Vrin.

Dover, K. 1968. *Aristophanes: Clouds*. Oxford: Clarendon Press.

Dover, K. 1988. "The Freedom of the Intellectual in Greek Society". In his *The Greeks and their Legacy*, 135–58. Oxford: Blackwell.

Engman, J. 1991. "Cosmic Justice in Anaximander". *Phronesis* 36: 1–25.

Faris, J. 1996. *The Paradoxes of Zeno*. Aldershot: Ashgate.

Farrar, C. 1988. *The Origins of Democratic Thinking*. Cambridge: Cambridge University Press.

Fränkel, H. 1974. "Xenophanes' Empiricism and his Critique of Knowledge (B34)". See Mourelatos (1974b), 118–31.

Fränkel, H. 1975a. "Studies in Parmenides". See Allen & Furley (1975), 1–47.

Fränkel, H. 1975b. *Early Greek Poetry and Philosophy*. Oxford: Blackwell.

Frede, M. 1992. "Plato's Sophist on False Statements". In *The Cambridge Companion to Plato*, R. Kraut (ed.), 397–424. Cambridge: Cambridge University Press.

Freudenthal, G. 1986. "The Theory of the Opposites and an Ordered Universe: Physics and Metaphysics in Anaximander". *Phronesis* 31: 197–228.

Furley, D. J. 1967. *Two Studies in the Greek Atomists*. Princeton, NJ: Princeton University Press.

Furley, D. J. 1969. "Aristotle and the Atomists on Infinity". In *Naturphilosophie bei Aristoteles und Theophrast*, Proceedings of the fourth Symposium Aristotelicum, I. Düring (ed.), 85–96. Heidelberg: Stiehm. Reprinted in Furley (1989e), 103–14.

Furley, D. J. 1976. "Aristotle and the Atomists on Motion in a Void". In *Motion and Time, Space and Matter*, P. K. Machamer & J. Turnbull (eds), 83–100. Columbus, OH: Ohio State University Press. Reprinted in Furley (1989e), 77–90.

Furley, D. J. 1987 *The Greek Cosmologists, Volume 1*. Cambridge: Cambridge University Press.

Furley, D. J. 1989a. "The Cosmological Crisis in Classical Antiquity". See Furley (1989e), 223–35.

Furley, D. J. 1989b. "The Dynamics of the Earth: Anaximander, Plato, and the Centrifocal Theory". See Furley (1989e), 14–26.

Furley, D. J. 1989c. "Anaxagoras in Response to Parmenides". See Furley (1989e), 47–65.

Furley, D. J. 1989d. "Notes on Parmenides". See Furley (1989e), 27–37.

Furley, D. J. 1989e. *Cosmic Problems*. Cambridge: Cambridge University Press.

Furley, D. J. 1993. "Democritus and Epicurus on Sensible Qualities". In *Passions and Perceptions*, J. Brunschwig & M. Nussbaum (eds), 72–94. Cambridge: Cambridge University Press.

Furley, D. J. 2002. "Anaxagoras, Plato and Naming of Parts". See Caston & Graham (2002), 119–26.

Furth, M. 1974. "Elements of Eleatic Ontology". See Mourelatos (1974b), 241–70.

Furth, M. 1991. "A Philosophical Hero? Anaxagoras and the Eleatics". *Oxford Studies in Ancient Philosophy* 9: 95–130.

Gallop, D. 1984. *Parmenides: Fragments*. Toronto: University of Toronto Press.

Gemelli-Marciano, L. 2002. "Le context culturel des Présocratiques: adversaires et destinataires". See Laks & Louguet (2002), 85–114.

Geuss, R. 2005. "On the Usefulness and Uselessness of Religious Illusions". In his *Outside Ethics*, 131–52. Princeton, NJ: Princeton University Press.

Gorman, V. B. 2001. *Miletos: The Ornament of Ionia*. Ann Arbor, MI: University of Michigan Press.

Gosling, J. C. B. & C. C. W. Taylor 1982. *The Greeks on Pleasure*. Oxford: Clarendon Press.

Gottschalk, H. 1965. "Anaximander's *Apeiron*". *Phronesis* 10: 37–53.

Graham, D. W. 1988. "Symmetry in the Empedoclean Cycle". *Classical Quarterly* 38: 297–312.

Graham, D. W. 1994. "The Postulates of Anaxagoras". *Apeiron* 27: 77–121.

Graham, D. W. 1997. "Heraclitus' Criticism of Ionian Philosophy". *Oxford Studies in Ancient Philosophy* 15: 1–50.

Graham, D. W. 1999. "Empedocles and Anaxagoras: Responses to Parmenides". See Long (1999a), 159–80.

Graham, D. W. 2002. "Heraclitus and Parmenides". See Caston & Graham (2002), 27–44.

Graham, D. W. 2005. "The Topology and Dynamics of Empedocles' Cycle". See Pierris (2005), 225–43.

Graham, D. W. 2006. *Explaining the Cosmos: The Ionian Tradition of Scientific Philosophy*. Princeton, NJ: Princeton University Press.

Granger, H. 2002. "The Cosmology of Mortals". See Caston & Graham (2002), 101–16.

Granger, H. 2004. "Argumentation and Heraclitus' Book". *Oxford Studies in Ancient Philosophy* 26: 1–17.

Greaves, A. 2002. *Miletos: A History*. London: Routledge.

Guthrie, W. K. C. 1957. "Aristotle as Historian". *Journal of Hellenic Studies* 77: 35–41.

Guthrie, W. K. C. 1962 *A History of Greek Philosophy Volume 1: The Earlier Presocratics and the Pythagoreans*. Cambridge: Cambridge University Press.

Guthrie, W. K. C. 1965. *A History of Greek Philosophy Volume 2: The Presocratic Tradition from Parmenides to Democritus*. Cambridge: Cambridge University Press.

Hankinson, R. J. 1995. *The Sceptics*. London: Routledge.

Hankinson, R. J. 1998. *Cause and Explanation in Ancient Greek Thought*. Oxford: Oxford University Press.

Harris, W. V. 1989. *Ancient Literacy*. Cambridge, MA: Harvard University Press.

Hasper, P. S. 1999. "The Foundations of Presocratic Atomism". *Oxford Studies in Ancient Philosophy* **17**: 1-14.

Hasper, P. S. 2006. "Zeno Unlimited". *Oxford Studies in Ancient Philosophy* **30**: 49-85.

Hölscher, U. 1974. "Paradox, Simile, and Gnomic Utterance in Heraclitus". In *The Pre-Socratics: A Collection of Critical Essays*, A. P. D. Mourelatos (ed.), 219-38. Garden City, NY: Anchor.

Huffman, C. A. 1993. *Philolaus of Croton: Pythagorean and Presocratic*. Cambridge: Cambridge University Press.

Huffman, C. A. 1999. "The Pythagorean Tradition". See Long (1999a), 66-87.

Inwood, B. 2001. *The Poem of Empedocles*, 2nd edn. Toronto: University of Toronto Press.

Inwood, B. 2006. "Who do We Think We Are?". In *The Virtuous Life in Greek Ethics*, B. Reis (ed.), 230-43. Cambridge: Cambridge University Press.

Johnson, W. A. 2000. "Toward a Sociology of Reading in Antiquity". *American Journal of Philology* **121**: 593-627.

Jordan, W. 1990. *Ancient Concepts of Philosophy*. London: Routledge.

Kahn, C. H. 1974. "Religion and Natural Philosophy in Empedocles' Doctrine of the Soul". See Mourelatos (1974b), 426-56.

Kahn, C. H. 1979. *The Art and Thought of Heraclitus*. Cambridge: Cambridge University Press.

Kahn, C. H. 1985. "Democritus and the Origins of Moral Psychology". *American Journal of Philology* **106**: 1-31.

Kahn, C. H. [1960] 1994. *Anaximander and the Origins of Greek Cosmology*. Indianapolis, IN: Hackett.

Kahn, C. H. 1998. "Pre-Platonic Ethics". In *Ethics*, S. Everson (ed.), 27-48. Cambridge: Cambridge University Press.

Kahn, C. H. 2001. *Pythagoras and the Pythagoreans: A Brief History*. Indianapolis, IN. Hackett.

Kahn, C. H. 2002. "Parmenides and Plato". See Caston & Graham (2002), 81-93.

Kahn, C. H. 2003. "Writing Philosophy: Prose and Poetry from Thales to Plato". In *Written Texts and the Rise of Literate Culture in Ancient Greece*, H. Yunis (ed.), 139-61. Cambridge: Cambridge University Press.

Kahn, C. H. 2005. "Parmenides and Being". See Rechenauer (2005), 217-26.

Kingsley, P. 1995. *Ancient Philosophy, Mystery and Magic: Empedocles and Pythagorean Tradition*. Oxford: Oxford University Press.

Kirk, G. S. 1962. *Heraclitus: The Cosmic Fragments*, corrected edn. Cambridge: Cambridge University Press.

Kirk, G. S., J. Raven & M. Schofield 1983. *The Presocratic Philosophers*, 2nd edn. Cambridge: Cambridge University Press.

Laks, A. 1983. *Diogène d'Apollonie, la dernière cosmologie présocratique*. Lille: Presses Universitaires de Lille.

Laks, A. 2002a. "'Philosophes présocratiques': Remarques sur la construction d'une catégorie de l'historiographie philosophique". See Laks & Louguet (2002), 17–38.

Laks, A. 2002b. "Reading the Readings: On the First Person Plurals in the Strasburg Empedocles". See Caston & Graham (2002), 127–37.

Laks, A. 2005a. "Some Thoughts about Empedoclean Cosmic and Demonic Cycles". See Pierris (2005), 265–82.

Laks, A. 2005b. "Remarks on the Differentiation of Early Greek Philosophy". In *Philosophy and the Sciences in Antiquity*, R. W. Sharples (ed.), 8–22. Aldershot: Ashgate.

Laks, A. & C. Louguet (eds) 2002. *Qu'est-ce que la philosophie présocratique?* Lille: Presses Universitaires du Septentrion.

Lear, J. 1981. "A Note on Zeno's Arrow". *Phronesis* **26**: 91–104.

Lee, M.-K. 2005. *Epistemology after Protagoras*. Oxford: Oxford University Press.

Le Poidevin, R. 2002. "Zeno's Arrow and the Significance of the Present". In *Time, Reality and Experience*, C. Callender (ed.), 57–72. Cambridge: Cambridge University Press.

Lesher, J. 1992. *Xenophanes of Colophon: Fragments*. Toronto: University of Toronto Press.

Lesher, J. 1999. "Early Interest in Knowledge". See Long (1999a), 225–49.

Lloyd, G. E. R. 1966. *Polarity and Analogy*. Cambridge: Cambridge University Press.

Lloyd, G. E. R. 1987. *The Revolutions of Wisdom*. Berkeley, CA: University of California Press.

Lloyd, G. E. R. 1991a. "The Debt of Greek Philosophy and Science to the Ancient Near East". In his *Methods and Problems in Greek Science*, 278–98. Cambridge: Cambridge University Press.

Lloyd, G. E. R. 1991b. "The Social Background of Early Greek Philosophy and Science". In his *Methods and Problems in Greek Science*, 121–40. Cambridge: Cambridge University Press.

Lloyd, G. E. R. 2002. "Le pluralisme de la vie intellectuelle avant Platon". See Laks & Louguet (2002), 39–53.

Long, A. A. 1974. "Empedocles Cosmic Cycle in the 'Sixties'". See Mourelatos (1974b), 397–425.

Long, A. A. 1978. "Timon of Phlius: Pyrrhonist and Satirist". *Proceedings of the Cambridge Philological Society* **24**: 68–91.

Long, A. A. 1996a. "Heraclitus and Stoicism". In his *Stoic Studies*, 35–57. Cambridge: Cambridge University Press.

Long, A. A. 1996b. "Parmenides on Thinking Being". *Proceedings of the Boston Area Colloquium in Ancient Philosophy* **12**: 125–51. Revised version in Rechenauer (2005), 227–51.

Long, A. A. (ed.) 1999a. *The Cambridge Companion to Early Greek Philosophy*. Cambridge: Cambridge University Press.

Long, A. A. 1999b. "The Scope of Early Greek Philosophy". See Long (1999a), 1–21.

Louguet, C. 2002. "Note sur le fragment B4a d'Anaxagore: pourquoi les autres mondes doivent-ils être semblables au nôtre?". See Laks & Louguet (2002), 497–530.

Mackenzie, M. M. 1982. "Parmenides' Dilemma". *Phronesis* **27**: 1–12.

Mackenzie, M. M. 1988. "Heraclitus and the Art of Paradox". *Oxford Studies in Ancient Philosophy* **6**: 1–39.

Makin, S. 1993. *Indifference Arguments*. Oxford: Blackwell.

Makin, S. 2005. "Melissus and his Opponents: The Argument of DK 30 B8". *Phronesis* **50**: 263–88.

Malcolm, J. 1991. "On Avoiding the Void". *Oxford Studies in Ancient Philosophy* **9**: 75–94.

Mann, W. 1980. "Anaxagoras and the *Homoiomerē*". *Phronesis* **25**: 228–49.

Mansfeld, J. 1979/1980. "The Chronology of Anaxagoras' Athenian Period and the Date of his Trial". *Mnemosyne* **32**: 39–69/**33**: 84–95.

Mansfeld, J. 1980. "Anaxagoras' Other World". *Phronesis* **25**: 1–3.

Mansfeld, J. 1986. "Aristotle, Plato, and the Preplatonic Doxography and Chronography". In *Storiografia e dossografia nella filosofia antica*, G. Cambiano (ed.), 1–59. Turin: Tirrenia Stampatori.

Mansfeld, J. 1999. "Sources". See Long (1999a), 22–44.

Mansfeld, J. & D. T. Runia 1997. *Aetiana*. Leiden: Brill.

Martin, A. & O. Primavesi 1999. *L'Empédocle de Strasbourg (P.Strasb. gr. Inv. 1665–1666). Introduction, édition et commentaire*. Berlin: de Gruyter.

McCabe, M. M. 2000. *Plato and his Predecessors*. Cambridge: Cambridge University Press.

McDowell, J. 1983 "Falsehood and not being in Plato's *Sophist*". In *Language and Logos*, M. Schofield & M. Nussbaum (eds), 115–34. Cambridge: Cambridge University Press.

McKirahan, R. D. 1999. "Zeno". See Long (1999a), 134–58.

McKirahan, R. D. 2001. "Anaximander's Infinite Worlds". See Preus (2001), 49–65.

McKirahan, R. D. 2005. "Assertion and Argument in Empedocles' Cosmology or, What did Empedocles Learn from Parmenides?". See Pierris (2005), 163–88.

Mogyoródi, E. 2002. "Xenophanes as a Philosopher: Theology and Theodicy". See Laks & Louguet (2002), 253–86.

Morel, P.-M. 1996. *Démocrite et la recherche des causes*. Paris: Klincksieck.

Morgan, K. 2000. *Myth and Philosophy from the Presocratics to Plato*. Cambridge: Cambridge University Press.

Most, G. 1999. "The Poetics of Early Greek philosophy". See Long (1999a), 332–62.

Mourelatos, A. 1970. *The Route of Parmenides*. New Haven, CT: Yale University Press.

Mourelatos, A. 1974a. "The Deceptive Words of Parmenides' '*Doxa*'". See Mourelatos (1974b), 312–49.

Mourelatos, A. (ed.) 1974b. *The Pre-Socratics*. Garden City, NY: Anchor.

Mourelatos, A. 1979. "Some Alternatives in Interpreting Parmenides". *Monist* **62**: 3–14.

Mourelatos, A. 1987. "Quality, Structure and Emergence in Later Pre-Socratic Philosophy". *Proceedings of the Boston Area Colloquium in Ancient Philosophy* **2**: 127–94.

Murray, O. (ed.) 1990. *Sympotica: A Symposium on the Symposium*. Oxford: Clarendon Press.

Nagy, G. 2002. *Plato's Rhapsody and Homer's Music: The Poetics of the Panathenaic Festival in Classical Athens*. Washington, DC: Center for Hellenic Studies.

Nehamas, A. 2002. "Parmenidean Being/Heraclitean Fire". In Caston & Graham (2002), 45–64.

Neils, J. (ed.) 1992. *Goddess and Polis: The Panathenaic Festival in Ancient Athens*. Princeton, NJ: Princeton University Press.

Nightingale, A. 1995. *Genres in Dialogue: Plato and the Construct of Philosophy*. Cambridge: Cambridge University Press.

O'Brien, D. 1968. "The Relation of Anaxagoras and Empedocles". *Journal of Hellenic Studies* **88**: 93–114.

O'Brien, D. 1994. "Démocrite d'Abdère". In *Dictionnaire des philosophes antiques*, R. Goulet (ed.), 649–715. Paris: Éditions du Centre National de la Recherche Scientifique.

O'Brien, D. 2001. "Empedocles: The Wandering Daimōn and the Two Proems". *Aevum antiquuum* new series **1**: 79–179.

O'Brien, D. 2005. "Empedocles: A Synopsis". See Rechenauer (2005), 316–42.

O'Keefe, T. 1997. "The Ontological Status of Sensible Qualities for Democritus and Epicurus". *Ancient Philosophy* **17**: 119–34.

Osborne, C. 1987a. "Empedocles Recycled". *Classical Quarterly* **37**: 24–50.

Osborne, C. 1987b. *Rethinking Early Greek Philosophy: Hippolytus of Rome and the Presocratics*. London: Duckworth.

Osborne, C. 1997. "Was Verse the Default Form for Presocratic Philosophy?". In *Form and Content in Didactic Poetry*, C. Atherton (ed.), 23–35. Bari: Levante.

Osborne, C. 2000. "Rummaging in the Recycling Bins of Upper Egypt: A Discussion on A. Martin and O. Primavesi, *L'Empédocle de Strasbourg*". *Oxford Studies in Ancient Philosophy* **18**: 329–56.

Osborne, C. 2005. "Sin and Moral Responsibility in Empedocles' Cosmic Cycle". See Pierris (2005), 283–308.

Osborne, C. 2006. "Was There an Eleatic Revolution in Philosophy?". In *Rethinking Revolutions through Ancient Greece*, S. Goldhill & R. Osborne (eds), 218–45. Cambridge: Cambridge University Press.

Osborne, R. 1996. *Greece in the Making, 1200–479BC*. London: Routledge.

Owen, G. E. L. 1957–58. "Zeno and the Mathematicians". *Proceedings of the*

Aristotelian society **58**: 199–222. Reprinted in Salmon (1970), 139–63; Allen & Furley (1975), 143–65; and Owen (1986a), 45–61.

Owen, G. E. L. 1960. "Eleatic Questions". *Classical Quarterly* **10**: 84–102. Reprinted in Allen & Furley (1975), 48–81 and Owen (1986a), 3–26.

Owen, G. E. L. 1966. "Plato and Parmenides on the Timeless Present". *Monist* **50**: 317–40. Reprinted in Owen (1986a), 27–44.

Owen, G. E. L. 1986a. *Logic, Science and Dialectic*. London: Duckworth.

Owen, G. E. L. 1986b. "Plato on not Being". See Owen (1986a), 104–37.

Palmer, J. 1998. "Xenophanes' Ouranian God in the Fourth Century". *Oxford Studies in Ancient Philosophy* **16**: 1–34.

Palmer, J. 1999. *Plato's Reception of Parmenides*. Oxford: Oxford University Press.

Palmer, J. 2004. "Melissus and Parmenides". *Oxford Studies in Ancient Philosophy* **26**: 19–54.

Pepe, L. 2002. "Le livre d'Anaxagore lu par Platon". In *Platon, Source des Présocratiques*, M. Dixsaut & A. Brancacci (eds), 107–28. Paris: Vrin.

Pierris, A. L. (ed.) 2005. *The Empedoclean Kosmos: Structure, Process and the Question of Cyclicity*. Patras: Institute for Philosophical Research.

Popper, K. 1998. "The Unknown Xenophanes: An Attempt to Establish his Greatness". In his *The World of Parmenides: Essays on the Presocratic Enlightenment*, 33–67. London: Routledge.

Preus, A. (ed.) 2001. *Before Plato: Essays in Ancient Greek Philosophy VI*. Albany, NY: SUNY Press.

Primavesi, O. 2005. "The Structure of Empedocles' Cosmic Cycle: Aristotle and the Byzantine Anonymous". See Pierris (2005), 245–64.

Procopé, J. 1989. "Democritus on Politics and the Care of the Soul". *Classical Quarterly* **39**: 307–31.

Procopé, J. 1990 "Democritus on Politics and the Care of the Soul: Appendix". *Classical Quarterly* **40**: 21–45.

Purcell, N. 1990. "Mobility and the Polis". In *The Greek City from Homer to Alexander*, O. Murray & S. Price (eds), 29–58. Oxford: Clarendon Press.

Pyle, A. 1997. *Atomism and its Critics: From Democritus to Newton*. Bristol: Thoemmes.

Rashed, M. 2001. "La Chronographie du système d'Empédocle: document byzantins inédits". *Aevum Antiquum* new series **1**: 237–59.

Rechenauer, G. (ed.) 2005. *Frühgriechisches Denken*. Göttingen: Vandenhoeck & Ruprecht.

Reinhardt, K. 1974. "The Relation Between the Two Parts of Parmenides' Poem". See Mourelatos (1974b): 293–311.

Ridings, D. 1995. *The Attic Moses: The Dependency Theme in some Early Christian Writers*. Göteborg: Acta Universitatis Gothoburgensis.

Romano, F. (ed.) 1980. *Democrito e l'atomismo antico*. Catania.

Rorty, R., J. Schneewind & Q. Skinner (eds) 1984. *Philosophy in History*. Cambridge: Cambridge University Press.

Russell, B. 1961. *History of Western Philosophy*, 2nd edn. London: Allen & Unwin.

Sainsbury, R. M. 1995. *Paradoxes*, 2nd edn. Cambridge: Cambridge University Press.

Salem, J. 1996. *Démocrite: Grains de poussière dans un rayon de soleil*. Paris: Vrin.

Salmon, W. C. (ed.) 1970. *Zeno's Paradoxes*. Indianapolis, IN: Hackett.

Schibli, H. S. 1990. *Pherecydes of Syros*. Oxford: Clarendon Press.

Schofield, M. 1970. "Did Parmenides Discover Eternity?" *Archiv für Geschichte der Philosophie* **52**: 113–35.

Schofield, M. 1980. *An Essay on Anaxagoras*. Cambridge: Cambridge University Press.

Schofield, M. 1991. "Heraclitus' Theory of Soul and its Antecedents". In *Psychology*, S. Everson (ed.), 13–34. Cambridge: Cambridge University Press.

Schofield, M. 1996. "Anaxagoras' Other Worlds Revisited". In *Polyhistor: Studies in the History and Historiography of Ancient Philosophy*, K. A. Algra, P. Van der Horst & D. T. Runia (eds), 3–19. Leiden: Brill.

Schofield, M. 1997. "The Ionians". In *Routledge History of Philosophy 1: From the Beginnings to Plato*, C. C. W. Taylor (ed.), 47–87. London: Routledge.

Scott, D. 2006. *Plato's Meno*. Cambridge: Cambridge University Press.

Sedley, D. N. 1982. "Two Conceptions of Vacuum". *Phronesis* **27**: 175–93.

Sedley, D. N. 1992. "Sextus Empiricus and the Atomist Criteria of Truth". *Elenchos* **13**: 19–56.

Sedley, D. N. 1995. "The *Dramatis Personae* of Plato's *Phaedo*". In *Philosophical Dialogues*, T. J. Smiley (ed.), 3–26. Oxford: Clarendon Press.

Sedley, D. N. 1998. *Lucretius and the Transformation of Greek Wisdom*. Cambridge: Cambridge University Press.

Sedley, D. N. 1999. "Parmenides and Melissus". See Long (1999a), 113–33.

Sedley, D. N. 2003. *Plato's Cratylus*. Cambridge: Cambridge University Press.

Sedley, D. N. 2004. "*On Generation and Corruption* I.2". In *Aristotle's On Generation and Corruption I*, F. de Haas & J. Mansfeld (eds), 65–89. Oxford: Oxford University Press.

Sedley, D. N. 2005. "Empedocles' Life Cycles". See Pierris (2005), 331–71.

Sedley, D. N. forthcoming. *Creationism and its Critics in Antiquity*. Berkeley, CA: University of California Press.

Sider, D. 2005. *The Fragments of Anaxagoras: Introduction, Text, and Commentary*, 2nd edn. Sankt Augustin: Academia.

Sorabji, R. R. K. 1983. *Time, Creation and the Continuum*. London: Duckworth.

Stokes, M. C. 1971. *One and Many in Presocratic Philosophy*. Washington, DC: Center for Hellenic Studies.

Strang, C. 1975. "The Physical Theory of Anaxagoras". See Allen & Furley (1975), 361–80. First published in *Archiv für Geschichte der Philosophie* **45** (1963): 101–18.

Stratton, G. M. 1917. *Theophrastus and the Greek Physiological Psychology before Aristotle*. London: Allen & Unwin.

Strauss–Clay, J. 2003. *Hesiod's Cosmos*. Cambridge: Cambridge University Press.

Tarán, L. 1979. "Perpetual Duration and Atemporal Eternity in Parmenides". *Monist* **62**: 43–53.

Tarán, L. 1999. "Heraclitus: The River-Fragments and their Implications". *Elenchos* **20**: 9–52.

Taylor, C. C. W. 1967. "Pleasure, Knowledge, and Sensation in Democritus". *Phronesis* **12**: 6–27.

Taylor, C. C. W. 1999. *The Atomists: Leucippus and Democritus*. Toronto: University of Toronto Press.

Thomas, R. 1992. *Literacy and Orality in Ancient Greece*. Cambridge: Cambridge University Press.

Thomas, R. 2000. *Herodotus in Context*. Cambridge: Cambridge University Press.

Trépanier, S. 2003. "Empedocles on the Ultimate Symmetry of the World". *Oxford Studies in Ancient Philosophy* **24**: 1–57.

Trépanier, S. 2004. *Empedocles: An Interpretation*. London: Routledge.

Vander Waerdt, P. A. 1989. "Colotes and the Epicurean Refutation of Scepticism". *Greek, Roman, and Byzantine Studies* **30**: 225–67.

Vlastos, G. 1945–6. "Ethics and Physics in Democritus". *Philosophical Review* **54**: 578–92/**55**: 53–64. Reprinted in Vlastos (1995), 328–58.

Vlastos, G. 1947. "Equality and Justice in early Greek Cosmologies". *Classical Philology* **41**: 156–78. Reprinted in Vlastos (1995), 57–88.

Vlastos, G. 1950. "The Physical Theory of Anaxagoras". *Philosophical Review* **59**: 31–57. Reprinted in Allen & Furely (1975), 323–53 and in Vlastos (1995), 303–27.

Vlastos, G. 1952. "Theology and Philosophy in Early Greek Thought". *Philosophical Quarterly* **2**: 97–123. Reprinted in Vlastos (1995), 3–31.

Vlastos, G. 1955. "On Heraclitus". *American Journal of Philology* **76**: 337–68. Reprinted in Allen & Furley (1970), 413–29 and Vlastos (1995), 127–50.

Vlastos, G. 1966a. "Zeno's Race-Course". *Journal of the History of Philosophy* **4**: 95–108. Reprinted in Allen & Furley (1975), 201–20 and Vlastos (1995), 189–204.

Vlastos, G. 1966b. "A Note on Zeno's Arrow". *Phronesis* **11**: 3–18. Reprinted in Allen & Furley (1975), 184–200 and Vlastos (1995), 205–18.

Vlastos, G. 1975. "One World or Many in Anaxagoras?". See Allen & Furley (1975), 354–60.

Vlastos, G. 1995. *Studies in Greek Philosophy*, vol. 1. Princeton, NJ: Princeton University Press.

Voros, F. K. 1973. "The Ethical Fragments of Democritus: The Problem of Authenticity". *Hellenika* **26**: 193–206.

Wallace, R. J. 1994. "Private Lives and Public Enemies: Freedom of Thought in Classical Athens". In *Athenian Identity and Civic Ideology*, A. Boegehold & A. Scafuro (eds), 127–53. Baltimore, MD: Johns Hopkins University Press.

Wardy, R. B. B. 1988. "Eleatic Pluralism". *Archiv für Geschichte der Philosophie* **70**: 125–46.

Wardy, R. B. B. 2002. "The Unity of Opposites in Plato's *Symposium*". *Oxford Studies in Ancient Philosophy* **23**: 1–61.

Warren, J. 2002. *Epicurus and Democritean Ethics: An Archaeology of Ataraxia.* Cambridge: Cambridge University Press.

Warren. J. 2004. "Ancient Atomists on the Plurality of Worlds". *Classical Quarterly* 54: 354–65.

Warren, J. 2006. "Democritus on Social and Psychological Harm". In *Democritus: Science, the Arts, and the Care of the Soul*, A. Brancacci & P.-M. Morel (eds), 87–104. Leiden: Brill.

Warren, J. 2007. "Diogenes Laërtius, Biographer of Philosophy". In *Ordering Knowledge in the Roman Empire*, J. König & T. Whitmarsh (eds), 133–49. Cambridge: Cambridge University Press.

West, M. L. 1971. *Early Greek Philosophy and the Orient.* Oxford: Clarendon Press.

White, S. 2002. "Thales and the Stars". See Caston & Graham (2002), 3–18.

Wiggins, D. 1982. "Heraclitus' Conceptions of Flux, Fire and Material Persistence". In *Language and Logos: Studies in Ancient Philosophy Presented to G. E. L. Owen*, M. Schofield & M. C. Nussbaum (eds), 1–32. Cambridge: Cambridge University Press.

Index of passages

Index